Pleasure Seeking - Antidotes

Galations 5:13

D1017265

CHANGE YOUR
HEART
CHANGE YOUR
LIFE

CHANGE YOUR
HEART
CHANGE YOUR
LIFE

How Changing What You Believe
Will Give You the Great Life You've Always Wanted

Dr. Gary Smalley

THOMAS NELSON
Since 1798

NASHVILLE   DALLAS   MEXICO CITY   RIO DE JANEIRO   BEIJING

© 2007 Gary Smalley

All rights reserved. No portion of this book may be reproduced, stored in a retrieval system, or transmitted in any form or by any means—electronic, mechanical, photocopy, recording, scanning, or other—except for brief quotations in critical reviews or articles, without the prior written permission of the publisher.

Published in Nashville, Tennessee, by Thomas Nelson. Thomas Nelson is a trademark of Thomas Nelson, Inc.

Thomas Nelson, Inc. titles may be purchased in bulk for educational, business, fund-raising, or sales promotional use. For information, please e-mail SpecialMarkets@ThomasNelson.com.

Unless otherwise noted, Scripture quotations are taken from the Holy Bible: New International Version®. © 1973, 1978, 1984 by International Bible Society. Used by permission of Zondervan Publishing House. All rights reserved.

Scripture quotations marked GNT are from The Good News Translation. © 1976, 1992 by The American Bible Society. Used by permission. All rights reserved.

Scripture quotations marked KJV are from the King James Version of the Bible.

Scripture quotations marked NASB are from the New American Standard Bible®. © The Lockman Foundation 1960, 1962, 1963, 1968, 1971, 1972, 1973, 1975, 1977. Used by permission.

Scripture quotations marked NLT are from the Holy Bible, New Living Translation. © 1996. Used by permission of Tyndale House Publishers, Inc., Wheaton, Illinois 60189. All rights reserved.

Scripture quotations marked NKJV are from the New King James Version®. © 1982 by Thomas Nelson, Inc. Used by permission. All rights reserved.

Page design: Walter Petrie

Library of Congress Cataloging-in-Publication Data

Smalley, Gary.
        Change your heart, change your life : how changing what you believe will give you the great life you've always wanted / Gary Smalley.
            p. cm.
        Includes bibliographical references.
        ISBN 978-0-8499-1964-0 (hardcover)
        1. Christian life. 2. Belief and doubt. I. Title.
BV4501.3.S625 2007
248.4—dc22   2007038627

Printed in the United States of America

1 2 3 4 5 6 QW 08 09 10 11

To my oldest son, Dr. Greg Smalley, who started me on the path to understanding personal responsibility, for his unending love and patience with me until I understood the truth of God's Word that set me free. He used to say, "Dad, why do you give those people the power over you to control your emotions?" I didn't get it for more than a year. He never lost the desire to help me. Then, when the truth of this book hit my heart, it changed me forever.

Love the King, your God, with all of your heart, soul, mind, and strength.

Love your neighbor in the same way you want to be loved.

Give thanks to God in all circumstances for this is his will.

Forgive those who trespass against you so that your heavenly Father will forgive you.

Contents

Acknowledgments

First and foremost, I would like to thank God for allowing me to understand his message to share with all of you. Without him, this book wouldn't have been written. To Mike Hyatt, my longtime friend at Thomas Nelson, it's great to be working with you again and I look forward to partnering on many books in the future. To Joey Paul, another dear friend at Thomas Nelson, thank you for your patience with me while I was perfecting each chapter. Your love comes shining through once again. To Tom Williams, you are an amazingly talented man. I love how you are so committed to making sure that readers understand my thoughts and ideas so clearly. My heart is filled with gratitude. To Paula Major, my editor at Thomas Nelson, thank you for your diligence in bringing even more clarity to my thoughts. To all of the people at Thomas Nelson who work behind the scenes, please know that you are thought of and I'm grateful for all you do. To my writing team, Terry Brown, Ted Cunningham, and Sue Parks, the challenges that we went through to get this book out to the readers were well worth their weight in gold. I love each and every one of you. And to my beautiful bride, Norma, thank you so much for helping me become more like Christ. I love you endlessly.

One
Hope for You in All Circumstances

I t seems normal today for people to feel discouraged, stressed out, hopeless, and even depressed. The pace of our lives is part of the problem. Everyone seems to be in a huge hurry to go everywhere, even if they're going nowhere. The tensions of the world add anxiety and uncertainty—terrorism, political turmoil, wars, and rumors of wars. And the disintegrating values of our nation don't help matters any. We are constantly egged on by advertising and our peers to want more and more things, entertainment, pleasure, and leisure, and this brings on the added stress of working harder in order to afford these things. These combined pressures bring many of us down, inducing more or less permanent feelings of discouragement, depression, envy, guilt, frustration, anger, and a host of other defeating emotions.

What if I could show you a way to rise above all that? What if I could show you a surefire way to live so that these pressures and negative influences would never interfere with your joy and satisfaction with life? What if I could show you a proven method of increasing your peace of mind, reducing stress to the point that it almost disappears, and increasing the satisfaction in your marriage beyond your wildest dreams? What if you were to hear negative words from your mate, experience difficulties in life as we all do, but you rebounded in less than a day? Would you be interested?

In fact, I can show you the secret to accomplishing all this and more. The secret is not original with me; I found the key to changing my life in God's Holy Scriptures. I discovered four awesome, God-given beliefs that, when embedded in my heart, brought about changes in my life far beyond what I ever dreamed possible. These principles work. I know they do because they worked miracles in my own life. And I know they can work in yours as well, because they are God's own principles for living and loving. They were written more than five thousand years ago, and I found them to be life changing for me. I've used them every day for over six years and I can't get enough. I suspect that you'll have the same response if what I write makes sense to you.

Wouldn't it be great if you suddenly found the willpower to lose all that unwanted weight in just six months? Wouldn't you love to achieve more of your goals and reap more benefits from your job? Wouldn't it be wonderful to experience the love and excitement in your marriage that you thought you had lost forever? It can happen. It provides more safety and love for your marriage than anything I know. As you fly through this book, you'll learn the secret to achieving all these dreams and so much more. And the secret is simple: all you have to do is change some of the beliefs that are lodged in your heart.

"Impossible!" you may say. "Surely just changing what I believe in my heart will not make such radical differences in my life." But it can. I am living proof that these four beliefs can change your life beyond measure. Discovering these beliefs has given me the most amazing and rewarding times in all my sixty-seven years, changing and enriching my life in ways I could never have imagined. Six years ago I didn't even know these principles existed. It was my psychologist son who introduced them to me. But when I began to put them into practice, the dramatic and exciting changes they produced in my own life led me to share them with people in my immediate circle. When I saw them change preteens, teens, and adults of all ages, I knew I had found something amazing that could turn a person's life around in just a few weeks. I couldn't wait to share these four beliefs with the world. That's why I have written this book.

The Power of Beliefs

To show you how putting the right beliefs in your heart can change you, let me tell you a story about my oldest grandson, Michael. The incident occurred when he was ten years old. I had just discovered the principle of beliefs, but at the time I didn't know just how broadly they would apply.

Michael walked into my house as discouraged as I've ever seen him. I greeted him and listened as he poured out his heart about how miserable he was.

"Grampa," he said, "Mom is driving me crazy. I can't live like this. Can you do something about it? Can you talk to her?"

The more I listened, the more I realized that his problem with his mom—Kari, my daughter—was nothing more than her insisting that he be responsible about her rules concerning household chores and homework. But what he wanted was my help in changing her so she wouldn't bug him any more and *cause* his *unhappiness*. I'm very close to Kari, and she is one of my best friends in life and a wonderful mother. I chose not to take his side or hers. I didn't talk with Michael about the need to be responsible and to give one's parents respect and obedience. Instead I decided to see if my newfound discovery of beliefs would work for a ten-year-old. So I asked him this question: "Is your mom making you unhappy or is she revealing some belief in your heart, which is the thing that is actually making you unhappy?"

He stared at me with that what-in-the-world-are-you-talking-about? look and asked me to repeat the question. I did, and then I went on. "Michael, would you do something with me that I'm almost sure will get you over your frustration, no matter what your mom says to you?" He agreed, and so I said, "You and I are going to learn three scripture verses and say them to each other every day until they sink in as new beliefs in our hearts.[1] Are you in?"

"Yes, I'll do it," he replied. "Are you sure this will really work?"

"It has for me, and I've seen it work for a few others who have tried it. You could be my youngest guinea pig." I prayed fervently that it would work for him. I didn't want to disappoint him further. He looked deeply into my eyes and said, "Gramp, I have seen changes in you over the last two years; yes, I'll try this with you."

We did learn those three scripture verses, and we helped each other rehearse them several times per day for over a year. And then I think I witnessed a miracle. Here's the story as he shared it.

His mom picked him up at school one day and asked him if he had brought everything he needed to do his homework. He said he had. But after she had driven two miles through difficult construction traffic, he suddenly remembered that he had left something very important in his locker.

"Mom, can you take me back?" he asked. "I left my spelling book, and I need it for a spelling test tomorrow. I can't do without it."

"Michael! What is wrong with you?" Kari exploded in frustration. "Why didn't you think of this when I asked? How can you be so irresponsible? You're just like your grampa!" She was really at the poor kid's throat, and she kept up the verbal barrage, using the *tough love* method.

When he arrived at home, Michael sprinted through the woods to my house to share what had happened. He banged on my door, yelling, "Total miracle, Grampa!"

He told me the entire story, and then he said, "Usually when Mom starts in on me like that, I talk back, saying something like, 'Just put a cork in it, Mom. You've told me this a million times, and I'm tired of hearing it.' But this time I didn't say a thing; I just listened because all three Bible verses rushed into my mind. Then in the middle of her angry lecture I interrupted and said, 'Mom! Mom, wait!' She stopped, glared at me, and demanded, 'What is it now?' I said to her, 'Mom, I can tell by your words how much you love me, and because you love me, you want me to do better in school, right? I just want you to know how much I really appreciate that, and I thank you for loving me so much. Would you please forgive me?'"

Kari told me later that when Michael said this, her jaw dropped to the steering wheel. She got goose bumps and had to pull the car over because she could no longer see for the tears in her eyes. She told him how much she loved him, and she forgave him. Being overwhelmed, she said she felt like handing Michael her purse and telling him to go buy whatever he wanted.

My experiment worked. Michael simply changed a couple of beliefs in his heart, and that change affected not only his behavior but also his attitude and relationship toward his mother. Things did not suddenly go perfectly for him, but with the change in his inner belief, his parents and I saw the dramatic changes in his life. His discouragements and frustrations were lowered significantly. And over the past three years, he has increased the changes in his heart, and his mom wrote me a letter outlining those changes.[2]

In this book I will tell you many other stories—several of them about my own experiences—showing how people with major life difficulties overcame them by going to the root of the problem and changing the beliefs in their hearts. I'll tell you of my own *water-to-wine* miracle of overcoming a lust problem, of marriages that seemed impossible to heal, of people caught in addictions they thought were hopeless, and many other examples of how changed beliefs produced changed lives. No matter what you are facing in your life, this could be your story as well.

Our beliefs usually come to us from our parents, or we pick them up from our culture. Thus we are likely to be as happy or unhappy as our parents were or as our culture is as a whole. But I don't want my happiness to be dependent on others, whether it's my parents or the culture in general. I know that God created me to be filled with joy (inner happiness that is not dependent upon my happenings), peace, and love; therefore, in the past few years I have learned to base my beliefs solely on Scripture. It is in Scripture that I have found the four major beliefs I am basing my life on today. I have many more I'm working on as you'll see in appendix 5, but these four beliefs are where I started to experience the best riches in life. These are the key beliefs I have been diligent to embed or *hide* in my heart so that they become guiding principles for everything I do in life. And I have found that they work. If we will conform our minds to these four key beliefs that were designed by our Maker, they will put us on top of everything that matters in life.[3]

The result of embedding these four beliefs in my heart has been an almost complete victory over worry, judging others, irritations, lust, eating habits, anger, complaining, disharmony with others, and ingratitude. My stress level is now almost nonexistent. My health is much better than it has been since I was a very young man. But even if my health fails and chronic aches and pains begin to wrack me, I will still be able to maintain a grateful heart and remain joyful—all because of these new beliefs I have implanted in my heart.

> To sum it up, the concept is how you can manage your own life and make improvements in any area you wish through changing a few beliefs by the power of our Designer and his words.

Learn these principles and you will discover how to manage your own heart and reap the wonderful consequences of a much closer walk with God and harmony with others. You'll be thrilled at the growing compassion in your heart toward all people. It all comes as a gift from God when you learn to adjust your deepest beliefs to only a few of the most powerful living words in his Scriptures. Just think of it. God's Word is truth (John 17:17), and you will know this truth, and it will set you free! (John 8:32).

In these pages I will touch on many important beliefs from God, but my main theme will center on the four beliefs that I explain fully, beginning in chapter 10, as well as the five steps that can set you free, explained in chapter 5. Everything in this book prior to chapter 10 is preparatory and introductory to these four beliefs. If you get too curious, feel free to skip to these chapters. But I urge you to read the preparatory material as well. You may find that you have some *bad* beliefs that will be rooted out as you open your heart to the empowering truth of godly beliefs.

You may be way beyond me in this journey. You may already know these four beliefs and have them firmly hidden in your own heart. If so, that's great. For you this book may be just a testimony of a person who has just learned to walk with God and take his words and beliefs seriously. If you already know and live by these principles, you will be able to influence others so that these amazing beliefs can spread across the world.

Beliefs: The Key to Your High Quality of Living

One of the most powerful truths to come out of my discovery is that no one can make you unhappy. Your ability to be happy or unhappy is entirely in your hands. You will be as happy as the beliefs in your heart allow you to be, and no person or circumstance can make you happier or unhappier than that.

The idea that you control your own happiness is such a foreign concept that many people find it simply unbelievable. Humans do terrible things to each other all the time. They lie, steal, hurt, deceive, and even maim and kill. How can one possibly say that having these things done to you wouldn't make you unhappy? That's the way most of us reason, but, as I will show you in this book, it's a huge lie that's stuck firmly in the hearts of men and women. And I, along with a lot of them, have been clueless that it is a lie.

The lie is that someone else—or something else—is the cause of your unhappiness. As you will see, this simply is not true. No one is making you miserable. You are never, ever, a victim of someone or something else. Your happiness is always in your own hands. You are and have always been 100 percent responsible for the quality of your life. As I said above, you will always be as happy as the beliefs in your heart allow you to be.

Nothing and no one can take away your happiness or joy unless you hand that job over to others or to your circumstances. To find enduring joy and peace, you must learn to recognize and accept the reality that your Designer created the best beliefs for you to store in your own heart, and those beliefs determine your level of happiness. I can see now why King Solomon warned all of us, "Above all else, guard your heart, for it is the wellspring of life" (Proverbs 4:23).

This truth seems so extreme that you may wonder if it will work in every situation. My answer is that if it can work for a person in a horrible World War II concentration camp, it can work for anyone. The now-famous Austrian neurologist Dr. Viktor Frankl suffered under Hitler in just such a camp. He endured terrible physical torture. And worse, his father and his wife died in these camps at the hands of the Germans. Yet he wrote, "The guards could control how much pain I was in, they could torture me, deny me food, but they could never control my thoughts."[4] After the war was over and Frankl was freed, guards in his prison section wrote that they had never met a happier person in their lives. Isn't that amazing? A mistreated, tortured prisoner was the happiest person they knew. Happier than the guards who maltreated him! What would give this man such control over his emotions and the quality of his life in a terrible concentration camp where pain and death were constant companions? He had learned one of the greatest lessons in life. His happiness came not from how he was treated, but from how he thought about his treatment. He was in control of what he allowed himself to think about all day long.

Frankl had discovered the key to changing one's life. He discovered that there is tremendous power in learning to control your thoughts. As the ancient Greek philosopher Epictetus said, "Men are disturbed, not by things, but by the view they take of them." When you learn the right thoughts and *chew on them* over and over, day after day, they will lodge in your heart as beliefs. Those new beliefs will become the controlling principles of your life. And

> What you think about all day long, over long periods, eventually seeps into your heart as a belief.

then no person, no circumstance, no amount of mistreatment can touch you at the center of your being, which is where true quality of life resides. You'll get knocked over from time to time, but it's amazing how fast you'll get back up on your feet.

The key to a fulfilling life is to find the best and most truthful thoughts to think on day and night and store them in your heart as beliefs.

God has already answered the question about what beliefs to store within our heart. It was recorded for us thousands of years ago in Deuteronomy 6:5: "Love the Lord your God with all your heart and with all your soul and with all your strength." This one belief will accomplish more in your life than any other belief I know.

If you've never been exposed to the concept of beliefs controlling your well-being, I know that it probably makes no sense to you right now. It's counterintuitive. It goes against the way people normally think and believe. It goes against the way people around you act and live all the time. It even causes some people to react negatively to me when I teach it. They have spent their entire lives blaming others or circumstances for the quality of their lives, and it's as if I have taken away their foundation for feeling discouraged.

You and I live in a fallen world where things tend to fall apart. No matter how carefully you construct your life, the seams tend to unravel: relationships go sour, company graphs go south, doctors' reports stun us, the air conditioning goes out, the car refuses to start, the commode stops up, rain ruins the vacation. Even a bad hair day wrecks the equilibrium of some people.

I want to show you that if your life or any part of it is miserable because of what someone has done to you or because of something you don't have or something you have lost or because something doesn't work, you have relinquished your innate power of control over your life. You need not remain in misery, however. You can get out of it, and getting out of it is really quite simple. All you have to do is change or revise some of your deepest beliefs. It's so miraculous that, at first, it seems impossible. But really, it is deceptively simple.

Simple, however, doesn't always mean easy. The concept of changing your beliefs is simple, but making the change stick and become deep and meaningful won't just happen. It will take some *want-to* on your part. It will mean replacing old beliefs that you have inherited or acquired—beliefs that have stuck to your heart like barnacles to a boat, beliefs that are lies and have no business being there. Beliefs that slow you down but can easily be gotten rid of once you understand how. I won't be asking you to dig deeply into your subconscious and discover those early childhood beliefs that may be wrecking your present life. I'll just add a few new beliefs that will wipe out or cover over the old ones that are *doing you in.*

This book is all about understanding how those powerful beliefs you already store in your heart are controlling your life in every way. I want you to understand how you acquired your beliefs and how they control you. I want to show you how to change your old destructive beliefs, especially the three *deadly* beliefs that are the most damaging to you and actually drain love from your life. And finally, I want to show you the four most important beliefs to store inside your heart and how to embed them deeply.

The next chapter starts the process by showing you how you got your beliefs and how your current beliefs are affecting everything you think, say, or do.

Two
How You Formed Your Beliefs

Everyone who is old enough to reason has developed deep beliefs. Where did we pick up those beliefs? We get them from what we think about every day, all day long. How do we pick up these thinking patterns? As we grow up, we tend to adopt the ways of thinking of everyone around us. When we're young, we can't discern right thoughts from wrong ones, and we simply pick up the thinking patterns of those in our environment. We feel constant pressure to conform to the thinking of the people from our *birth group*, and when we deviate from these patterns, our parents or friends are likely to hit us over the head to get us back in line. Even where we live can determine a lot about our long-held deep beliefs. But here's the great thing: no matter how wrong those beliefs may be and no matter how ingrained they have become, you can change them in just a few short weeks.

In fact, let me offer you even more hope. If you follow the principles I outline in this book, you can change old beliefs and improve your life in as little as two weeks. But so we will understand our beliefs better, let's briefly explore where most of them come from.

Early Experiences Can Cause Bad Beliefs

I started my life as a wild kid, and many of my early experiences shaped damaging beliefs that I unwittingly held into late middle age. In my earliest years my family lived in Downey, California. Some of my first memories are of when I was five years old, playing with other children on the huge lawn of a church near our tract home. In the house behind ours lived an eight-year-old girl named Ginger, who was very pretty and full of life. She was the neighborhood leader. I don't know what kind of parents she had, but they seemed to be gone most of the time. She was able to lead the rest of us young kids around like a pied piper. She regularly took us into her garage in the afternoons, where she taught us some of our favorite games. Some of the games were typical blindfold hide-and-seek, but some included exciting doctor, patient, and nurse experiments.

I know that some people have early sexual experiences when they are forced, intimidated, or coerced by friends or family members who are stronger than they are. My experiences in Ginger's garage were not like that. It never occurred to me that innocently experimenting with sex would be wrong or have any lasting effect on me. What we did seemed normal, and we all followed this girl willingly. In fact, I'll not lie to you and pretend I didn't enjoy these experiences. Maybe somewhere in the back of my mind I should have known that what we were doing was wrong, but it was so pleasurable and exciting that I apparently snuffed out that thought and kept on going into that garage with Ginger.

Yet these experiences did have inevitable negative consequences. They stuck in my mind and affected my attitudes and behavior for much of the rest of my life. Whenever you have a major emotional experience like this, you tend to remember it for life, whether you want to or not. Those memories embedded themselves into my mind and became thoughts I entertained so often that they inevitably seeped into my heart as beliefs that greatly affected my later behavior.

> I had an early belief that life should be pleasurable and thrilling most of the time.

For example, I vividly remember my gang of best friends in junior high school—all boys—who hung out together after school. None of us attended a church or had an active belief in or any relationship whatever with God. We were always looking for a thrill and were willing to try anything that would bring us excitement or pleasure. On some nights we painted our faces black, donned old clothes, and crawled through tall grass and shot out streetlights with our BB guns. The moment a car came down the street we took off running. What a rush that was! You can be sure our list of exciting and pleasurable things included girls. Our hormones were screaming, and we heeded their call. Such escapades satisfied my hunger for thrills and pleasures.

Today I recall those memories with sickening regret, but I'm dredging them up now in order to show you just how influential experiences can be in formulating your beliefs. And what beliefs did my early experiences with Ginger and my guy friends form in me? The belief that life should be pleasurable and thrilling most of the time.

I was out of balance as a kid with no guidance from adults helping me build accurate beliefs that would enable me to see life from God's viewpoint. My early experiences led me to continuously seek pleasure, thrills, excitement, and fun. These experiences dominated my mind, and I had no idea that the things I thought about all day and night would wind up settling into my heart as major, powerful beliefs. Do you know what the world calls this pleasure-craving, thrill-seeking belief? Hedonism. And I'm convinced that hedonism is the dominant belief that permeates our society. I will explain in chapter 5 how I changed this belief, but suffice it to say for now that early experiences are one source of the beliefs we hold, often for the rest of our lives.

You Can Inherit Bad Beliefs

My early home life was typical of families back in the 1940s. I grew up watching my father work at various jobs, trying to provide more for his family. Yet in spite of his hard work, we were dirt poor. How clearly I remember a Christmas tree in our living room with hardly any presents beneath it. I remember sitting at the dinner table hearing my mom apologize for the skimpy meals, usually followed by, "Won't it be great someday when Mom and Dad can buy our own house and live in a nicer neighborhood?" "Yes," we kids agreed, "that will be wonderful." The idea of having more and better things got me excited because it excited everyone else in my family. Kids pick up many of the beliefs of their parents and siblings without even knowing it.

In the late 1940s, I entered a raffle at a carnival and actually won the first TV on our block. We kids sat in front of that tiny screen and watched those black-and-white shows for hours. And what did we see? Television commercials urging us to buy more things so we would have a better life, interspersed with thrilling entertainment. I wanted the things those commercials dangled before me, and I wanted more entertainment. And that meant I needed money.

And why shouldn't I want more money? Everyone around me often talked about how important money is, so the belief sank into my heart that life must be all about making money. I added this belief to the belief I already held that life was all about fun, excitement, thrills, and pleasures. I suppose that even at my young age, my mind must have made the connection between the thrills that Ginger gave me and having money. I reasoned that money buys more of those things that bring pleasure and thrills. My inherited belief that life was about acquiring money, coupled with my belief that life was meant to be pleasurable, plunged me headfirst into the two-headed American belief system: hedonism and materialism.

My parents inherited beliefs from their families who had inherited them from their families from who knows how far back. I know that our two families produced at least four generations of children who reflected the core beliefs that their great-great-grandparents passed down. The children picked up the family beliefs, and, [as Jesus told us, out of the beliefs in their hearts flowed their thoughts, words, and actions (Matthew 15:19).

My father inherited beliefs other than the materialism that he passed on to me, and many of them were not good at all. For example, he believed that the world of his family should essentially revolve around him and his wants and comfort. When this didn't happen to suit him, he would explode in anger, and all of us suffered from the fallout of his volatile temper.

Naturally, I picked up my father's belief as well as his reaction when his belief was violated. As a young father, when my family crossed my wishes, like my father, I sometimes blew up all over them in anger. As a Christian I came to know that this was wrong and I wanted to change. But I didn't know what to do. I tried my best, I thought, to take a different path from that of my father. I even told my kids that I didn't like the way my dad raised me, and I gave them permission to point out anything I did that sounded or looked like what my angry father would do. But in spite of my efforts at control, that old anger could rise up and grab hold of me at any time.

Like the time we went on our big family vacation to Hawaii.

We had been in Hawaii for only a couple of days when one morning we all decided to walk down the beach and gather shells. I was a little delayed for some reason, and so my wife and three children took off walking ahead of me. They agreed to wait for me at a certain place. By the time I reached the beach, I couldn't find them. They weren't where they were supposed to be. For over an hour I searched for them, walking first in one direction and then the other. No family. Irritated and disappointed, I walked back to our hotel as hurt and hostility built up inside me. They were not at the hotel. *Where could they be?* I wondered. I even imagined that they were trying intentionally to lose me so that they could enjoy their time without the "angry old man." Those thoughts added fuel to my anger, and I became even more upset. About two hours later, here they came, all excited about the shells they had gathered.

"Look, Dad, this must be a rare one," said my little daughter Kari, happily.

Instead of sharing her excitement, I glared at all of them. "Where in the world have you been?" I demanded. "Why did you take off and leave me?"

"We told you we'd be walking up the beach."

"You told me no such thing!" My anger kept rising.

"Hold on," they said, "it's not our fault. We did what we said we'd do. We waited and you didn't come. So we walked up the beach just like we told you we would." They reacted to my anger and turned on me for an old-fashioned argument. Finally my son Greg found a moment of sanity.

"Dad," he said, "didn't you tell us to help you see when you're acting like your own father?"

All of my breath escaped from my lungs and I hung my head. "Yes, I did ask you to help me."

"Well, are you acting like him now?"

"Yes," I responded. I was always amazed at how Greg could turn me around so fast. "And I hate it when I act like him. I'm very sorry. It was wrong of me to blow up like this. Can you guys forgive me?"

Just as Greg was always the first to defuse my anger, little Michael was always the first to run to my arms and hug me. His forgiveness was always instantaneous because he so disliked feeling the rejection of estrangement. Each one of the family followed, coming to me with tears, eager to reconnect. Their quick forgiveness always humbled me and made me feel so blessed to have my family's love.

I wish I had known then what I know now about getting in charge of one's beliefs. I wish I had known how to change my destructive beliefs. What I love most about being in charge of my own beliefs is that I can change a whole new generation by changing my own beliefs. I can pass on a new kind of inheritance, altogether different from the one my father passed to me. How I act will reflect what I believe, and in turn those beliefs will be reflected within my own children and grandchildren and their children for generations. What often blows me away is the promise from God that if I love him with all of my heart as my King, he'll show lovingkindness to a thousand generations, but he'll also visit the iniquity of a father on at least four generations if the father hates or rejects him. I don't know about you, but I get extremely interested in forming the beliefs in my heart that God intended me to have.

That day in Hawaii I could have explored what beliefs inside caused me to blow up on my family, and I could have begun working to change them. Instead, we did the only thing I knew to do. We actually got on our knees together and prayed that God would somehow break the hold my dad and his relatives had on me and keep it from being transferred to my kids. I suppose I was on the right track—praying is always a worthwhile activity—but I didn't know how to get to the core of the problem.

I did see the need for making deep changes, and that resulted in an alteration of some of my beliefs. But it was done pretty much by accident—by feeling and groping toward a solution to my problem. I could have made lasting and amazing changes if I had known what I know now about the power of reaching down to my deepest beliefs and making the first change there.

Over the years I discovered that much of my anger came from a deep belief that bad things happening to me are actually *bad*. And I would ask, "Why me, God?" I even believed I shouldn't have to go through bad experiences as severe or as often as an unbeliever. I reacted to bad events in anger because they robbed me of pleasure, good times, and good things I thought I deserved.

Years later I realized that a belief that attaches a negative meaning to all bad or difficult events is not from God. I had inherited that belief from past generations of my family. My father, who was a believer but did not allow God to lead him in his daily life, believed all negative events were to be avoided, and he struck back at them in anger. I was hurting my family because I carried this belief forward. Like my father, I also reacted in anger or hurt when negative events intruded on the good life I wanted. No wonder the apostle Paul told us not to be conformed to this world but to be transformed by the renewing of our minds (Romans 12:2). This renewing means taking the beliefs we have picked up over the years and replacing them with the teachings of Christ. In chapter 11 I'll expand on the concept that trials are, in fact, good for us and bring some of the best character and spiritual growth possible.

Bad Beliefs Can Come from Your Culture

While in South Africa recently, I was shocked to see a man beating his wife in plain daylight. Years before in Rockford, Illinois, I counseled an amazing number of wives who had been physically hit by their husbands. In every country of the world, I have either witnessed such selfish cruelty from men or have read, as you have, about the violence men often inflict on their wives. A dad recently told me about his twenty-seven-year-old daughter who was teaching kids in a foreign country how to read. When it came time for her to return to the United States for a brief visit with her parents, several children literally fell down in front of the van taking her to the airport. She explained that she would return in only a few short weeks, but the children pleaded with her not to leave at all. They explained that their fathers did not beat their mothers as much while she was actually present in their small village.

United Nations workers have been sent to Uganda to protect women from abuse, and now many of these same men are being tried there for cruel treatment of hundreds of little girls.

It's estimated that nearly one hundred thousand reported rapes occurred in the United States in 2003, and if you add that number to those abuses inflicted in the rest of the world, it's easy to imagine that number rising into the millions. Then think of the painful stories about the precious little girls who are molested by their fathers or relatives. It breaks my heart to read even of a single case of such abuse. The overwhelming prevalence of it is simply staggering. Even my small town has many registered pedophiles.

Where did all this evil come from? Could it be that we have not been guarding the hearts of our children and many are growing up with the same love-killing belief in "pleasurism" that contaminated my childhood? Even if that is the case, it's never too late to reach out and help our society. We can start by changing our own beliefs and then help our children in the formation of theirs. If enough Christians would just take those two steps, they would go far in showing our school and government leaders a better way than conforming to the powerful standards of the world that currently dominate our nation. Let's begin by changing the three deadly beliefs, which I'll tell you about later, and wake up those around us with our example.

There is far, far too much damage to women and children taking place everywhere in this world. I'm confronted with it every day, just as you are. And I'm convinced that most of this violence comes from a deep-seated belief in the heart of the perpetrators. They hold to an insidiously wrong belief that women are inferior and subject to men's every whim. In many societies this belief is long-standing and even supported by religious beliefs. Because the culture holds the belief as true, many men hold it unthinkingly in their hearts and find it acceptable to abuse women.

This is only one example of how the culture we live in can embed wrong beliefs into our hearts. In America today, the culture persistently pushes us toward ever more ungodly and destructive beliefs. And I fear that many Christians are completely clueless, as I have been, that they have bought into these beliefs lock, stock, and barrel. America is awash with the idea that everyone has a right to have whatever he or she wants and to be free from any kind of misfortune. It's essentially the same idea I grew up with gone wild. Almost everyone seems to believe they have a right to pleasure, excitement, luxury, ease, and freedom from any kind of discomfort. Many of us have come to believe the lie that what I have and how other people treat me are what make me happy or unhappy. It's a formula for disaster at every level.

Wrong Beliefs Are the Source of All Evils

What happens in a society dominated by the prevalent belief that happiness comes from having all needs and wants continually met? Any news report on any given day gives us the answer—violence, murders, immorality, and crimes of every imaginable sort. Most of these crimes are committed because of three deceptive beliefs: what our eyes lust for, what our senses lust for, and what we think we need, we can't live without. A perpetrator believes that his or her happiness depends upon having a certain thing, or getting a certain pleasure, or avoiding a certain disagreeable situation. When this expectation is not met, violence can erupt. And the sad thing is that our society can see no solution. As a result, all our prisons are overflowing.

What is the source of all this evil? Did not Jesus tell us that evil actions come from the beliefs stored in a person's heart (Matthew 15:18–20)? It's true. Everything anyone does is a reflection of what is in his or her heart. These actions come from beliefs picked up early in life from experience, family, or the culture. And those beliefs produce the selfishness, violence, and greed we see rampant around us.

People can learn to believe almost anything. They can grow up believing that women are worthless, that people of different faiths or color are less valuable, or, as in Nazi Germany, that certain people do not deserve to live. Any culture can come up with thousands of destructive beliefs that can seep into a person's heart.

What is the solution? How can we stem this devastating tide? Can we help these evil or abusive people change their hearts and their behavior? Yes, we can. This is one of my main goals for the rest of my life, and it's my purpose in writing this book. I want to show people where and how to find great beliefs—beliefs that will lead them to a happier, more loving, and more fulfilling life. I want to show how people unwittingly lock on to beliefs early that will last a lifetime and cause misery and grief unless they are changed. Who wants to live sixty-plus years, as I did, and finally discover that some of his beliefs were lies? They held me back and robbed me of experiencing God's full love.

I want to show you what happened in my life as I dug into the beliefs of my heart and discovered thoughts and motives that were false and destructive. I want to show you how to isolate those beliefs and root them out, replacing them with time-tested, absolutely true beliefs designed by our Maker and guaranteed to work. These beliefs not only will change your life but also will lead you to the purposes you were designed for: more love for God and others and more of God's worth within yourself.

Wouldn't it be great to see a whole new generation of kids growing up with parents who know how to guard their own hearts and who will instill into their children's lives our Designer's most important beliefs? Now, that's a dream worth living for!

You may find it hard to believe, but I assure you that even the most ingrained and destructive lifetime habits you thought you could never change will give way when you learn to change the beliefs of your heart. I wouldn't have believed it either, but in the pages that follow I will give you numerous examples showing how it happened to me. In the very next chapter, I'll show you what I did to experience my first really wonderful, miraculous change. And I'll show you how it can happen in your life as well.

Three
The Amazing Power of Your Beliefs

I used to wonder why I said such hurtful words to my wife, Norma, for so many years of our marriage. Some of what I said in anger was terrible: "If you don't stop being negative and trying to block my lifetime dreams, I'm going to quit writing and speaking and just take a regular job. I'm sick of your being a drag, a heavy weight on my legs as I try to serve God, couples, and families all over this world. I'm sick of it, do you hear me?"

I can't count how many times I used this trump card in the first twenty years of my life's work. Today my stomach turns inside when I think of how I treated her. And I'm embarrassed that I didn't know how damaging these statements were. I certainly know now about the terrible pain she felt with my degrading attitude. Don't you wish you could take back many of the words you have spoken to people over the years?

Two things were happening here. First, I was out of control. I was being controlled by my beliefs, and my beliefs were pulling and pushing me around, causing me to say things that I thought would help me, but that actually inflicted pain—not only on Norma, but ultimately on me as well. Second, I was trying to control her. My beliefs made me think she should be completely subservient to my needs and supportive of every little thing I wanted to do. After all, I was serving the Lord, wasn't I? I believed that my ministry gave me the holy right to demand that she place my needs (or supposed needs) above all

18

others. I believed I should have my perceived needs met and that I should be in control of her, at least, to some degree and bend her into the mode of meeting those needs. My wrong beliefs were causing all kinds of grief. But can you see that since two of my strongest beliefs were excitement and pleasure along with minimizing difficulties, when she didn't make my life more pleasurable and less difficult, I was upset with her?

Today I see the logic in how I came to these false beliefs. Ephesians 5:22 clearly says, "Wives, submit to your husbands as to the Lord." Who can miss that command for wives? It's pretty straightforward, isn't it? But why on earth didn't I see the next verses? It would have made a huge difference in my behavior if I had paid as much attention to Ephesians 5:25: "Husbands, love your wives, just as Christ loved the church and gave himself up for her." Wow! My wife could have experienced so much more love from me if I had believed from the start of my marriage that I was required to love her so much I would be willing to get up on a cross as if to die for her and lay down my life for her in every way. God is the God of love, and I could have cried out to him for his love, and when he gave it to me, I could have given it to her. I never hid that belief in my heart until years later. We both would have reaped much more enjoyment from our time together. But no, not me! I took only the one part of the instructions for a marriage that looked good to me and put that thought into my heart. And I did it to my wife's hurt.

And that was not the worst of it. Not only did I harp on her for not meeting my needs, I took it on myself to impose my beliefs on her. I used to try to convince her to exercise with me more often. I complained that the food she served was not healthy enough, and I went out and bought certain foods I deemed to be better for both of us. I couldn't understand why she reacted so badly to my attempt to take over what went on in the kitchen. It was for the benefit of both of us, wasn't it? I thought she should be glad that I would impose my superior beliefs on her inferior ones. Stupid me! Where on earth did I come up with the belief that it was my responsibility to improve her?

I learned a few things over the years (even a blind hog finds an acorn once in a while), and as my heart changed, I spoke these hurtful words to her less often until they finally died during our forty-four years together. But in the first few years, I still spoke them occasionally because, sadly, I *believed* I was serving God, and he expected her to obey me in everything. She may have been willing to obey me if I had loved her as Christ loves the church.

So I maintained that holy attitude: "Wife, don't get between me and my God." How blind I was. She has had so many great things to share with me as a woman and wife. Why didn't I learn early to recognize what I had in her? As I look back I can see that she tried to warn me about almost every major mistake I made with money, in work-related areas, and with family and friends. And I often ignored her. Or worse, I sometimes tried to silence her with hurtful words. This hurt not only her but me as well because I was blocking out the benefit of a major asset God had given me through the insights of my wife.

I did not understand at the time that my words were coming straight out of deep-seated beliefs hidden in my own heart. I didn't even know I had beliefs that caused me to strike out at her with hurtful words. I thought she was the cause of my frustration, that she was the one who was trying to make my life miserable with her lack of support. I thought my frustration was all her fault and had no idea I was bringing it on myself by acting on erroneous beliefs. I blamed her for my unhappiness, never once realizing my happiness could easily be under my own control if I would simply change the beliefs I held in my heart.

I can't remember the last time I spoke those hurtful words to my wife because I'm constantly thinking day and night on adjusting my own beliefs to be more consistent with God's greatest commands: loving him and others (Ephesians 5:17, 21). Many of these truths have already reached my heart and are *branded* there. As a result my words and actions are constantly changing. No longer do I feel any need to complain, gripe, or blame her or others for my unhappiness or displeasure. I have watched my life become what I have always desired it to be—more loving, understanding, even-keeled, and compassionate. Even stress is at my all-time lowest. And if I get upset or stressed out now, it only lasts for a few hours. The change is the result of my doing just one thing: changing the beliefs in my own heart and reaping some of the results of the change in as little as two weeks.

Whenever Norma and I used to drive on a trip together, her loving reminders concerning my driving skills (or lack of them) used to drive me up the wall. Then I found Matthew 7:1–4 and reviewed it for weeks until it reached my heart and gave me a new belief about not judging others or reacting to people who irritate me. I am happy to say that now (and this is the truth) she can correct anything about my driving abilities and I literally think to myself how fortunate I am to have at least one person who irritates me. How else can we know what God wants to change about our character? Irritations are reflections of the logs in our own eyes. I now thank God for those irritations and instantly try to connect the irritation to something in my own life that needs work. When anyone corrects my driving, I know that God wants me to learn how to be in deeper submission to him. I tend to resist submitting to anyone, but how else can I become the servant God wants me to be unless I allow him to remind me through irritations? God's ways are so amazing. I'll cover this more later, but if you remember that irritations are within yourself and not in the other person, it really helps as you start working on your own faults.

You see what a simple change of belief can do? I looked into my heart and found beliefs that were making life miserable not only for me but also for my wife. I believed that she should support me. I believed that I should control certain things about her. But believing these things was putting my well-being out of my control. I could not be happy because my beliefs put my happiness in the hands of circumstances that I had no real control over. I believed I would be happy *if* my wife supported me in the way I thought she should. She did not support me in that way, therefore I was not happy. I would be happy *if* my wife allowed me to control certain areas of her life. She would not allow that, therefore I was not happy. My beliefs put happiness out of my control. It was only when I changed those beliefs that I gained control of the quality of my own life, and that comes through adopting the beliefs our Creator intended us to have. I can only change one person on this earth and you are reading that person's words.

Today there is more love in my house than there has ever been. As a husband, I am changing faster every day and becoming more and more alert to Norma, listening better and loving her more than ever before. And it's all because I changed my beliefs by managing what I think about all day long (Philippians 4:6–9). Let's look more closely at how this works.

The Amazing Power of Belief

Neuroscientists tell us that our emotional center is actually the subconscious or the limbic section of our brain. I prefer to use the warmer term *heart* to designate this inner storehouse of our beliefs and the seat of our emotions. This term follows the scriptural teaching that our spiritual heart is the center of our being, the wellspring of who we are (Proverbs 4:23). The embedded beliefs in your heart control everything about you—what you eat, how you rest, how you take care of yourself, what you say and think, what your job is, and how much money you make. Dr. William Backus says that "you feel the way you think; you think the way the way you believe. Beliefs are the primary source of your attitudes, reactions, feelings, and behavior. Isn't that just about everything you are?"[1] In short, these beliefs determine the entire scope of your life. Best-selling author and psychologist Dr. Gary J. Oliver says the following about your beliefs:

Most people aren't aware of and haven't identified the core beliefs that have an unbelievably powerful impact on virtually every area of their life. In addition to being powerful and complex, your core beliefs, including your level of emotional intelligence, influence virtually every aspect of your life, including the social, mental, physical, and spiritual dimensions. They impact your loves, hates, worries, fears, values, priorities, goals, what you enjoy, who you can trust, the friends that you choose, what you will achieve, what you live for, and what you would be willing to die for. In fact, there is virtually nothing in your life that does not have your core beliefs, including your emotional makeup, as its mainspring.[2]

You have no beliefs in your heart that you did not put there, either of your own volition or by inheritance from your family or by absorbing them from your culture. So if you don't like an area of your life, it's up to you to find better beliefs to improve that area. Your life will change just as fast as your beliefs change.

What Really Causes Your Emotions?

If we want to be strictly accurate, we can never say, "You make me sad," or "You make me afraid with your terrible driving," or "What you said really upset me." Not one of these statements—as well as others like them—is ever true. What happens to you or even what someone does to you never *makes* you happy or sad. There is a step between the event and the emotion that is the true cause of how you feel.

To explain this phenomenon, let's turn to Dr. Albert Ellis, the founder of cognitive therapy. Dr. Ellis developed the famous ABC model to explain how our experiences, beliefs, and actions interact. His model of a three-event sequence that happens every time you feel an emotion such as fear, worry, sadness, or discouragement follows:

A = the **event** that happens to you—good or bad.
B = what you **think** about the event that happens to you.
C = the **feelings** that result from what you think of the event.[3]

Here's how the interaction between belief and action works. When the event happens to you, your brain perceives the experience through one or more of your five senses. In a matter of milliseconds, so fast that you are not aware of the procedure, your brain processes the experience using information stored in the limbic area of your brain or your subconscious mind, which, as previously stated, I like to call your heart, a term we all understand. Your heart interprets the experience by the information it has stored within it. That interpretation produces your feelings about the experience, and your feelings produce your resulting action.

It almost takes a book to describe the process, but it happens instantaneously —faster than the blink of an eye. Because it happens so fast, we are not even aware of a process going on. To our conscious minds it seems that we simply had something happen to us and we responded naturally. It seems to us that only two of the three steps described above were involved—A and C. We experienced the event, which caused us to feel a surge of emotion and react in a certain way. We are unaware that step B was even involved—the invisible step that is really the key to the entire episode. But the truth is, it was actually this intermediate step B that determined our reaction, *and not the original event itself.*

Let me illustrate the process with an example. Let's say you are hurrying outside into your backyard to move your lawn sprinkler. You notice something moving in the grass just beneath your feet, and you freeze. You instantly step back as you realize that you are face to fang with a large black snake. Immediately you feel a surge of fear as adrenalin pumps into your system. Snakes are dangerous. They can kill you. The snake slithers under a small pile of brush you cleaned from the yard, and if you're really brave or stupid, you run to the shed for a hoe. You come back, flush the critter from the brush, and try to dispose of it.

You were aware of only two things happening in your mind: the sensory experience and the emotion. The sensory experience occurred when your eyes saw the movement. The emotion of fear occurred when you identified the movement as a snake. And the fear motivated you to kill the snake. You experienced event A—the sight of the snake—and you felt emotion C—the fear that drove you to action. What you were not aware of was the involvement of step B—the thoughts that came from your *belief*. In spite of the way it seemed, it was not really the seeing of the snake that caused your fear; *it was your belief that some snakes are deadly and this might be one of them.* That belief was lodged in your subconscious—your heart—even before you saw the snake. And it was that belief that caused you to react in fear and kill the snake. To make the concept clearer, let's repeat the same scene, but this time instead of you, it's the head herpetologist at the local zoo who hurries out into his backyard to move his lawn sprinkler. He notices something moving in the grass, and as he draws cautiously closer, he sees that it is a large black snake. Immediately he relaxes, smiles, ignores the reptile, and moves his sprinkler, stepping over the brush pile where the snake hid without giving it a second thought.

Here we have exactly the same sensory experience, but the experience produced an altogether different emotion. Why the difference? The herpetologist had a different belief in his heart. He knew snakes. He knew that there are only four species of harmful snakes in the U.S., and only two of those inhabited his area of the country. He knew the shape and color of all harmful snakes, and the snake in his yard didn't match any of them. Furthermore, he knew that most snakes are not only harmless but also beneficial, keeping certain kinds of rodents and other small pests under control. So he was happy to have such a snake in his backyard.

The same event produced heart-pounding fear in one person and a smile of pleasure in the other. The difference was in their belief systems. One believed most snakes were harmful and had a deathly fear of them; whereas, the other believed that most snakes were beneficial and was happy to have one of the good ones around.

Do you see the point? Our reactions are not caused by what happens to us; they are caused by our beliefs. Emotion C is not caused by experience A; it is caused by belief B. The identical experience can cause a fearful, destructive reaction in a person with a wrong belief and a positive reaction in a person with a right belief. As I quoted earlier from the ancient Greek philosopher Epictetus: "Men are disturbed, not by things, but by *the view* they take of them." Now we can add, "And the view they take of them is determined by their beliefs."

Can you see what a difference your beliefs can make in your life? If you replace your wrong beliefs with right ones, true ones, you will no longer be the victim of your emotions. Changing your beliefs puts you in control of your emotions. Your controlled emotions will produce corrected reactions, which will ensure your own equilibrium and quality of life. No longer will emotions spring untamed from wrong beliefs and take control of you. No longer will you react in fear and damage relationships. You will be in control, and you will react to every situation with proper measure and proper responses.

But, you may wonder, what if a person knows the right belief yet simply can't control what he thinks when the event happens? He knows that most snakes are not dangerous, and he knows the difference between those that are and those that are not. But perhaps he had a bad experience with a dangerous snake in childhood. Perhaps he was bitten and almost died. Or perhaps a close friend or family member was bitten. This person is so conditioned by a long-held belief about snakes that his reaction is automatic and overrides his corrected belief.

Learning new information about snakes is not enough for him to overcome the intuitive reaction to his traumatic childhood experience.

That is, in fact, the case with most of us. We may learn that our old beliefs are wrong and want to replace them. But we find that those old beliefs are so deeply embedded and glued into place by bad experiences that simply knowing better does not immediately change our behavior. That's why I say the concept of changing your beliefs is both simple and hard. It's simple for an open-minded person to learn a new principle or to find that an old belief is wrong. It's not always so simple to make that new belief operational in his or her life. That may take time and concentrated effort. But I can tell you from my own experience, it is well worth every ounce of effort and every minute of time you invest. It can change your life. And you'll know specifically how to change your beliefs and what ones to change by the time you finish this book.

It took me almost a year to really understand how to apply this new truth to my everyday life. But after I learned to apply it to my deepest beliefs, I was amazed to find that I was managing my own emotions any time I chose to. The big change for me came when I faced a big, traumatic event in my life. A heart attack. That was my letter A—the event—a 100 percent blockage of my heart. My letter C—my emotional reaction—was pretty bad at first. My emotions were in shambles. I had just experienced a heart attack, and now I faced major heart surgery. I was scared. I could die!

But then I remembered what I was learning about beliefs and decided to apply it to my present situation. What was the letter B here? What beliefs did I have in my heart that were causing my feelings of panic? As I examined those beliefs, I realized that they did not square up with principles that I knew to be true. As a Christian, I knew I was in God's hands. I knew a better life awaited me at death and, like the apostle Paul, it didn't matter whether I lived or died; I would be with the Lord either way. And I knew that all things work together for the good of those who love the Lord. Live or die, I couldn't lose. I knew these things, yet there I lay in that hospital bed, feeling panic and distress at my upcoming heart surgery. I knew the truth; I believed the right things; yet like most people who don't know these truths, I had skipped from letter A to letter C and ignored letter B. If I knew the truth and believed it, why couldn't I control my own thinking?

This is where my journey became fun for me. I stumbled upon three verses in the Bible that really made a difference. I began to experiment with these verses to see how long it would take to get them embedded into my heart as beliefs.

We can rejoice, too, when we run into problems and trials, for we know that they help us develop endurance. And endurance develops strength of character, and character strengthens our confident hope . . . And this hope will not lead to disappointment. For we know how dearly God loves us, because he has given us the Holy Spirit to fill our hearts with his love [*through this trial*].

—Romans 5:3–5 NLT

These verses told me that enduring trials is like winning a trophy. When you endure difficulties with God's grace, you accomplish something really important and wonderful. What? Difficulties and trails are good for me? Well, I guess I knew that. After all, it was in the Bible, and I had read it many times. But I had never needed to stop and think about what it really meant. I suppose I vaguely thought that trials are really bad things, but when they come, Christians should make the best of them. But here Paul tells us that they are really, really, really positive things. So positive that we should not merely endure them but rejoice that they came our way. But I was facing open-heart surgery. Surely God didn't expect me to rejoice in *that*.

Yet as I reread this passage over and over, the truth began to penetrate my mind. The apostle himself tells us in the passage exactly what kind of good comes from trials. Anyone who experiences a bad time or difficulty actually receives more of the qualities of endurance and patience, more of God's character especially (give that a thought for a few seconds), and more hope about the future. You will always get more of God's *love* poured into your heart by God's Spirit. Is that good or what?

I liked and agreed with those ideas, but just knowing them didn't seem to help me. I also found other Bible passages with a similar message about rejoicing in the pain of trials.[4] I memorized and reviewed them over and over, day after day. I kept this up until I knew each verse perfectly and understood what each word meant in the original language. I became passionate about memorizing these simple but powerful verses. Mind you, in all my sixty-plus years, I had never done this before. I had certainly memorized a lot of Bible verses, but never had I *chewed* on them day and night as I did these (Jeremiah 15:16). The result was that these passages began to seep into my heart. Their meaning became much more than merely principles I knew to be true; they became deep beliefs, thoroughly embedded in my heart. And within a few weeks, most of my fears slipped away. Why? Because I had inserted a sound B between my A and C, and that new belief enabled me to gain control of my negative and fearful emotions about any future surgery or any of the other trials I was experiencing.

After my recovery, when I had been back on the job for more than a month, some of my staff and family members commented that they hadn't heard me complain in a while. I paused to reflect and realized that I couldn't remember when I had last complained, griped, or blamed someone for my problems.

This discovery excited me. If I could make this kind of dramatic change in one area of my life, I could make it in others. Just think of the new life I would have if in all areas I got in control of my automatic negative feelings and acted accordingly. I would be a new man—never again the victim of out-of-control emotions but always in control of my own happiness. And best of all, I would know that God must be pleased because I was hiding his words within my heart. Therefore, I knew that he would be in control of my thoughts, words, and actions. I could then truly call him my King. I would trust him, submit to his ways, and thus love him with all of my heart. Immediately I rushed to look at other problem areas of my life and found Bible verses that would help me get those areas under control. For the next two years I did this consistently. I kept meditating or thinking deeply about just a few Bible verses each day until their words and meaning became embedded in my heart. Today I'm still rehearsing those same Bible verses, and my past negative attitudes that led to complaining, harmful words, angry reactions, worry, and other negative emotions have virtually disappeared. (You can see my list of more than one hundred powerful, life-changing verses in appendix 5.)

> It seemed that it had taken only a month for my revitalized thoughts to reach my heart as new beliefs. The key is rehearsing the few verses you know over and over again as it's explained in Deuteronomy 6:4–9.

Don't get me wrong; I don't mean I have perfectly conquered all my negative emotions or actions. To think that would be foolish and unbiblical. Read the apostle Paul's struggle in Romans 7. Once in a while I do get irritated at someone or something, but those irritated feelings now last only seconds because, immediately, my faithful verses rush into my mind, and I begin to feel the effects of my new beliefs that control my new thoughts. The result is a feeling of peace I never imagined I could experience. Am I excited about this new life of mine or what?

Let me tell you a little more about what it's like. Because of my new beliefs, this old man in his late sixties feels like he's forty again. I've been through several surgeries and even a kidney transplant. My weight is exactly where I want it today because I found that my weight problems for more than fifty years had been caused by my erroneous beliefs. I discovered some of the main beliefs that keep people overweight, and I changed the overweight beliefs I harbored. As a result, my weight dropped exactly to where it should be for a person of my height.[5]

I woke up the other morning with a major worry attack racking my stomach, and within seconds I was able to overcome it and go right back to sleep with calmness and peace. What enabled me to do this? I have been changing my fear-and-worry beliefs over the past three years. This is the truth: I simply don't worry anymore for more than a few seconds. Then it's gone so fast that I sort of miss all those old feelings of anxiety and fear in which I used to wallow. (Not really.) When you reach chapter 12, you'll discover that expressing gratefulness in all circumstances vaporizes worry. I have found it impossible to hold thanksgiving and worry within at the same time.[6]

The Key to Changing Your Beliefs

In the account of my own personal experience above, did you pick up on the key to turning my life around? Yes, I had to change my beliefs, but it took more than that. Even when I had consciously changed my beliefs, I still fought with negative emotions. It was only when those new beliefs really settled deeply into my subconscious mind—into my heart—that I experienced real transformation. I can say that I believe something and yet never think about it, never make it a part of me, and go on letting my mind dwell on things inconsistent with that belief. If this is all I do, no change will come. Those beliefs you need in your heart will never help you unless you embed them deeply and meaningfully. When your consistent, passionate thoughts are exercised consciously over and over for days, weeks, and months, they will become branded on your heart, and that's when they will form your true beliefs.

You've heard people say, "Be careful what you ask for; you just might get it." Well, it can also be said, "Be careful what you think about; you just might get it." Your consistent thoughts become your beliefs, and your beliefs control everything about you. Picture your subconscious mind—your spiritual heart—as a valentine's heart.

Then picture that every time you have a thought, that thought causes a small scratch on your heart. That scratch is the start of your belief. Week after week or month after month with that same thought repeating itself over and over, the scratch becomes a groove (a stronger belief). Then the grooves become paths (powerful beliefs), and the paths become roads, and the roads become four-lane freeways (strongholds). When our key beliefs are set within our hearts like four-lane freeways, they control everything about us.

Thoughts Turning into Beliefs

I read a sad story of a man whose mother died of cancer when he was about forty-five. Knowing that her type of cancer was hereditary, he panicked and began to believe that he might have this same cancer. Doctors assured him that there were no signs of cancer in his body, but his belief was so strong and passionate that within a year he was dead from the same kind of cancer that killed his mother.[7] When we think of life today with all its complexities, and when we see news about kids becoming more unruly, more marriages melting down, more sexual predators stalking about, more acts of violence, and more depression and suicides, it can be discouraging. But if we could help create a society, schools, and churches where people were more tolerant, kinder and patient, and less angry with each other and had more control over sexual thoughts and actions, wouldn't life be a lot brighter for all of us? Wouldn't you like to be able to walk anywhere in America and feel safe? It could happen if people would merely adopt this simple concept of changing bad or destructive beliefs.

> You are as happy as the beliefs you have created in your own heart! If you're not happy, you have no one to blame but yourself.

What would you like to see changed about yourself? Are your eating habits out of control?[8] Do you say hurtful things to your loved ones? Do you lust or immerse yourself in pornography and wish you could stop? (In chapter 5, you'll read about how I ended lustful thoughts.) How would you like to complain less, gripe less, or worry less? Maybe you are married and experience too many arguments, or your kids are too disrespectful of you. Maybe you are in a second marriage and wish you could lessen the hurtful words from your mate about many of the blending problems with your kids or soften some of the major conflicts commonly associated with second marriages. Wouldn't you like to see such a refreshing change of behavior in your children that you want to check their foreheads for a fever? All of this can happen. You can get new control over so many areas of your life simply by changing your beliefs.

Our Designer Has Given Us the Method to Change

You are in charge of all your thoughts. I know this statement flies in the face of some modern deterministic psychological studies of the brain. They would have you believe that the spiritual heart does not exist; that it's merely a function of the brain, which is merely an organic machine that operates according to immutable laws of science. They leave no place for the power of a God or a conscious heart that chooses independently of the brain what subjects to which the mind will attend.

Some modern scientific psychology theories can become a person's deeply held beliefs, which then can force God from a person's life. But for me, I have seen such wonderful changes, I have chosen to believe what my choice of God has been saying for thousands of years: love me and love others; this is the greatest belief you can have. You *can* choose. You *can* change. You can believe what you choose to believe. If you doubt this, all you have to do is try it. Do as I did. See for yourself how *chewing* on powerful, selected Bible verses day after day throws out your old destructive beliefs and leaves you more empowered to manage your own life and be happier and more satisfied than you ever imagined.

If you are unhappy about anything in your life, discover what erroneous belief you have stored within your heart and begin changing your thoughts. Do this and you will begin to see major changes as soon as your new thoughts reach the branding stage in your heart. If you can't figure out exactly what your old destructive beliefs are, that's okay. Just start hiding a few of God's main powerful and living words within, and not only will you start reflecting more of God's character, but you'll also see the very things you don't like about yourself fading away. Just this week, in the middle of editing this book, I had an experience with my staff members in which I interpreted their actions as trying to sabotage one of my major passions. I thought they were trying to get out of working with a major company that teaches kids better than anyone how to memorize God's words: Awana. It really upset me, and I scolded all of them. But by about nine o'clock that evening, I sat alone in my favorite chair and listened to my emotions. Emotions are only data telling us what we believe. As I gathered the facts, I realized that I was traveling to meet the staff at Awana in just four days, and my accusation was not true—my stress just melted away within seconds. "Then you will know the truth, and the truth will set you free" (John 8:32). As I sat there for a few more minutes, I got up and e-mailed my apology to everyone on my staff and went peacefully to bed. My point here is that whether you like it or not, what you hide within your heart will come to your mind and either calm you or further upset you.

The kind of new thoughts you put into your heart are very important, of course. It will do you no good to replace one false belief with another. You can't just take any thought that comes from today's experts, psychological researchers, TV commentators, world leaders, or even most religions. I use only those thoughts that were given to mankind from the God of the Bible. I take his most important thoughts into my heart and form my new beliefs from his words.

It's worth mentioning again: "I have hidden your word in my heart that I might not sin against you" (Psalm 119:11).

Our society is disintegrating, and many Christians are unwittingly caught up in its thinking. Do you know what your children see and hear all day long on TV, radio, iPods, and the Internet or even from their peers? Let me assure you that the music kids listen to is reaching their hearts. Just last week I asked my granddaughter Hannah to sing and dance to a new tune she was learning from *Hannah Montana*. I really liked the words about how a kid can choose to do what is right. But have *you* listened to what your kids are listening to?

What they see on TV or on the Internet is affecting the way they think and react. Please don't put your head in the sand when it comes to regulating what your kids are exposed to. This is deadly serious. Most of us realize that our society is in big trouble. Many Christians are in big trouble because the world's values have become embedded in their hearts. But they have no idea that it's happened, and so they're oblivious to the danger.

Most people in our nation see no real difference between themselves and the way many Christians live today. The lives of Christians and non-Christians alike are filled with worry, anxiety, fear, anger, revenge, boasting, pride, judging, divorces, and the list can go on and on. It saddens me that most Christians demonstrate about the same self-control over the basic areas of life as the world does.

I want the world to see me as I am becoming and understand how powerful Scripture can be in managing how we act and live. Our task is to warn, alert, and spread the idea that the solution is found in what we put into our hearts. Just as Solomon warned us, above all else, guard your heart. Please pause to consider just what the wisest man who ever lived was telling us. King Solomon had everything a person could want; he could do anything he wanted to do and experience any pleasure he chose to experience. And yet he told us that above all else, nothing is more important in life than to *guard your heart*. Why? Because your heart is the wellspring of your life. Out of it flows the essence of who you are (Proverbs 4:23).

Today we are in a fierce battle for the heart, and I'm afraid that, on the whole, many Christians are losing that battle. Let's stop running in the rat race and begin doing what Solomon told us to do. Start doing the one important thing that can make a real difference in your life. Start guarding your heart.

You may feel like despairing because you feel you can't make a difference in the battle for the heart. You might not be able to change the destructive beliefs that saturate our culture, but you can make a difference. You can change yourself. You can set the example. You can become a beacon, a lighthouse for others who will see how you got your life under control. And they will wonder how you did it. When you truly desire to reflect the character of Christ, you will begin a personal campaign to change the beliefs in your own heart. And believe me, the world will see the difference. Don't be concerned about changing the hearts of others—your mate, children, siblings, parents, or friends. You can change only one person—yourself. Start there, and when you change yourself, you may be surprised at the change you begin to see in others around you.

Along those lines is a great quote by an unknown monk from AD 1100:

When I was a young man, I wanted to change the world. I found it was difficult to change the world, so I tried to change my nation. When I found I couldn't change the nation, I began to focus on my town. I couldn't change the town, and as an older man, I tried to change my family.

Now, as an old man, I realize the only thing I can change is myself, and suddenly I realize that if long ago I had changed myself, I could have made an impact on my family. My family and I could have made an impact on our town. Their impact could have changed the nation, and I could indeed have changed the world.

In this chapter, I have shown you the basic principle of changing your beliefs and how that change will put you in control of your emotions and actions. Read on, and I will show you how to prepare your life before you start branding new beliefs on your heart. You'll see how to make the *soil* of your life ready to receive those all-important new beliefs.

Four
Preparing Your Heart for Powerful Changes

There is nothing more important in life than getting ready to improve your heart. If you desire to be a lawyer, you prepare yourself with years of study; if you want to learn how to swim, you learn the strokes, learn to breathe properly, and practice. If you want to date the homecoming queen, forget it, unless you've learned from your mom how to treat a girl. Anything worth having requires preparation.

It's the same when you desire to change your heart. You don't just snap your fingers and expect it to happen. It requires careful preparation. When you want new flowers to come up in your flowerbed, you don't just go to Wal-Mart, buy the seeds, come back home, and scatter them over the place where you want them to grow. If that's all you do, you're doing nothing but feeding birds. You know you have to prepare the ground to receive the seeds. You dig it up, pull out all the grass and weeds that have encroached on the space, add a few bags of rich soil, add a little fertilizer, dig furrows for the seeds at just the right depth, then drop them in place, cover them up, and water them.

Then you come back day after day to add more water and pull out the weeds, and as the little sprigs begin to grow, you protect them from weather and keep your dog and cat out of the flowerbed. It takes considerable time and trouble to grow flowers. But you don't mind doing it because when those brilliant blooms come up, adding dazzling accents to your house and yard, you know it's worth every ounce of effort. (By the way, I've never planted flowers, but people who have time and do tell me this is how it's done.)

We think nothing of spending just a little time and trouble every day to get flowers to grow, but isn't it strange that when it comes to making major changes in our lives, we often seem to expect instant results with little effort? We want to toss the new belief into our hearts and expect it to blossom spontaneously and immediately, changing our thinking, our responses, and our actions with no cultivating and preparatory work at all. I'm not telling you anything new; you know that it just doesn't work that way. Your heart must be prepared to receive new beliefs, and that will take a little work on your part. But I assure you, the result will be worth the effort. As you plant a new belief, it will take root and produce brilliant blossoms in your life. You'll be willing to do it because God tells us through Solomon that it is the number one thing to do each and every day of our lives.

Replacing old bad beliefs is like replacing old bad habits. They become engrained, and they don't root out easily. You bring the new belief into your heart and begin to consciously act on it, but the old one is still there, and it keeps rearing its ugly head on every occasion that could activate it. For a while you must consciously repress, ignore, or tolerate the old belief and keep building the new one until it replaces the old. This is because memorizing and chewing on a new Bible verse to form the new belief doesn't come naturally at first. According to psychologist Dr. Archibald Hart, it usually takes more than three weeks of constant effort before a new habit can replace an old one.[1] That is true no matter how long you have held the old habit. The same is also true with beliefs, which are really the bases of our habits. You can replace the old ones with new ones but not without effort and not without a period of time in which you consciously and repeatedly exercise the new words that form your new belief. In time the new belief seeps into the subconscious and the old belief gives up, lets go, and withers away like a dried-up weed. At that point, the new belief is like a new habit. You no longer have to attend to it consciously. It becomes part of who you are and part of your mode of behavior.

I have discovered three important factors that can speed up the process of embedding a new belief in your heart and getting rid of the old one. Those factors are surrender, passion, and daily immersion.

Surrender

I began my ministry with passion, conviction, and total focus on God. As a result, he was faithful to reward me in every area of my life. I had money, national television fame, prosperity, widespread distribution of my books and tapes, grandchildren, and more rewards than I could ever count. The blessings came so fast and so abundantly that I didn't have the wisdom to manage all of it. Before long, my focus began to shift. I began to spend more of my time managing and planning how to get more of these rewards instead of seeking the Rewarder. I had too much money and too much property—too much of everything for my brain and personality type to manage. As a result, it began to ruin me. It came to the point where most of my time was consumed with managing what I had. As I took my eyes off God, I began to lose my sparkle, and his light dimmed within me.

It took a few disasters to wake me up to what was happening. But when it hit me, I did what our presidents do when they are elected to office. They put all they own into a blind trust so they can concentrate solely on their new responsibility— the welfare of the country. I put my possessions out of my hands and turned them over to my wife and a committee so I could concentrate solely on my service to Christ and others. In other words, I surrendered. I quit trying to be in control of my possessions and essentially gave them up. I did this so I could surrender myself to him, submitting to his control. My life was no longer my own. I surrendered it to God and put myself in his hands.[2]

In our culture the emphasis is always on winning. If there's anything we Americans want to be, it's winners. We don't like the idea of surrender because it seems the opposite of winning. It looks to us like loss or weakness. When we surrender we wave the white flag and concede that the fight is over. In World War II, Japan and Germany surrendered when they realized that America and its allies were stronger than they were, and to continue the fight could mean total annihilation. But when you surrender to God, the opposite happens. You don't lose; you win. You become strong. When you give up and surrender, you find your life instead of losing it.

This is another of those wonderful paradoxes we find when we come to God. He is always fresh and surprising. In the spiritual world, if you want to gain your life, you must lose it. If you want to be first, you must position yourself to be last. If you want to be rich, you must become poor in spirit (an attitude of being humble, helpless, a beggar). On Sundays our pastor loves to say, "Grab a cup of Starbucks in our coffee shop, find a seat, then *die*." It sounds shocking, but dying to all of your selfish desires is the only way to live. The only true way we can find the fulfillment Jesus offers in the Christian life is to die daily to ourselves and accept the real life he offers. That's what it means to surrender. In other words, you die to life as you want it or as the world advises you to live, and live only by what God says in his Word. He designed us and he wrote the instruction manual. When you and I brand his words upon our hearts, we begin to enjoy the life God designed us to have. The bottom line—and I will mention this over and over so that it sticks in your mind—is this: his highest will for us is twofold—to love and crave him and to love and crave to serve others. That's it. To surrender to these two commands is to find life at its best. The apostle Paul said it this way: "The entire law is summed up in a single command: 'Love your neighbor as yourself.'"³ Life becomes so much simpler when we realize that this one thing pleases God, and we're loving him when we love others.⁴

When we surrender to him we give up trying to figure out the best and most fruitful ways of living our lives. When we surrender we give up and admit that our way has gotten us into a deep rut, or even into addictions, misery, unhappiness, bitterness, or a destructive lifestyle. When we go our own way we are fighting against God, for he designed us to function with him in the driver's seat. All I'm really describing here is the word *sin*. Sin is doing life your way and ignoring God's ways. When you're the driver, you are in sin, plain and simple. So when we surrender, we stop fighting against God. We realize he is more powerful, and he has us pinned to the mat. The greatest part of doing his will is that not only does he give us his *love* when we ask him, but we get to use his *love* to love him and others. To me, that's a no-brainer.

When you surrender to God, you discover the Creator's Manual of how you were designed to live. You admit that many of those beliefs you have accumulated and embedded in your heart are wrong. You may have picked them up from the culture, your parents, your friends, or your teachers. When you surrender, you willingly choose to embed into your heart the beliefs God gives you and start all over again, this time living where those new beliefs lead you—to a more loving and eternal life.

In spite of Oprah Winfrey's success as host of a Chicago morning talk show, one ambition of hers had remained unfulfilled. She had always wanted to be an actress, but that goal had eluded her. She had tried and tried, but the doors remained closed. So finally, with great sadness, she gave it up. One day while doing her daily walk on a running track, tears ran uncontrolled down her face as she told God that she was giving up her long-held dream of acting. She was through trying. If God wanted her to act, he would have to open the door. To affirm her decision, she sang the song made popular in the Billy Graham crusades, "All to Jesus, I surrender . . . I surrender all."[5] While she was singing out loud and alone, a phone call came from Steven Spielberg, inviting Oprah to play a part in his upcoming movie, *The Color Purple*. As we all know she got the part. And the rest—the story of her extraordinary career—is history. Oprah is now one of the most popular and successful women in the world.[6]

Surrendering to God is like opening your hand to receive his gift. As long as you keep your hand clutched on those few stones you've managed to buy or earn, he can't give you the diamonds he has for you. You must open your hand, which means dropping everything you hold in it. You must surrender those beliefs about you that come from the world in order to receive the beliefs that come from God.

So if you are to open your hand and surrender to God, just how and what should you surrender? Let's explore the answers to this question.

Surrender daily.

This is of huge importance. I find that my natural tendency is to return to my old nature or to the beliefs of the world in a relatively short time if I'm not reviewing God's words daily.

I finally understand that *daily* is the key to success in changing your beliefs. You must chew on God's words daily in order to embed them into your heart. And leave it to a thirteen-year-old to teach me this lesson. My grandson Michael had memorized five sections of Scripture. Then because of school activities, his parents' vacations, and his golfing, he neglected reviewing these verses. He thought, as I did a few years ago, that it's okay to take a break from reminding ourselves of our most important Bible verses each day. Some of us think, *Once God's words are in my heart, I don't have to review them every day, do I?* But to neglect

> *Daily* is the key to this entire book!

his words for even a week can lead us back to our old ways. It's what we think about all day long that reaches our hearts as beliefs, and if your mind is not dwelling on God's words, it's dwelling on the concerns of the world. This is exactly what I did in the nineties when I almost lost my entire relationship with God because I spent so much time managing the financial rewards God had given me.

Several sections of Scripture warn us about neglecting his words and not having a daily habit of reviewing them. Oh, how easy it is to allow the weeds, cares, and lack of watering and nurturing to choke out God's words from our hearts. When this happens, the world's beliefs and our natural flesh take over our lives quickly. Carefully ponder the powerful admonition that Moses gave us to heed if we are to bloom as God designed us.

In Deuteronomy 6:4–9 he essentially says that parents are to teach their kids God's number one commandment of loving him with all their heart and loving his words each day while they drive with them in the car, walk with them, sit down to eat, lie down to sleep, or walk into the house. It's hard to miss the *daily* idea here, isn't it? And there are three other powerful scripture passages that remind us to daily review God's most important truths in order to enjoy his successes and abundance.[7]

Surrender your mind.

No, this doesn't mean you are to give up thinking. God gave us minds, and he expects us to use them for his glory. He wants to think through you, but not for you. The power of your thoughts is what changes your beliefs. And as I have already pointed out, your beliefs control your thoughts, moods, words, and actions. Your mate, boss, children, or parents do not control what you think or believe. Scripture tells us that out of our *hearts* come the issues of life.[8] Your thoughts directly affect what is in your heart. What you think all day long eventually is what you become. When you grab hold of this truth, you'll stop trying to change others and better accept your circumstances. Only you can change your thought patterns.

The only way to change your thought patterns for the better is to surrender your own thoughts and replace them with God's. It's like throwing out all the old mismatched, worn, uncomfortable, and unsightly furniture in your mind and replacing it with matched pieces from God's warehouse. When I realized that I needed to completely refurnish my mind, I determined to clean out all the junk thoughts and bring in only those that were God-approved. To guide my refurnishing I turned to Philippians 4:8: "Whatever is true, whatever is noble, whatever is right, whatever is pure, whatever is lovely, whatever is admirable—if anything is excellent or praiseworthy—*think [only] about such things*" (emphasis mine). I determined never to bring in a new thought without running it through this eight-point checklist:

☐ Is it true?	☐ Is it beautiful?
☐ Is it noble?	☐ Is it admirable?
☐ Is it right?	☐ Is it excellent?
☐ Is it pure?	☐ Is it praiseworthy?

If the thought passes these tests I know it's from God, and I furnish my mind with it. If any thought is not consistent with these criteria, I throw the thought out and go on to thoughts that meet God's standard. I like thinking the truth all day long, every day.

If you fail to surrender your mind to God and furnish your mind with thoughts that do not meet his standard, you will be vulnerable to what I teach as the "Confirmation Bias Principle." Without a standard of right thinking, we tend to make decisions without a solid basis and then seek evidence to support those decisions. In other words, we confirm our biases. For example, if you decide that your wife is an intolerable nag, then every time she opens her mouth your mind will hear whatever she says as a constant, bothersome drip. You will not hear the truth; you will hear only what you believe. If she straightens your collar before you leave for work, you will not see the act as helpful, but as critical of your ability to dress. Your erroneous belief will confirm your bias, and you will interpret everything that happens according to that belief, even if the belief is wrong.

If, on the other hand, you furnish your mind with beliefs that pass the eight-point test above, you will believe your wife is a masterpiece, personally autographed by God, who overlooks no detail to present you at your best. And you will see real and true evidence to support that belief that you were blind to before. Later in chapter 12, I'll show you how to develop the belief that an irritating mate can actually be very good for you. Once you see this truth and apply it for a little while, your mate's irritating habits will no longer bother you. I know that sounds hard to believe, but I will show you how it happened with me.

By refurnishing my mind with God's truth, I am now able to manage all my moods. I wake up each morning with the overwhelming peace that comes from knowing that nothing or no one can control how I feel today. Because my beliefs are solidly based in God's own truth, I don't give away to others or to circumstances the power *to make me* happy or unhappy.

Surrender your expectations.

In the 1990s, I reached a point where I did a really dumb thing. I told God that I had done enough for him. It was time for me to reap the rewards for all the work I'd done for him and retire, turning my ministry over to others. But while I retired, I didn't let go of my expectations for how all I had built over my career would be run. Therefore I hovered over those who were now running my ministry, worrying when decisions were made that went against my better judgment or when debts were incurred that I felt overburdened the ministry and jeopardized its stability. As you can imagine, the result of these expectations was stress. Serious stress. I worried myself into a major heart attack and kidney failure, resulting in a kidney transplant from my son Michael.

The transplant got my attention. After the surgery I resurrendered my life to God for the third time. I opened my heart and mind to him again, probably because I had no other options. He let me know that I can never retire from his service. I cannot find happiness sitting on my accomplishments and claiming to have done my share. So I surrendered my retirement, my self-will, my needless worry, and my expectations for my ministry, and turned back to God—which is where he wanted me in the first place. He wanted me back where I had started, seeking him and him alone. So I went back to my ministry work, and within a few months my wife and I took over the headship of our ministry for the second time, and the stress eased. I was back where I belonged—serving others full-time. Had I not gone through all that stress and difficulty and then surrendered my life back to him, I probably would not have understood the principles I'm setting forth in this book.

Here's the simple definition of what stress is: the gap between what you expect in each area of your life and what you are actually getting in each of those areas. For example, you expect your mate to hug you ten times per day. But if you're only getting two hugs per day, you'll be stressed because you're missing eight hugs. My stress was caused by the gap between what I expected within my ministry and what was actually happening. If reality does not meet your expectations, worry and concern set in and cause unhealthy changes in body chemistry. We are all familiar with the effects of adrenaline on the body in moments of immediate stress when we are in danger or when we are called on to perform a serious action. The pulse races, neck hairs stand on end, and energy seems packed into every fiber of our body. What is less apparent to us is another stress hormone called cortisol, which is also produced by the adrenal glands. Cortisol enters the bloodstream more slowly but lingers longer. Normally, after the stress-inducing incident is over or dealt with, cortisol levels drop back to normal. But if the stress lingers, so does the cortisol, throwing body chemistry out of balance and doing damage to tissues and organs.[9]

Short bursts of cortisol in brief moments of stress won't hurt you. If you are driving to an important meeting and expect to arrive five minutes before ten but you get stuck in traffic, your stress will be relatively short—amounting to the time between ten o'clock and your actual arrival at ten fifteen. The cortisol infusion dissipates and no damage is done. But suppose you expect your company to give you the next promotion because you're in line for it. Instead, it goes to a person who works under you. That's a huge gap between

CHANGE YOUR HEART, CHANGE YOUR LIFE

expectation and reality. Your bitterness, anger, or disappointment over missing the promotion may produce long-lasting stress, causing cortisol to seep into your bloodstream and linger there.

We can't avoid long periods of stress. It's with us all the time as part of our everyday living. Even getting up in the morning produces stress, and stressful incidents, small or large, will happen throughout every day. But while we can't avoid stress, we can manage it. The idea is to shorten your stress time as much as possible. Health manuals offer fine techniques for relieving stress—breathe deeply, take time off, mix with friends, get enough sleep, exercise regularly, eat right, and do what you love. These are all good suggestions, but I've found a better way, and it has brought my stress level down to zero most of the time.

Not long after my health crisis, I was strongly drawn to Colossians 3:1–17. The first three verses in particular helped me reduce my stress by reducing my expectations: "Since, then, you have been raised with Christ, set your hearts on things above, where Christ is seated at the right hand of God. *Set your minds on things above, not on earthly things.* For you died, and your life is now hidden with Christ in God" (emphasis mine). If I have died to myself and have placed my life in the hands of God, then I have surrendered to him. I have given over to him all my expectations, and now I trust him with the results. If you give yourself over to God, does it make sense to worry about what comes next? I could lose everything and it wouldn't matter for long, because I would still have God. He is now all I really want. He can give me whatever success he wishes in his own good time. I'm not expecting anything, nor do I have a timetable for my future dreams of ministry. That also used to kill me: "I need it now, God. Hurry up!" I have surrendered to his timetable. He is in control.

You cannot imagine how much that surrender relaxed me and took the pressure from my life. I wanted to seek God and God alone, even if it meant I would never make another dime publishing a book, speaking, or running my ministry. He is now everything to me. I wait for him to meet all my needs and fill me up with the fullness of himself. And when I learned to relax in him and focus on living with and for him alone, everything else in life became less important to me, and the stress of expecting my own wants to be met simply slipped away. It happened to me, and it can happen to you. It's absolutely true that if you seek God and his righteousness, then everything else will be added to you.[10]

Once this principle lodges in your heart, it can give you a virtually stress-free life.

I surrendered to the reality that God is my protector and is aware of everything in my life. I accept as literal truth the fact that God is always filtering what hits me daily. Now as I go through my normal share of stressful difficulties every day, my heart relaxes when I come to my senses and realize that God is really in control of my life. He knows and understands what's best for me. In no way can I totally understand why certain things happen to me, but I can know that he is concerned about me in every way and is guiding me toward transformation into his image. He is constantly molding me into a more loving person so that I can love others with greater effectiveness.

No matter what happens in the course of a day, a week, or a year, ultimately I need not worry. My time is in his hands, and I trust him to guide my every step. I now see that those things in my past that seemed so terrible at the moment happened for a reason greater than I could know. As I've said, it hasn't been possible for me to worry while at the same time I'm expressing gratefulness to him for all of my circumstances.

In all circumstances, I can trust in God's sovereignty. He knows and cares for each sparrow he created, and I can easily trust that whatever happens to me does not escape his knowledge.[11] Not only is he taking care of me, but he also has a plan to use everything that happens—even the bad things—for my good and his glory, which means all the bad things that happen to us are really for our own good. I'll have much more to say about this in chapter 12.

Surrendering to God is the best thing you can do for yourself and those around you. He has the best plan for your life, so why not put him in control?

Passion

After surrender, passion is the second factor that can facilitate the process of embedding a new belief into your heart. I'm sure you remember falling head-over-heels in love with a new girlfriend or boyfriend in high school. It happened to me many times. And when it did, she would consume all my waking thoughts and even my dreams. I remember loving to drive by the house of a new girlfriend just to see where she lived. My heart would pound like a drum as I passed by. For that moment, I was so in love that nothing in the world was as important to me as that one girl. She was—even if temporarily—my passion.

Your passion is what means the most to you, what consumes your being and occupies most of your waking thoughts. You can identify your passion by what you think about as you drift off to asleep at night and when you wake up in the morning. Our lives get out of kilter when we invest our passions in the wrong things. This is why the Bible tells us that a wealthy man often has trouble falling asleep at night. "The abundance of a rich man permits him no sleep" (Ecclesiastes 5:12). His passion is often invested in all his stuff, and it can easily consume him.

Whatever consumes you is your passion, and all too often we place our passion in things that do us harm. That is why it is so important to examine our deepest beliefs and discover whether what we hold as valuable in our hearts is really worthy of our passion.

As I've told you, when I surrendered to God, new beliefs entered my heart. I began to believe that my life was not my own to control, and I placed myself in God's hands and trusted him. At about this time I remembered something I had read in the book *Think and Grow Rich* by Napoleon Hill. He said that one of the major factors in producing wealth is passion. You have to go for it with all your heart. Wealth was no longer my primary interest, but I have found that the principle of passion works equally well in any pursuit. So I made the pursuit of God my passion. I decided it was not enough merely to passively surrender to him; I determined to crave him with all my heart, soul, mind, and strength. Oh, by the way, isn't that God's greatest commandment?

With my new passion I plunged into reading the Bible as never before. I began to memorize verses that would help me overcome the wrong beliefs I held in my heart. I repeated key verses over and over, every time I had the slightest break when my mind was free. In the past I would always turn on the radio every time I drove my car. But now if I find myself stuck in traffic or waiting for a light to change, I review my scripture verses. I do the same at other odd moments when my mind is free, such as waiting for my wife to finish shopping, taking a morning walk, or even walking out to the mailbox. I repeat scripture verses that I want lodged in my heart or I continue reviewing verses already branded to my heart.

It may surprise you that I don't have to make myself do this. I never tell myself, "Now, Gary, you have to become more disciplined and memorize more Scripture." No, when your values start changing, you have a new belief about the crucially important truth of guarding your heart; you do these things out of *want to*, not from *got to*. When you develop passion, it replaces the need for deliberate effort. Just as it was a joy for me as a high school kid to drive miles out of the way just to pass by my girlfriend's house, it's now a joy for me to spend every available moment drinking God's words into my heart. The belief of guarding my heart has become the key to my new passion.

I know that if you have not had the experiences or seen the same needs I have, all this may not resonate with you, at least not yet. You may be thinking— as I used to think—that scripture memory is a real chore and has little value other than being able to show off your Bible knowledge to your small group. I understand. Been there, done that. But I hope as you read on through this book, I can show you just how life changing it can be to hide God's Word in your heart. So don't despair. Your passion will come when you see the need clearly. If you do this, trust me, a time will come in your life when you'll find the time and expend the effort, and it won't even seem like work. You will actually want to focus on God and his will for you all the time.

You do have to put out the effort at first, of course. You have to want those new beliefs in your heart, and you have to want to change your life so that the old beliefs don't keep messing up your relationships and your joy. Once you see the value in surrendering to God and allowing him to move into your life, your passion will begin to come. Your passion for anything will always emerge naturally in equal proportion to the value you put on it. That's why it's so crucially important for you to value the right thing. "For where your treasure is, there your heart will be also."[12] Passion builds upon itself. The more passionate you become, the more passionate you will become.

Immersion in Your New Beliefs

I want to briefly make one more point before I leave this chapter on preparing your heart to receive new beliefs. You can't embed new beliefs into your heart by giving sporadic attention to them. You must attend to the content of your new beliefs often and continually, and you must really expose yourself to their full meaning and immerse yourself in the fullness of your new belief.

It's like what I see many people do when they decide they want to experience nature. They want to get out into the wilds of campsites and mountains and rivers and really get close to the natural elements of our planet in their raw form. So what do they do? They buy a big motor home and furnish it with everything they have in their house—a big bed, a refrigerator, a TV complete with satellite dish, hot and cold running water, a shower, air conditioning, and a bathroom with a flushing toilet. Then they go to the campsite at the national park, park their motor home on a concrete slab, and hook up to the water line, sewer line, and electricity. They can now experience nature without having to bother with the inconvenience of sleeping bags, getting dirty, and campfire smoke stinging their eyes or with hauling water from the stream. In fact, they can now go camping without ever having to step outside their camper. And when they return home they commend themselves for having gotten away from it all and really experiencing nature.

But if they didn't sit by a campfire at night, take a long walk through the quiet pine trees, and smell cedar bark, did they *get away from it all?* They may have taken it all with them. Carrying their furnishings and previous comforts completely insulated them from nature. While they may have looked at the pine trees from their window or viewed the lake from their window, they always returned to their insulated environment where nature could have no effect on them.

It pains me when I see people treating their new beliefs in the same way. They realize the need to get away from their old patterns, and this means submitting themselves to fresh, new beliefs. But instead of getting away from the old beliefs, they refuse to leave them behind. They have grown used to them and find it comforting to keep them around. So while they may make brief forays into their new beliefs, they are never really affected by them because they take their old beliefs with them and continue thinking about them day and night. The newness has no effect because they carry along their old setting. It's no wonder their life doesn't change.

As David Roher has written in a sermon illustration on the topic of transformation, "The adventure of new life in Christ begins when the comfortable patterns of the old life are left behind."[13] That is surrender, and it takes passion to keep it going. That means you must decide what is important and dedicate yourself to it. It's like what the guide said to the character Tangle in George MacDonald's story "The Golden Key," when their journey led them to a deep, dark hole in the ground. The guide assured Tangle that it was safe to enter.

"But there are no stairs," she replied.

"You must throw yourself in," said the guide. "There is no other way."[14]

It may seem hard to leave the comfortable old beliefs behind and throw yourself fully into something new and unknown. But if you truly want to change your life, there is no other way. You can't do it by half measures. It requires utter dedication, a complete overhaul, a total makeover. You must reprogram your mind, and this means a willingness to plunge into something new and erase the old, virus-infected programs that caused recurrent crashes to your relationships and happiness. It may even feel as though you are abandoning your folks or your family's way of living, but God's way will always lead you to the truth, and the truth will set you free.

You must throw yourself in.

I urge you to surrender to God and throw yourself into his way for you with passion. Commit yourself to a willingness to immerse yourself fully in his will for you, and I assure you that you will find a new life of love, completeness, peace, and fulfillment.[15]

Finally, we have reached the place where you'll see the powerful steps you can take to begin changing your beliefs. And you'll read about my most exciting change—my water-to-wine miracle.

Five
Five Steps to Changing Your Beliefs

I've told you how my early experiences and heritage formed damaging beliefs that dogged me most of my life. The lustful thoughts that began in Ginger's garage when I was five years old continued well into my sixties. Many people think lustful thoughts are simply inevitable in men, and there's nothing we can do about them. But I'm happy to tell you, that simply is not so. I briefly mentioned this incident in my previous book, *I Promise*, but now I want to explore it in more detail and use it to show you how you can change even the most deeply embedded beliefs of your heart.

I remember the time and place very well. It was in January 2006. I was speaking to several thousand ministers at a four-day conference in a huge church in Orlando, Florida. The mornings were beautiful in Orlando, so I had been getting up at six to spend time on my daily Bible verses as I took my morning walk. I walked for an hour or so each morning through the neighborhoods around the hotel.

On this particular morning I was probably reviewing my key verses about loving God and our fellow humans. I'm sure I prayed to God, thanking and praising him. I was quite happy and relaxed as I strolled leisurely down the sidewalk.

Up ahead I noticed a girl walking toward me. There was nothing unusual about that. It was a neighborhood, and I had already encountered several morning walkers. As she came closer I noticed that she was an exceptionally beautiful girl in her mid-twenties, and she wore very short, hot pink, silky shorts and a tightly fitting T-shirt. Basically everything on her body was moving as she walked briskly toward me. Any red-blooded man would have noticed her, and I am a red-blooded man. She was an outstanding creation of God. And to top it off, she was friendly. As she drew near she dazzled me with a big smile and said, "Hi." Utterly fascinated, I returned the greeting as she walked on past me, never breaking her stride.

As if on autopilot my head turned instantly to gaze at her as I continued walking. I finally had to turn forward again to keep from falling over the curb. I'm sure I thought something like, *Whoa, God, you really did a great job there.* Even after another fifty or one hundred steps, I was still thinking about this girl. And then I began having lustful thoughts about her. Mind you, I didn't even know this girl. I had never seen her before, and yet here I was, imagining being with her in—well, you know what I was imagining. Of course my thoughts did not include all the terrible consequences and all the goofed-up stuff that happens to your life when a man actually follows through on what I was thinking. I was simply thinking of the pleasure. It was those old beliefs rising up—those beliefs I had harbored in my heart ever since those afternoons in Ginger's garage sixty years ago.

Then I paused. I was appalled to realize that I had just been praying and working on key sections of Scripture that I wanted to hide in my heart, and here I was lusting for this girl just seconds after seeing her. And I asked God, "Lord, is it possible to be over these thoughts?" All my life I had lusted in my mind over various female acquaintances or women I had met. The habit went back as far as I could remember and included girls I had worked with or gone to school with or played with as a child. I have read statistics that say most men lust and that most of us resort to masturbation on a regular basis. (I also heard that the rest of us are liars!)

I can't refute the findings; it has been true of almost every man I have ever known—even those in full-time ministry. I tell you this to show you just how pervasive lust is, which leads many people to assume it simply can't be overcome. It seems that almost every secular and religious institution has problems with sexual situations in which the leaders are either fired or severely admonished. I am not suggesting that all men have lustful thoughts; only 99.99 percent of them do.

Why do men do these things? It's because of the beliefs written in their hearts. And it's no wonder. Most of the men I have known have been exposed to the same world beliefs that rubbed off on me. No matter what they say, and no matter even what they may think they believe on the surface of their minds, deep down in their heart of hearts they believe that life is about pleasure and thrills. And they believe they can find better pleasure and a fresh thrill by being with another woman sexually. If they don't act on this fantasy in reality, they act on it in their minds, using porn as a stimulus or regularly resorting to masturbation.

I never would have admitted what I'm about to tell you before I experienced my own freedom from lust. I can remember sitting on the stage in the front of a church one Sunday morning just before preaching and looking out over the audience, only to find a woman on the front row wearing a low-cut blouse. Much of her upper body was hanging out for all to see, especially me, because when I got up to speak she gazed up at me with a big smile. I wanted to walk down off the platform, throw my suit coat over her, and say, "Excuse me, ma'am, but I'm trying to preach about the sins of man, and I can't get my mind on the subject with you sitting there flashing all that flesh. Would you mind buttoning up your blouse?"

Many women seem not to understand how men react to the way they dress—or undress. It's hard for a man speaking in a church to have some babe sitting on one of the front rows with her clothes falling off. But today I'm happy to tell you, I don't care how they dress. I have found the key to overcoming my lust and distractions.

After I passed that girl on that morning in Orlando, I said to God, "I really don't like repeatedly dealing with these kinds of thoughts. Am I always going to be lusting for women? Even when I'm seventy, eighty, or ninety years old?" I am my own research machine. I am always trying to figure out the questions of life and where I need improvement, so I determined to get to the bottom of my reasons for continual lust and see if I couldn't find a way to put it behind me. Now I have ended it, and I understand what I have done to end it. And I have learned that I can use the same principle to overcome the dozens of other problem areas in my life that need changing or improving—any area that does not reflect the love and character of Jesus. In the rest of this chapter, I will share with you the key—the five steps I take every day to change my own behavior when it does not reflect the character of God.

Step One: Identify Your Behavior
That Needs to Change

My goal for my life—and it is the goal of every follower of Christ—is to be transformed into his image, the kind of person whom God intended me to be. And what he intended me to be is quite simple: he created me in his image, which means I am to be like him, which means I am to be loving as he is. That means I must change all the motivations within my heart so that my every action reflects the loving nature of God. So if I'm serious about my commitment to him, I must do an inventory of my heart, as revealed by my actions, and identify the behaviors that must change.

Lusting for women on the front row of church or on a morning walk is obviously not a reflection of God's nature. It's not loving them; it's imagining a way to use them for my pleasure. When my inconsistency hit me that morning in Orlando—lusting only a few minutes after diligently reviewing the Bible—I saw the vast chasm between my claims and my behavior, and I was appalled at my failure to reflect God's nature. I identified the problem. I agreed with God that my behavior did not reflect him and admitted that I needed his transforming power. I humbled myself and admitted to God that I had a major problem that needed healing. In a sense, I was like King David asking God to know my heart and to see if there are any beliefs within it that he's not pleased with.

At this time I had been studying about the heart and how beliefs lodged in the heart form one's behavior. So as I continued walking that morning in Orlando, I decided that I had to probe deeper. Simply identifying the wrong behavior was not enough; I needed to identify the belief that caused the behavior. I said, "Okay, God, Jesus said that out of my heart flow my thoughts, so what belief do I harbor in my heart that is bringing these thoughts about?"

I had not gone another fifty steps before it hit me like a ton of bricks. *Whoa, Smalley, you still cling to the belief that life should be mainly pleasurable, fun, thrilling, and full of adventure. You think you should experience all the good life has to offer—pleasurable food, sex, stimulants, luxuries, entertainment, hang gliding, skiing, and just anything you want to try. You're out for all the gusto you can get.*

Everyone has some hedonism within them, but on a scale from zero to ten, with ten being an out-of-control hedonist, I was about a seven or eight. Certainly, life is pleasurable, and if you're married, sex can and should be very pleasurable. But at an early age I had developed a belief that was out of balance. My pleasure-seeking went to thoughts about women outside of my marriage. I placed great emphasis on receiving personal pleasure. It was all about me. I really wanted pleasure more than I wanted to serve others by loving them.

As I listened to these thoughts I realized that I was a full-blown hedonist. As I already mentioned, a hedonist is a person who lives for pleasure, thrills, fun, and excitement—someone who feels that life is to be highly sensual and enjoyed to the maximum. That fit me like a glove. I had a huge hedonistic belief *written on my heart*. No wonder I had lusted my entire life. It all started back in Ginger's garage, and I have kept it going ever since.

You may not have known a Ginger, but you may have picked up the same hedonistic beliefs from teachers, parents, friends, or the culture in general. We live with hedonism running rampant all about us. It's hard not to be influenced, and it's hard not to rationalize that when anything is so prevalent, God must somehow relax the restrictions and ease judgment. But his truth has not changed. He doesn't take into account the philosophies that dominate society and adjust his scale accordingly. We must learn the key to resisting society's pervasive attitudes to keep them from becoming embedded in our hearts. The key is in what you think about every day with deep interest and enthusiasm. What is on your mind when you lie down at night and awaken in the morning? Whatever your mind dwells on will eventually reach your heart and lodge there as a belief.

When Ginger taught me and her other little friends the pleasures of the body, we didn't have the slightest understanding that our experimenting would lead to a rampant pursuit of pleasure and thrills, but it did. Having acquired the hedonist mind-set, I went on to pursue other pleasures. Not all those pleasures were bad, but that didn't matter; the point is that the focus of my heart was on thrills and pleasure, certainly not serving others with compassion.

Please understand that I am not knocking pleasure. As Dr. Ed Wheat tells us, we are intended for pleasure.[1] Pleasure is God's idea. He made our bodies and minds to experience all the pleasures he gave to us. Problems become attached to pleasure because we live in a fallen world where our desires get out of balance and we tend to go for pleasure in unhealthy and ungodly ways. We want too much pleasure, pleasure that belongs to someone else, pleasure in wrong ways, and pleasure that may hurt other people. And the result is pain, addiction, complications, disease, and even death. In a fallen world God puts controls on pleasure, not because it's wrong, but because our desire for it is abnormally strong, like it's pumped up on steroids. God's controls on pleasure are not meant to keep us from having it. They are there for our benefit, pointing us toward the best use of pleasurable gifts such as sex, food, and drink. The controls are another of God's gifts. They show us how to get the most out of pleasure.

In fact, when a man submits to God's way and is true to his wife, focusing on her needs rather than his own, he will discover that sex is ten times more pleasurable for him as well as for her. It gives an added dimension to the idea expressed in Matthew 10: when a man loses his life for God and others, he truly gains more than he loses.

I've shown you here the principles I used to identify one particular problem in my life. First I uncovered the problem. Next I identified the deeper belief that led to it. Then I explored the source of that belief in order to understand how it got into my heart. Now let's go on to the next step.

Step Two: Admit the Behaviors in Your Life That Are Not Godly

I fear that many Christians today are reluctant to admit that their actions are deeply sinful. Even if they realize that certain things they do are not really best, they want to rationalize the behavior or charge it off to some circumstance or event that relieves them of responsibility for it: "It's not really my fault." When they do this, they rob themselves of this vital second step that will lead to cleansing.

To return to the problem of lust that I'm using as an illustration for this chapter, I spent years ogling and lusting without ever pausing to take inventory and peg this behavior as a real problem. We are helped along in that comfortable illusion by common attitudes in our culture and even in the church. We tend to think that lust in men is inevitable. Our sex drive is strong and women are beautiful, so what else can we expect? It's just the way we're wired. I remember my Dallas Theological Seminary professor Howard Hendricks saying that all men struggle with lust, or if they don't, they have another problem. He's right. If men don't find the natural beauty of women appealing, somewhere there may be faulty wiring in their hearts.

Yet a strong sex drive combined with a natural attraction to women does not excuse lust. To think that imaginary sex along with masturbation is inevitable is simply a myth. The key, as Dr. Hendricks hinted, is in the word *struggle*. If we functioned as God intended before the fall, we could legitimately appreciate the beauty of women without the contamination of lust. Our desire would not strain at the leash in the presence of beautiful women. The sin is not in our visual attraction to women; God instilled that into men at creation. It's our failure to enjoy feminine beauty without the impulse to do more than merely enjoy it. To adapt an analogy from C. S. Lewis, we must appreciate the glory of a woman without feeling the impulse to use her body for our pleasure, just as we can appreciate the glory of Niagara Falls without feeling the impulse to make it all into cups of tea.[2]

I had fallen into the trap of believing that lust was unavoidable. I was justifying this behavior instead of admitting that it was ungodly.

Another rationalization is our tendency to shift the blame. *That little stinker, Ginger—look what she did to me—gave me exciting, pleasurable experiences early in life that saddled me with a destructive belief for over sixty years.* No, that is not true. I could easily think that way and fit right in with the mind-set of our present "it's not my fault" culture. But the truth is Ginger didn't cause my problem. I'm the one who thought about sex every day since those experiences. It was my brain doing the dirty work, not hers. To blame her would be a cop-out that would prevent me from identifying my problem as mine alone, thus preventing me from doing something about it.

The only way to get free from the bondage of lust is to admit that the problem is real, wrong, and ugly. In no way does it reflect the nature of God. When this fact becomes real to you, you must present it to God with no rationalization, no hiding, and no excuses. It's called confession. Did Jesus not say that even thinking about having sex with another person's mate is adultery? Imagining being with another mate other than your own is breaking the commitment you made at the marriage altar of "do you take your mate to be your *only*, until death separates you?" If a man spends a great deal of his time imagining sex with another woman, he becomes what he thinks about over a period of time.

Here is the really amazing truth that I learned from my own freedom experience. I read in 1 John 1:9 that if I am willing to confess my sins, God will forgive me and cleanse me from *all* of my unrighteousness. The key here is that it is God who cleanses me. I can't do it myself. When I admit that my actions, words, or thoughts are not pleasing to my God, he is willing and able to cleanse me of *all* unrighteousness. That still amazes me. When I admitted my lust and the hedonism in my heart that spawned it, God began healing and cleaning me.

Let's talk about that word *unrighteousness.* It's not a word we use in ordinary conversation. Basically, it means not being like God. To simplify what it means to be like God, I turn to the two main teachings of Christ. He told us that we are being like God when we love God our King with all our heart, soul, mind, and strength, and when we love others in the same way that we want to be loved. Jesus told us that these two commands cover all the laws of Scripture. That does it for me. I judge everything I do on the basis of those two commands. Righteousness is simply being like God, and since God is love, we are like him when we love. As we noted at the first of this chapter, the goal of every authentic Christian is to be transformed into the image of God: to be like him. When we are unrighteous, we are not like him.

Sin is simply trying to be the lord of your own life. The essence of sin is self-ishness, which is the opposite of love. It's like insisting on being your own boss when you're hired to work under the management of a company. It's a kind of rebellion against the proper order. Every sin we commit flows from the basic sin of Adam and Eve when they chose to reject God as boss and become managers of their own lives. As sinners, we simply follow in their footsteps. Sinners are simply people who say to God, "My life is mine; I'll live it the way I want. I'll do what I want, when I want, and how I want. Don't bother me, God; don't try to force any of your stuffy advice down my throat. I know what makes me happy, so I'll do things my way, thank you very much."

If I am willing to admit this basic it's-all-about-me sin and the reflections of it that show up in beliefs like hedonism, God is willing and able to forgive me and cleanse me from all unrighteousness. When that happens, I'm free to begin to live righteously (within his great boundaries of love). It pleases God when I choose to live my life as a reflection of him because he designed me and will lead me to the lifestyle that makes life fulfilling and satisfying. God created us, and he wrote the how-to manual, showing us how to live in a way that not only delights him but also brings us the best life possible.

On my walk back to the hotel in Orlando, I confessed that I was a hedonist. I said, "God, I admit out loud to you that I hold in my heart this huge belief that seeking pleasure is the way to joy instead of seeking to love you. I can't even count the number of times that I have sought excitement from women in my imagination. Now I want to love you and others with all the passion I have been pouring into lusting."

I arrived back to my hotel room feeling a freedom I had never felt before. I knew a huge cesspool had started draining from my heart. And my confession that day began my own transformation and healing that took place in only two weeks. It could never have happened had I not faced the fact of real sin in my life and admitted before God that I was not living a life of righteousness.

Step Three: Locate Scripture Verses
That Address the Problem Behavior

The thought of having God cleanse my heart of the contamination of lust was a wonderful thing. My heart felt free and clean. It was exhilarating, and at that moment I felt extremely grateful to God and closer to him, but I had to realize that this cleansing was only a step. The process of transformation in me was not complete. Had I gone on my way, happy to have my heart cleaned out, and failed to take the next step, the result would have been disastrous. God had rid my heart of its condemnation, but it was important that I not leave it empty. He emptied it to be filled again. An empty heart, even a clean empty heart, is a dangerous thing.

Jesus warned the Pharisees about this danger when he told them of casting out an evil spirit from a man. The spirit roamed about seeking a new home, but finding none, it returned to the person from whom it had been exiled. Finding that person's heart empty, swept, and clean, the spirit simply walked in and made his home there again. And worse, he brought with him seven more demonic spirits, each more evil than himself.[3] If you neglect and fail to care for your clean, empty heart, the evil will simply come back. And worse, it can multiply itself, becoming more malignant and destructive than before.

I determined, therefore, to actively fill my heart with positive reinforcement to maintain my newfound awareness of the causes of lust. Knowing that the Word of God is alive, powerful, sharper than a two-edged sword, true, able to convict and bring transformation to my life, I turned to the Bible to find verses that addressed freedom from sexual sin. I found what I was looking for in Galatians 5. The entire chapter is about slavery to the pleasures of the flesh versus enjoying the freedom that comes from placing yourself under the control of God's Spirit.

It was verse 13 that really exploded off of the page: "You, my brothers, were called to be free. But do not use your freedom to indulge the sinful nature [for me, my sexual imagination pleasures]; rather serve one another in love." God gives me freedom through the power of his Spirit living within me. Not only does he desire for me to be free, he provides his Spirit within me to make that freedom and his love possible. Is that a great verse or what?

Verse 14 adds another dimension as Paul reaffirms Jesus' reminder that the second greatest commandment in the Bible covers all the other commandments in just five words: "Love your neighbor as yourself." Couple this great verse with Matthew 22:37 telling us to "Love the Lord your God with all your heart and with all your soul and with all your mind," and you have a powerful combination. The essence of living is to love God and love each other. When these giant truths reach your heart as beliefs, the power of God's words and his Spirit living within you start working major changes in your life. Simply hiding these verses in my heart is now my ultimate goal in life. I want to love God with all my heart, soul, mind, and strength. And I want to love others as I love myself.

Galatians 5 describes the life we'll have if we retain hedonist beliefs within our hearts: "The acts of the sinful nature are obvious: sexual immorality, impurity and debauchery; idolatry and witchcraft; hatred, discord, jealousy, fits of rage, selfish ambition, dissensions, factions and envy; drunkenness, orgies, and the like" (vv. 19–21). If we fail to submit to God's Spirit, we will submit to our sinful nature and become enslaved by our unbridled desires, which will lead us to constant discord and great unhappiness. We will become sexual predators looking for pleasure wherever we can get it.

As if that were not terrible enough, giving ourselves over to hedonism leads to an even worse result. In the last sentence of Galatians 5:21, Paul warns us that if we pursue these hedonistic activities, we are excluded from the kingdom of God. The reason for this exclusion is perfectly clear when we think about it. As King of his kingdom, God has the right to set the laws by which his people live. If his law tells us to love, it's the same as if he told us to jump; there should be no question except to ask, "How high?" If, on the other hand, we say, "Oh, no, forget that. I'm looking out for number one—me!" then we are simply excluding ourselves from God's kingdom. We are refusing to recognize him as our King. If we refuse to let God reign over us, it follows that we are not a part of the kingdom of God.

When I surrendered to the King, his Spirit within me worked great changes in my life. He gave me a natural desire to follow his commands. I was set free from lust, complaining, and many other sins that had bound me like a slave to my own wants and desires. A free man is one who is free from his own selfishness, which, as Galatians 5:13 tells us, frees us to love others by serving them.

Again, we encounter those delightful paradoxes we find in the Bible. Freedom comes from being under control; forgetting yourself and seeking the pleasure of others results in the greatest pleasure for yourself. It doesn't seem to make sense, but when you put it to the test you find that it really works. The continual grasping for sexual and other pleasures results in compulsions, addictions, obsessions, diminishing satisfaction, and the perpetual need for greater stimulation in more varied experiences. Seeking the things of the Spirit, on the other hand, means giving up focus on the self and focusing instead on compassion and the well-being of others, which brings you love, joy, and peace. The Spirit of God leads you to think in ways that are just the opposite of self-seeking. Instead of thinking what can I *get* from people to increase my pleasure, I now think of what I can *give* to them to increase their well-being.

How did I apply this to my battle with lust? Instead of using mental images of women to pleasure myself, I now think of women as glorious fellow beings who reflect the beauty of God. They live in the same fallen world and face many challenges and evils that men never face—evils that deserve my compassion, protection, and concern for their safety, honor, purity, and well-being. The Holy Spirit wants me to enrich women, to see their great value and try to serve them in ways that build them up and help them become stronger spiritually.

The next step explains how this truth entered my life. But if you're a woman reading this book, you can have your own list of addictions and struggles with lust. You may be struggling with sexual imaginations with other men beside your husband; you may be lusting for more clothing, a bigger house, and a host of other struggles you face just like me but in different areas. Love for God and love for others are my new guiding principles, and I learned them by finding passages in the Bible that I placed in my heart to replace the old selfish hedonism that sought mainly my own pleasure. As a result of the influence of these scriptures, I'm happy that today I can say, "Hello, I'm Gary Smalley. I'm a recovering out-of-balance pleasure-seeker."

Step Four: Memorize
Your Selected Scriptures

You may wonder how latching on to Bible verses admonishing us to love God and love others can give us freedom from lust. Follow my logic here. Common sense says that what Jesus told us is obviously true: out of my heart flow my words, thoughts, and actions.[4] It follows, then, that since my beliefs live within my heart, as my beliefs change, so will my words, thoughts, and actions. If I want to be God's servant, obeying him naturally, I can embed his words in my heart, and those words will become my new beliefs. He actually becomes my boss, my Lord, and my King automatically when his words form my new beliefs. And as my new beliefs dictate my behavior, sin vanishes little by little from my life because my behavior conforms to the ideal of God's words.

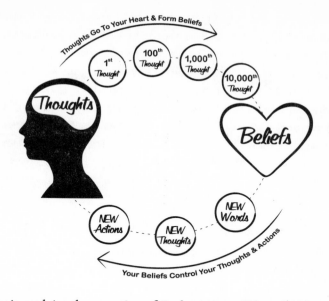

This logic explains the meaning of Psalm 119:11: "I have hidden your word in my heart that I might not sin against you." That is why hiding God's Word in my heart has become so important to me. It is the basis for all the beliefs that will conform my behavior to the image of God.

As long as my heart was filled with the hedonistic belief that life is mainly for experiencing pleasure, that belief drove my lustful thoughts. But when I discovered the antidote to hedonism in Galatians 5:13, I eagerly memorized that verse and, like the psalmist, began to meditate on it day and night.[5] It worked! I found that as I hid God's Word in my heart, I sinned against him less and less. In fact, I found that I actually cannot sin against him in certain areas when specific Bible verses reach my heart and form my new deep-seated beliefs. God's Word and sin are mutually exclusive. If you hold to his Word, then sin flees. I cannot sin against God in certain aspects of my life because my new beliefs now control my behavior.

Therefore, God truly is my Lord today, my boss. It is so exciting to experience what's happening to me. Having found the key to conquering lust, I'm now searching my life to find what else I'm doing that does not reflect God. When I locate such an activity, I find a powerful section of Scripture to address the problem and start memorizing it to embed into my heart as my new operational belief.

When I speak of memorizing, I don't mean simply getting the words down so I can recite them by rote like punching a button to play a tape. I mean I chew on these verses, each word, one at a time and I chew on the meaning of each word daily until they are not just words in my brain; they are new beliefs deeply branded on my heart. That is so important that I will explain it more fully in the next section. As I said, it's essential to find the meaning of each word in every verse. I live the meanings consciously long before they become part of my natural behavior. I repeat the behavior I know to be right until those behaviors are absorbed into my heart to the point that God's ways become my ways. His ways become normal actions within me, and I no longer have to force myself to act according to his words.

Step Five: Deepen the Imprint of God's Words on Your Heart

When I discovered the huge change that came about in my life from hiding God's Word in my heart, I became like the prophet Jeremiah. He wrote that when he found God's words, he *ate* them. And he went on to say that those words were his joy and his heart's delight.[6]

A little after Jeremiah wrote this, he was beaten and imprisoned. He became discouraged and ready to give up on ministry. He cursed the day he was born and even cursed the man that came out of the delivery room to announce his birth. But wait; read on. Jeremiah couldn't give up because God's words flowed through his veins in such a way that he could not keep from thinking about them. God's words became part of him—a vital component of his spiritual DNA, ultimately changing everything about his life.

I'm glad to see many Christians who get on programs to read the entire Bible in one year. But if this is all they do—spend fifteen minutes in daily reading, check it off the schedule chart, then close the Bible until tomorrow, its truth will never become hidden in their hearts. If you want God's principles to become deeply embedded beliefs that change your life, you have to take deliberate steps to make it happen. This means spending time meditating on a given passage and delving into the meaning of the verse until you know it through and through.

So that is what I began to do with Galatians 5:13. Like Jeremiah, I ate it. I chewed on that verse day and night. Not only did I memorize it, I looked up each key word in the verse to discover its meaning. To show you what I mean, I will identify the key words of that verse and show you how I delved into the meaning of each word:

You, my brothers, were called to be free. But do not use your *freedom* to *indulge* the *sinful [sexual] nature*; rather, *serve one another* in *love* (emphasis mine).

Freedom. What does that word mean in this text? Freedom is not merely the absence of responsibility. When you free yourself from responsibility, appetites move into the vacuum and you become a slave to your desires. When God frees us from this slavery, he frees us to serve one another. We're free to do what is right, but even better, we're free from doing what we do not want to do.

Indulge. This means to give one's self to pleasure. It seems like freedom, but it's really slavery to selfish desire.

Sinful nature. Since the fall of Adam and Eve, every human born has been saddled with a selfish impulse to gratify the self and reject the ways of God. That nature cannot be changed; it must be replaced by the Spirit of God within our lives.

Serve one another. This means to follow the example of Christ in John 13 when he took up a towel and performed the menial task of a servant and washed his disciples' dirty feet. It means to discover people's deepest needs and serve them from the overflow we receive from God's Spirit.

Love. This is what motivates service to one another. It's putting the well-being of others above the well-being, comfort, and pleasure of self. Real, lasting love is a gift from God. He alone gives his love away for our use and enrichment, and he only gives it away to the *humble* (a beggar's helpless, bankrupted attitude).[7]

This gives you a sampling of how I immersed myself into Galatians 5:13. The idea is not merely to memorize, but to plunge in with all your heart, making God's principles the prime component of your spiritual DNA.

I meditate and chew on each word of each verse because that is how its words and ideas begin to press their meaning into my heart. Each time I rehearse the verses mentally, the words are impressed more deeply. It's like deepening the embossing on a book cover or an invitation. The first time I meditate, the impression is faint, maybe hardly even visible. But each time I review the words, the image becomes deeper and clearer. Finally, after I have gone over and over the verse, discovering more about it with each meditative chewing, it becomes so deeply embossed that it is there to stay.

Other mental pictures may work better for you. Maybe you prefer to think of the process as printing the words on your heart, with each meditation making the ink darker. Or maybe you prefer to think of it as engraving the words into the surface of your heart, with each meditation grooving the words deeper and deeper. Or maybe you're from out west and you like the image of branding God's Word into your heart.

To make the process real to you, I encourage you to pick your favorite image from those above or make up your own to visualize a Bible verse becoming embedded in your heart. If you choose the image of engraving, for example, close your eyes and imagine your hands holding a hammer and chisel, chipping that verse into the surface. Each time you meditate, think of the letters becoming deeper and clearer. The idea is to think of God's words becoming permanent—so much a part of you that they will always be there, always indelibly present as the belief from which your thoughts and actions will flow, making your new behavior become natural for you.

That's what I did with Galatians 5:13. Even now, not a day passes that I don't review that verse. I don't take any chances that my new beliefs about love and service will ever fade from me.

> The point is, by meditating, ruminating, chewing, and eating your verses on a regular basis, you are making them a part of you. You are making God's way of doing things the real beliefs of your heart from which all your thoughts and actions will spring.

My Amazing Changed Actions

Two weeks after my immersion into that verse, I experienced my water-to-wine miracle. I had traveled with part of my family to Idaho. My daughter, her husband, and their two children were staying with my wife and me in this beautiful hotel while I spoke in the area. One afternoon my nine-year-old granddaughter, Hannah, asked me to take her to the swimming pool. I was in the Jacuzzi playing and splashing with Hannah when into the pool area walked two beautiful women in their early twenties. They looked like swimsuit models and wore nothing more than little patches held in place by strings. And they were headed toward the Jacuzzi.

Hannah, who loves dolls, leaned close to me and whispered, "Granddad, there are two real live Barbie dolls." I responded by whispering the obvious: "Yes, I see them." No man could miss those two girls.

The two Barbies smiled and greeted us, and then came the miracle. The very first thought that entered my mind was, *I wonder if these girls know how much God loves them?* Startled, I looked around as if to discover where that thought came from because I had never thought anything like that in my whole life. Then came my second thought—which almost brought tears to my eyes. I wondered if their daddy loved them the way they should have been loved as little girls. Then the third thought hit, which was to wonder if they were married and if their husbands placed on them the high value that God did and loved them as they needed to be loved. I felt stunned.

These thoughts had me almost crying as the two beauties got into the Jacuzzi right next to me. I was absolutely thrilled that these three unexpected and uncharacteristic thoughts came to my mind instantly and naturally. I was (and still am) convinced that God's Word had worked a miracle in my heart.

Eventually I got out, dried off, and went back to my room. Even then I was still in a daze. I just sat in the chair and let this miracle sink in. *Dear God*, I prayed in love and adoration, *thank you so much that the very first thoughts that came to my mind were thoughts of love and honor for these girls. Thank you for healing the lust that has been in my heart for sixty years.*

That was in February 2006. From that February all the way to the writing of this book, I have not had one lustful thought toward another woman. In fact, I have had no lustful thoughts at all. What a miracle! And what's more, not one bit of interest in masturbation. I know that it may be hard for you to imagine Gary Smalley thinking the thoughts he had been thinking for so long. Even my own family wasn't sure that I should put this much information within these pages. But you know what? I'm 67 now, and I'm experiencing freedoms in several areas of life that are worth shouting over, and I didn't want to hold anything back. I feel so much like the blind man who shouted, "I was blind but now I see!" (John 9:25) How can I keep that silent?

In my own spiritual experiment, I'm watching this new freedom continue and based on God's words, I'll be successful in keeping this freedom as I delight in it day and night.[8] It's as if Galatians 5:13 replaced my old hedonism with a new belief. It grabbed the old belief, stamped over it on my heart, blotted it out, replaced it with a belief about the high value of women, and freed me to love them as God does, utterly without lust.

I simply cannot use my freedom for lust anymore. It no longer matters where I am—in the swimming pool, on the beach, at work, or even in the pulpit. And it no longer matters what a girl is wearing—low-cut blouse, short shorts, tight pants, or a teeny string bikini. It no longer matters whether she is beautiful as Eve or curvy as a mountain road, I simply don't have lustful thoughts anymore. Nor do they plague me when I wake up in the morning or go to bed at night. They are gone. As you can see, embedding God's words deeply has made them a delight to my heart. They have somehow replaced my old hedonistic belief with a desire to love and serve women instead of using them in my imagination. I now become literally choked up when I see a woman not being cared for and loved as God designed men to do for women. I like to imagine a host of God's children loving each other as God intended. This is his ultimate will for us. Make the words of God part of your spiritual DNA and they will transform every attitude and behavior in your being.

Hedonism was certainly a deadly belief for me. So what other beliefs should we avoid branding upon our hearts that cause the most damage on this earth and take the most love away from our hearts? The next section can open your eyes to three deadly beliefs that you may already have within your heart, and then, if so, you can use the lessons from this past chapter to *blot them out* to whatever degree you have them.

Scriptures to Hide in Your Heart

You, my brothers [and sisters], were called to be free. But do not use your freedom to indulge the sinful nature; rather, serve one another in love. (Galatians 5:13)

Jesus replied: "Love the Lord your God with all your heart and with all your soul and with all your mind."

And the second is like it: "Love your neighbor as yourself." (Matthew 22:37, 39)

Blessed is the man
who does not walk in the counsel of the wicked
or stand in the way of sinners
or sit in the seat of mockers.
But his delight is in the law of the LORD,
and on his law he meditates day and night.
He is like a tree planted by streams of water,
which yields its fruit in season
and whose leaf does not wither.
Whatever he does prospers. (Psalm 1:1–3)

How can a young man keep his way pure?
By living according to your word.
I seek you with all my heart;
do not let me stray from your commands.
I have hidden your word in my heart
that I might not sin against you. (Psalm 119:9–11)

Six
Coming to Grips with the Three "Deadlies"

The next three chapters show you not only why evil is so prevalent in our world today but also what destructive beliefs may have seeped into your own heart without your awareness. These chapters will help you understand why you may be acting in ways that are hurtful to yourself and others, and why you haven't been able to change those behaviors.

I understand, however, that some people do not want to read about negative influences on their lives. It may be too discouraging for you. If you are that type of person, you may prefer to skip this section and go on to the next, which addresses the four most important beliefs you need to hide in your heart in order to see real godly changes in your life. Those great beliefs are addressed beginning in chapter 10. The three deadly beliefs you're about to encounter will *naturally* move out of your life when you replace them with the four essential beliefs God directs us to "hide" within our hearts. So, skipping the following three chapters won't hurt you, but you eventually need to understand what ugly beliefs these three are. The choice is yours.

Beliefs That Dominate Our Culture

Now, let's look at those three ugly beliefs that can slip into your life unnoticed and spread their poison without your realizing anything bad is happening. These three insidious and destructive beliefs are so widespread and accepted in our culture that their danger is often hidden. When *everybody's doing it*, it's hard to see what's wrong with it. You could have some deadly belief eating away at your life right now and not even be aware of it.

Obviously what goes on in our culture today is hardly a valid guide for behaviors that reflect the nature of God. And remember, that is our goal—to transform our beliefs so that everything we do and say reflects God's design, because he knows which beliefs will bring us freedom and which will lead us to destruction. Many behaviors that today's culture trips all over itself to endorse reflect beliefs and attitudes that are far from the character of God. That is why I want to introduce you to three very toxic beliefs so widely accepted that they hardly seem wrong at all. They are *stealth* beliefs that slip in under our spiritual radar. I call them *the three deadlies*.

I call the three deadlies stealth beliefs because they so easily slip into your life unnoticed. You could have any or all of these deadlies eating away at your heart and be as unaware of them as many are unaware of a growing cancer in their bodies. That is why I hope you will pause at the end of this chapter long enough to take three self-evaluations that I have included in the appendices of this book. These tests are designed to help you assess your life to determine whether these stealth beliefs may have slipped into your heart and embedded themselves as established beliefs. Taking these evaluations could make a big difference in the way you read the rest of this book. But first, I want to specifically introduce you to the three deadlies in order to help you identify and avoid them.

The Three Deadlies

The apostle John addressed the three deadlies in his first letter to churches when he wrote, "Do not love the world or the things in the world. If anyone loves the world, the love of the Father is not in him. For all that is in the world—

the lust of the flesh,
the lust of the eyes,
and the pride of life—

is not of the Father but is of the world. And the world is passing away, and the lust of it; but he who does the will of God abides forever" (1 John 2:15–17 NKJV, emphasis mine).

To paraphrase these verses in today's terminology, John is saying: Don't crave the things the average person in the world craves. Don't take on the beliefs of the world, which are:

1. the deep cravings to stimulate your bodies with never-ending pleasures, excitements, or thrills;

2. the cravings to buy more and more stuff, playthings, and tasty foods to fill your houses and stomachs; and

3. bragging about all you have and all you accomplish and taking the credit for it all, instead of giving glory and thanks to God.

None of these beliefs are from God; they are all the thoughts and beliefs in *the world*. When these three deadlies lodge inside your heart as beliefs, they cause all kinds of problems in your life.

These three beliefs that John warns us to avoid are deadly because they turn us away from God and keep us from receiving and reflecting him and his love. When you turn away from God, you cut yourself off from the source of life, and that's deadly. Yet these are the beliefs that our culture as a whole lives by. The norm for most people today is the pursuit of pleasure (the lust of the flesh), the accumulation of things (the lust of the eyes), and defining ourselves by what we have and what we've accomplished (the pride of life).

Notice that each of these three pursuits is utterly selfish and has little regard for reflecting the character of God, which is love. God wants us to focus outward on loving others, not inward on pleasure and accumulation and pride. They drain your heart of love, shriveling it to where there is no room for God. That's deadly. When you read on and see the destructive results of these three deadlies, you'll want to move heaven and earth to root them out of your life.

That is what Dave did. All three of the deadlies had infested Dave's life; he was an off-the-charts pleasure-seeker. His scores on all three of the self-assessment tests in the appendices soared into the stratosphere. He was an over-the-top workaholic, holding three jobs to maintain the lifestyle he wanted. He acquired new toys every week—sports equipment, cars, electronic devices, and new clothing. He was a high achiever who took pride in his accomplishments, and he was overly involved in competitive sports, which left little time for his family.

Dave was very talented, industrious, and goal oriented, but it was clear that all his energy and abilities were being directed by the deep-seated beliefs he held within his heart—which were essentially the three deadlies. The crash that soon followed was inevitable.

Dave was married to an absolutely beautiful and loving woman. They had two terrific boys. He and his wife had been in one of my loving marriage support groups for more than three years. Though he came regularly and participated, he seldom followed through on the simple weekly assignments, which usually consisted of finding practical ways of showing love to his wife. One night during our small group meeting his wife set off a bombshell. There in the safety of that supportive group, she told us she had just discovered that Dave had been seeing an eighteen-year-old girl for sex about twenty miles from our town. He had used a fake name and told the girl that he was single. Dave's wife had actually called her and confirmed that the man the girl had been seeing was indeed Dave.

As you can imagine, the group was stunned. As the full story unfolded, she learned that Dave was not only having sex with this girl, but he was also contacting other girls through the Internet, sharing pictures of himself, and having sexual encounters with them on out-of-town trips. He had told his wife that these were business trips, of course. Fully caught up in rampant hedonism, Dave was totally under the influence of the deadly beliefs in his heart on every level—the lust of the eyes, the lust of the flesh, and the pride of life.

Dave's world came crashing down. His wife left him immediately, taking the kids with her. She had no hope at all of ever reconciling, so that was the end of Dave's relationship with his family. He also lost his high-paying job when his employer learned of his sexual activities. No more family, no more means of maintaining his pleasure-driven lifestyle.

Dave was utterly devastated. He immediately admitted to the group and to God that he was guilty of all of the charges. He began to meet with an expert in sexual addictions, who explained to Dave that his sins were the outgrowth of deeply embedded beliefs that ran counter to God's words. All three of his deadly activities were a direct result of his lack of relationship with God and his family. He joined a church support group for sexually addicted men and began immediately to memorize Galatians 5:13, Matthew 22:37–39, and Romans 5:3–5. The Romans passage helped him deal with the intense pain he suffered from losing his wife and family.

Dave now faced a recurring nightmare of pain and regret. He could hardly stand to live with himself after what he had done, and this kept him totally dependent upon the grace and mercy of God. In fact, he cried out to God for freedom and strength day and night, and slowly, it began to pay off. It wasn't long before I could see changes in his spirit and in his love for God and his family. He kept coming to church, and his wife saw him there week after week, month after month. Their contacts were rare and tentative, but she finally accepted a "date" with him, which was a big step that has brought hope back to Dave's life.

Dave and his wife have not yet reconciled completely, but everyone in the church is still supporting them as a couple and family. I see it coming, though, and sooner rather than later. She is showing signs of forgiveness and even hope, and she desires for her children to be reunited with their dad. But first she wants Dave to be free from the bondage of the three deadlies—free to love her and the kids as God ordained a man to love a woman—wholeheartedly, unselfishly, and sacrificially, as God loves us.

The Deception of the Deadlies

At the time all this exploded, neither Dave nor I understood the powerful effect of the three deadly beliefs on a person's life. But in today's wildly hedonistic culture the effect has become obvious; the deadlies are seriously infecting our society and our churches to the point that relationships and lifestyles are destroying the stability of lives at every level. Thousands upon thousands— even millions—of stories like Dave's exist all over this land, in the church as well as out of it. And most Christians are not even aware of the danger.

I fear that a majority of Christians are infected to some degree with these deadlies. I know this because I see the evidence in what they think about, what they say, and what they do. Remember, whatever beliefs are branded in one's heart will come out in his or her life in words and activities. How often do we hear stories of upstanding men, even pastors and church leaders, who have problems with pornography and lust? How many stories must we read about incest, pedophilia, or illicit affairs among church people before we wake up to the fact that there is a serious problem of the heart among too many professing Christians?

I know firsthand that people can hide the sordid fact from themselves that one or more of the deadlies has invaded their lives. A person can have several different beliefs in his or her heart, all of which play a role in one's thoughts, words, and actions. You can be openly a Christian with visibly exemplary behavior and at the same time harbor deadly stealth beliefs. I took the hedonistic assessment test (appendix 2) a few years ago and, good Christian though I thought myself to be, I scored appallingly high on the test. I may have projected my Christian beliefs outwardly, but buried deep within my heart, those deadlies were burrowing, contaminating all my thoughts and undermining my relationship with God and my love for others. It's not that I lacked a deep belief in God and his ways; I just allowed my hedonistic beliefs to keep growing over the years because I fed them weekly through lustful thoughts. And the repetition of those thoughts deepened the groove of pleasure-seeking in my own heart. I now understand firsthand that God's truth, his powerful, sharper-than-a-two-edged-sword Word, can brand over those old beliefs as I keep hiding more and more of his words in my heart.

Care deeply for your heart and your relationship with others and God. Allow yourself to see what deadly beliefs you might have within you. Then, when you reach chapter 10, you can begin to hide a few of the key sections of Scripture within your heart and you, too, can start watching your old patterns disappear.

Now that I have introduced the three deadlies and painted a dark picture of what they can do to you, this is a good time for you to take the three easy inventory assessment tests in the appendices to see how much these deadlies may have infiltrated your life. Some of the questions may make you squirm. I certainly did. You will not want to answer them honestly, but it's important that you do so. No one needs to see your scores. Don't worry about where you land with your score at this point. Good or bad, you need to know the facts. Just remember that if your score is not where you want it to be, you need not despair; there is a solution. God's Word can brand over any belief you harbor in your heart, even if you have carried it there for most of your life.

These inventory tests were developed by my son, Dr. Greg Smalley, and he was assisted by his team of researchers at John Brown University.

So take a deep breath, work up your courage, pick up a pencil, and take the three tests before you continue reading this book. And keep in mind that when you discover what level you are on with each one of the three assessments, just admit it to God, and he promises to forgive you if you confess it and admit your own weaknesses and sins. He is faithful and just to forgive you and then, to cleanse you from all unrighteousness (1 John 1:9). And also, don't forget that God only gives his grace to the humble and resists the proud. He gives his power to those who admit they are beggars, bankrupt, or helpless, but he resists the people who won't admit their own sins and pretend that they'll make it on their own somehow.

Seven
The Deadly Lust of the Eyes

God's world is about balance and love. What takes us away from God's love and loving people? We all need to shop, but if shopping gets out of balance and preoccupies our thoughts, words, or actions, maybe we have too much lust of the eyes in our hearts.

I am noticing how my heart is changing when I have certain thoughts and emotions I never would have had before I began changing my beliefs. I remember in the past being irritated by older people who held up the checkout line while they hunted for their few dollar bills in their purse or wallet. I was in a hurry to get on through, and I would think, *Get a life, lady, and stop making me wait. I've got important things to do. I can't stand here all day while you take your good old time.* But recently I stood in the grocery store checkout line and saw an older woman rummaging through her small purse for extra coins. I watched her sadly put aside a can of peas because she couldn't afford them. My eyes started watering so much I had to walk away for a moment and gather myself before heading back quickly so that I could buy all of her food.

Why was I so irritated by people who held me up in the past? It was because I had too many of the world's beliefs in my heart. When I analyzed it and brought it down to the basic problem, I realized I was impatient because I had the I'm-in-a-hurry-to-gather-more-stuff-into-my-life-because-I-want-to- at-least-keep-up-with-the-Joneses syndrome. I was always in a rush to do more so I could get more. I couldn't even drive in my hometown without getting upset by slow drivers. My wife would say to me every time, "Why are you so impatient?" Now I know. I had the lust-of-the-eyes belief buried in my heart, and that drove me every day to move faster so I could get more. I'm happy to say now that those days are almost gone for me. The more of his words that reach my heart, the more my heart aches for those who suffer in every area of life.

So far in this book I have used the term *lust* in its most common application, which is an illicit desire for sex or an imagination focused on sexual pleasure. But lust doesn't always have to do with drooling over some hot body. Lust can be any illicit or inordinate desire for anything. It can be for something that belongs to someone else, for something we should not have at all, or for too much of something we could legitimately have in moderation. The desire to have your neighbor's new sixteen-foot Bass Tracker pontoon party boat is lust for something that belongs to someone else. The desire for a snort of crack cocaine is lust for something you should not have at all. The desire for a third slice of key lime pie is lust for too much of something that one could legitimately enjoy in moderation. The desire for more clothing than you need, for someone else's husband, for a bigger and more expensive house when the present one is adequate, or for a bigger, faster, more luxurious car than you need may involve some form of unwholesome desire or lust.

Many, if not most, of these desires come through the eyes. What we see arouses the desire to have it. We see it and we want it, like the man who told me he was on a seafood diet. I had never heard of such a diet, so he explained, "A seafood diet means whenever I see food, I eat it." That's the lust of the eyes. And it gets us into a ton of trouble.

You can determine how deeply you're affected by the lust of the eyes by how you score on the materialism text in the appendix. The higher the score, the more you are infected with the problem, and the more you'll be tempted to visit the malls, the sporting shops, or the car dealerships. I have known people who tell me that they can't watch TV's QVC without buying some piece of jewelry.

The lust of the eyes leads most of us into that great American folly, materialism. Now, I want to be careful with definitions here. *Materialism* can mean two things. It is the name of a philosophy that claims matter to be the only reality. The materialist in this sense believes there is no such thing as spirit or anything supernatural. The world that science describes—the physical world we can see, hear, touch, and measure—is all that exists. Philosophical materialists have no use for God's ways simply because they do not believe in God.

The second definition of *materialism* designates a lifestyle in which the accumulation of things is a primary pursuit of life. The person who is a materialist in this sense may or may not be a philosophical materialist. He or she may believe in the existence of a spiritual, supernatural realm and yet be caught up in the idea that the best happiness is found in the accumulation of things. This second definition is the one I use in this chapter.

I've also heard this kind of materialism called *shopperism,* and maybe this is a better definition because aimless shopping can lead to a materialistic lifestyle. We might live more godly lives if we would stay away from the malls, the dress shops, and the sporting goods stores, because just seeing all this stuff displayed in its glory can make our mouths water to have it. And when the tags show hefty markdowns and rebates, it can seem too much to resist. We're caught by the lust of the eyes. If your heart harbors that old selfish belief that life is all about pleasure and pampering, it kicks in, pulls the plastic from your pocket, and propels you to the checkout stand.

My question is this: Is a person who is out of balance in this area focused on the love and care of others?

Just how much stuff does it take to bring you a full and satisfying life? Each of the following men and women have told me that having more things does not add to one's happiness: Billy Graham; his daughter, Anne Graham Lotz; Zig Ziglar; television personalities John Tesh, Kathy Lee Gifford, and Michael Landon Jr.; successful TV infomercial producers Steven Scott and Jimmy Shaughnessy; professional football hall of famer, Steve Largent; and world-famous speaker and survivor of the German concentration camps Corrie ten Boom.

If you try to find fulfillment and happiness in life through things, you'll face the same disappointment that these people have warned us against. It's inevitable because God tells us that the only thing we need for happiness and well-being is him. Seek only him and his will for us, which is loving others, and everything else we need for a joyful life will be added to us (Matthew 6:33). He gives us *all* we need by giving us himself. Can there be any more than *all*? As a very wise person once said, "He who has God and everything else has no more than he who has God only." When you have God at the center of your life, whatever else you gain in material goods is simply overflow.

When you're serving God and serving others in love, sometimes you get rewarded with more *stuff* than you ever dreamed of. That's okay because you can give away the excess. Whether you have more stuff or not doesn't really matter. The important thing is to get filled up with God alone. The other stuff that's added to your life is simply the *run off*. I have and have had more than I ever dreamed of, and nothing I have has ever added one thing to my own quality of life. So I no longer believe that things make me happy, and I now believe that only God is my true source of a meaningful and quality life.

Is my life really better because of all the things I own? Is it of ultimate importance how big my house is, how much disposable income I have, and how many boats, clothes, cars, monster TVs, tennis courts, golf carts, or swimming pools I can buy? As the apostle John said, all this stuff will pass away. It is of no lasting importance. It has all the endurance of a soap bubble, and only what I've invested in God and others will last forever (1 John 2:17).

The average Christian man I meet would say he believes all this, but what I often see in his life proves otherwise. In spite of what he says, what he owns and how he spends his time and money demonstrate his real belief: "If I had just a little more money, a few more acres, a house with just a few more rooms and a home theater, and that sleek, black Lexus I saw in the showroom last week, then I would have to be happier, wouldn't I?" It's no different with the average woman. She may want a little more money, a few more pairs of shoes and dresses, a better coat, new furniture that matches her new carpet, and then she would have the best life she could ask for. It's okay to have everything in moderation, but when the things we want crowd out God and loving others, do we have too much of the lust-of-the-eyes belief?

If you want to see real happiness, come with me as I recount my recent visit to the home of Normlydaylo, a ten-year-old orphan girl in South Africa. My wife and I had to plod almost a mile through tall grass to reach her grass-thatched hut. We entered the hut and found living quarters as sparse as you can imagine— mud walls, dirt floors, a few crude furnishings, no running water, and no bathrooms. The tall grass surrounding the hut provided Normlydaylo's privacy, her playground, and even her main source of food. We had the privilege of eating pottage, a kind of sticky, brownish watery mix made from a local grain. This girl had no clothing except for what World Vision had given her. She lived with her little sister and ailing grandmother, taking care of both of them.

You might think Normlydaylo would be miserable. According to American materialistic standards, she certainly ought to be. But she was not. Not at all. In fact, as we watched her gentle care of her grandmother and her delight in her little sister, we had seldom seen such love and joy reflected in the eyes of anyone. I knew at that moment that it was not my upscale affluent friends back in the States who held the secret of happiness in their wealth; it was this girl and people like her who invest themselves wholeheartedly and lovingly in the service of others. Norma and I walked away from that hut with a deeper sense of dependence on the Spirit of God. We had seen the happy result of such dependence dramatically demonstrated in action.

My daughter, Kari, has been telling us that when it comes to material goods, less is more. Each thing you own turns around and owns you. Think about it. The more stuff you have around you, the more it consumes your time, your worry, your money, your stress, and your heart. Just taking care of the equipment and stuff we own can take up a lot of our spare time. The pool won't be usable unless it has expensive and complex cleaning machinery. This machinery requires care and repair, which requires attention and time. It's the same with all that yard equipment you keep to maintain the several acres you don't need that surrounds your house that's much too big for your family's needs. Your riding mower, leaf blower, edger, sprinkler system, hedge trimmer, fertilizer spreader, weed trimmer, garden tiller—just keeping all that stuff running keeps you running. So much stuff means so much more maintenance, more worry, and more fear. Who wants those negative emotions anyway? Yet we bring those emotions into our lives by the "I have to have that" belief in our hearts. If you've found yourself with much fewer material possessions these days, trust me and the many rich friends I have—you have more time to do the most important things in life: loving God and others.

The more you have, the more you depend on it, and the more you depend on it, the more you fear that you will lose it, which brings on a whole new round of purchases such as a fence and a security system—which brings on another new round of maintenance and attention. It can come to the point where you hardly have time for anything but keeping up with all your stuff. And suddenly you have to work more hours to pay for what you already have or think you need more of.

But the worst thing about materialism is that it can divert you from loving God and others and undermine your dependence on him. His highest command for you is not to crave silver and gold but to crave him as you would silver and gold. He wants nothing more for you than true happiness, joy, fulfillment, and satisfaction, and he knows you can find these qualities only by becoming like him. Becoming like him means to love as dearly as he does. If we want to be truly happy, we must let go of our stuff so we can forget ourselves and make our highest goal loving and serving others. God clearly states that if we hunger and thirst for his righteousness, he will fill us. I love that promise and chew on it every day.

What do you really need to maintain your physical life on this earth? Water, air, food, shelter, and occasional medical care. Instead of seeking these things for yourself, as you change your deepest beliefs, you'll start seeking them for others. See what a difference it makes in your joy. Sometimes in the wee morning hours, I get a picture of the millions of folks around the world who have very little and some who have nothing, and even that is being taken from them. It breaks my heart that in Darfur people are being driven from their homes into pathetic refugee camps. I see them and feel some of their pain, and a sense of compassion fills me with the desire to do more for people in such great need. Do they have water, food, shelter, clothing—the bare basics? I am filled with a desire to help these people in some way. That's why I love partnering with World Vision, the organization that cares for others all over the world.

If you don't naturally desire to help feed and clothe others, ask yourself why. I can assure you it is because you have self-centered beliefs in your heart that need changing. You will not enjoy helping and feeding the poor as long as you harbor the self-seeking belief that your own pleasure is the highest pursuit. This belief will not change unless you take steps to change it. Unless you replace your pleasure-seeking belief with one or all four of the God-ordained beliefs discussed in this book, you will remain more selfish than you want to be. I want to help you change those beliefs in your heart. At the end of every chapter, I will give you a list of key Bible verses that you can begin to hide within your heart to enable you to become more loving and more like God. Like me, you'll start seeing many changes seeping into your life as a result of branding your heart with his words. I would never want you to feel any guilt from me, but if God's words convict you, well, that's another story.

It is important that you change your heart because it seldom works when you do good to others simply out of a sense of duty. If you start serving others without changing your heart, you might find that you resent the intrusion on your time and energy. But if you change your deepest beliefs and become caring and sensitive to their plight, just seeing their gratefulness

> We show by our actions the true belief in our hearts: that love and service are more important than the things we have. You can't have a greater belief branded on your heart. When you have it, your life exhibits how much you love God.

and the difference your help made in their lives might reach your heart and embed your new belief more deeply.

If you can make love for others and a desire to serve them the new belief of your heart, your life will change, and you'll find freedom from all the things that entangle you in materialism. You'll become freer from the lust of the eyes. And I can't say it enough: God is love, and he will give his love to each person who humbly cries out to him. Don't make up your own love. Cry out for the real thing: his love.

The scripture passage that helped me avoid materialism and increase compassion is in Colossians 3:1–17. These are the verses I chose to hide in my heart, making them a part of me and changing my beliefs from materialism to compassion.

> Since, then, you have been raised with Christ [by the power of God], set your hearts on things above, where Christ is seated at the right hand of God. Set your minds on things above, not on earthly things. For you died, and your life is now hidden with Christ in God.
>
> Therefore, as God's chosen people, holy and dearly loved, clothe yourselves with [his] compassion, kindness, humility, gentleness and patience. Bear with each other and forgive whatever grievances you may have against one another. Forgive as the Lord forgave you. And over all these virtues put on love [the best and only true love comes as a gift from God], which binds them all together in perfect unity. (vv. 1–3, 12–14)

C. S. Lewis, the English author of *The Chronicles of Narnia*, once wrote a fanciful little tidbit that gives us a good way to think about our things, unselfishness, and heaven. A great reader and lover of good books, he wrote, "You will find that your library in Heaven contains only some of the books you had on earth . . . The ones you gave away or lent."[1] I love this idea because it gives me a way of thinking not only about books but also about all our material possessions. When we lend or give away our possessions—that is, when we care for others enough to part with what we own for their benefit— we put our material things in proper perspective.

So you see, the stuff we own demonstrates the beliefs in our hearts. Our things can be used either to benefit ourselves, or they can be used to benefit others. And, as Lewis indicates, when we arrive in heaven, we'll find that nothing we gave away or used for others is truly lost. We will ultimately reap great benefits from giving to others.

Scriptures to Hide in Your Heart

"The most important one," answered Jesus, "is this: 'Hear, O Israel, the Lord [King] our God, the Lord is one. [Our God is number one, and no one is above him.] Love the Lord your God with all your heart and with all your soul and with all your mind and with all your strength.' The second is this: 'Love your neighbor as yourself.' [Love others as you want to be loved or as if your neighbor were you.] There is no commandment greater than these." (Mark 12:29–31)

You, my brothers, were called to be free. But do not use your freedom to indulge the sinful nature; rather, serve one another in love. (Galatians 5:13)

But seek first his kingdom and his righteousness, and all these things will be given to you as well. [God knows everything you need; rest in him and seek him with all of your heart as if he were silver and gold.] (Matthew 6:33)

Eight
The Deadly Lust of the Flesh

As I have been moving the Ten Commandments into my heart, I realize that the lust area of life must be grieving our God the most as his eyes move across our world. I'm sure he was saddened by all of my own struggles. We're not to lust and take another man's wife, and neither are we to lust for anything in another man's household: his children, car, goods, and on and on. Lust really is at the heart of not understanding that God's will is to give each one of us all that we need through his riches in glory. But so many of us neglect to hide that truth within our hearts.

A good definition of lust is the desire for that which is forbidden. The desire doesn't have to be for sex; it can be for any pleasure. Lust springs from the belief hidden deep in the heart that the way to get the most out of life is to seek a never-ending flow of pleasure, fun, thrills, and excitement of any kind. Keep the senses happy. Keep the nerves tingling. Keep them stirred up and excited as often as possible.

I have labeled this belief as hedonism, and I'm sticking by that definition. That's what the lust of the flesh really is—outright hedonism, even though our pleasure-seeking culture would have us believe that it's really the essence of enjoying life. I'm aware that a hedonistic person may have only a little of this belief. But whatever amount you have, you'll see the reflection of it in your thoughts, words, and actions. Just be aware, others can see and hear how much hedonism you have. When I was struggling to overcome hedonism, I found a scripture passage that told me that pleasure-seeking is not a key factor in happiness:

> Now the deeds of the flesh are evident, which are: immorality, impurity, sensuality, idolatry, sorcery, enmities, strife, jealousy, outbursts of anger, disputes, dissensions, factions, envying, drunkenness, carousing, and things like these, of which I forewarn you, just as I have forewarned you, that those who practice such things will not inherit the kingdom of God. (Galatians 5:19–21 NASB)

If you have any doubts about how seriously off-track today's culture has gotten, this passage should wake you up. Several items in this list of problem behaviors are blatantly hedonistic, such as sexual immorality, impurity, sensuality, drunkenness, and carousing. Many of the other items may spring indirectly from hedonism, but for the sake of focus, let's look briefly just at those relating to the lust of the flesh.

Sexual immorality is the most obvious lust of the flesh. Our eyes see an attractive member of the opposite sex, and the sight triggers desire. *Impurity* results when we allow lusts for what we should not have to rule our lives, keeping our hearts contaminated with beliefs that prod us to seek pleasure continually.

Sensuality is often associated with sex, but its meaning is much broader than that. The word indicates a complete focus on the pleasure of the senses—all the senses. I don't think it does injustice to Paul's meaning to expand the scope of lust of the eyes to include the desire of any of the senses for continual pleasure. For a person whose greatest pleasure is eating tasty foods, sensuality means *lust of the tongue*. People so addicted to music that they cannot go anywhere without their iPods stuffed into their ears or their car radio booming a heavy bass-driven beat are guilty of *lust of the ears*. (Just a few days ago I pulled up to a stoplight, and my car literally shook from the bass volume blaring from a teen's car next to mine. I wondered how he could possibly understand the words of the music. But then, maybe it's better if he didn't.) The principle of lust for the sensual is the same whether it's your ears, your eyes, or your taste buds that lure you. Just as the adulterer is lured through his senses by the lust of the eyes, we can be drawn into other sins of sensuality by anything that stimulates any of our senses.

The lust of the eyes in this broader sense is responsible for the two other specifically hedonistic sins on Paul's list in Galatians 5. *Drunkenness* comes about from overindulgence in the hedonistic desire for the high that alcohol brings as does indulgence in mind-altering drugs. *Carousing* means essentially wild partying with a no-holds-barred indulgence in drink, sex, and lascivious behavior designed to provoke lust and sensual thrills. As a kid, I could hardly wait to do what the adults whom I admired were doing.

We can fool ourselves into thinking we're not hedonists because we don't engage in such immoral behaviors. But other pursuits often show that indeed we really are hedonists to a degree in pursuit of sensual thrills. We just do it in areas more socially acceptable. I have no idea how much time and money Christians spend on ski trips, golf equipment, snowmobiles, jet skis, motorcycles, bigger and better cars, RVs, cruises, trips to Vegas, movies, videos, live shows, sports events, CDs, DVDs, sound equipment, theme parks—the list is endless. The problem comes when we expect life to be filled with all the fun and thrills these things bring, and it becomes a major focus. Don't kid yourself; it's happening. It happened to me, and it may be happening to you. You must examine your heart.

There's nothing wrong with any of these things until they overpower our hearts and slow us down in our pursuit of loving God and others. And when they lead us into worry, fear, loneliness, discouragement, depression, and the like, this is where we suffer and lose our opportunity of displaying to the world just how powerful God's words are at keeping us at peace and experiencing his joy and happiness. I believe hedonism may be the most destructive force in the world today. It saturates America, and it can seep silently into the heart of each of us. The result can be devastating because the lust of the flesh—the pull toward continual pleasure—leads to dissatisfaction with what we have and the pursuit of more and better. A wife can say to her husband, "I'm tired of you. You don't turn me on any more." A father can say of his children, "I'm sick of putting up with these kids. They really put a damper on my fun and thrills. I think I'll just walk out." An employee can say, "I'm quitting this stupid job! It's too much work, the hours are too long, and it's just not as fun anymore."

When people think like this—and many do—the damage to our nation, our homes, our schools, and our psyches, is beyond calculation. Unless checked, this trend will lead individuals in only one direction: toward the incessant search for more and more stimulating thrills and pleasures. This is because constant sensual stimulation actually increases the desire and raises the satisfaction threshold. It's the nature of pleasure indulged for its own sake to diminish with repetition. The fun gets old, the thrill dulls. Therefore to satisfy the continuing expectation of pleasure, the over-the-top hedonist will expand his or her search to find increasing doses of stimulation. That's why today we have epidemics of pornography, teen sex, high-school teachers making sexual advances on students, drug addictions, pedophilia, alcoholism, gambling addictions, and rampant materialism.

I remember in college walking into the men's washroom and hearing a student tell his friend that his present girlfriend no longer satisfied him sexually. "Tonight I'm going to tell her it's over," he said. He was about to break that poor girl's heart so he could connect with a new girl—whose heart he would also break before too long. Then what would he do after disposing of another girl or two who didn't satisfy him? Try two girls at the same time? Wow, that should be really thrilling. But when that ceased to satisfy, what then? When seeking pleasure is your primary goal, you're on the road to deep disappointment because there is no end to the pleasure search until you're deep into gross immorality and perversion. Then you either have a major sexual addiction with porn or seriously depraved behaviors, or you cope with deep despair because nothing gives you the old kick anymore.

I recently spent a week speaking to a group of Christians on a tropical cruise. One section of the ship was designated for gambling. Each time I wandered through that noisy room, I noticed that most of the people were smoking, drinking alcohol, and of course playing to win big money. A man in our group who had formerly owned a gambling establishment told me that the one-armed bandits are programmed with payoff limits guaranteed to make big bucks for the owners. But each person who feeds quarters to that machine hopes to be that one person who beats the odds and wins a fortune.

I decided to wander around asking the various gamblers why they wanted to win. Their replies varied, but they all had a common thread: to take more pleasure trips; to buy a bigger house; to accumulate more fun toys; to buy bigger and faster cars; to have their own home bar. As I listened, I saw myself in most of their responses. I realized that most of these people had the same pleasure-seeking belief that I had carried to a degree within me for almost sixty years.

It's no wonder that these beliefs seep into us. Our entire nation is out of balance with a deeply engrained belief that pleasures, thrills, excitements, and fun are natural rewards for living on this earth. We deserve it just because we are alive. Pleasure-seeking is normal and right. It sounds a little like the culture Paul describes in the first chapter of Romans, where the people had completely inverted right and wrong. They believed that no one should be denied all the gusto he or she could experience.

It sounds disturbingly like America today, where the widespread belief is that everyone is entitled to a pain-free life of pleasure and comfort, and if that entitlement is thwarted, the responsible party is likely to be sued. I deserve a pain-free, pleasure-filled, warm and cozy life complete with medical care that covers me even if I've ruined my health with my irresponsible, hedonistic lifestyle. If I gain pleasure from smoking, the government should cover the medical costs resulting from my habit. If sex is my highest pleasure, the government has no right to regulate my sexual behavior and it should pay for any inconvenience my actions may cause me in the future, such as disease, an unwanted child, or contraception. If drugs bring me pleasure, the government has no right to punish me for my actions. But if I do go to jail, they had better take great care of me while I'm there, providing good food, entertainment, comfort, good medical care, and good sleeping conditions, because the fact that I was caught doesn't mean I shouldn't have my share of pleasure while incarcerated. Hedonism saturates the entire culture from top to bottom. It's all about how much pleasure I can cram into my life.

The sole purpose of the commercials you see on TV is to stimulate the lust of the flesh. They intend to attract you to more and more pleasure, excitement, fun, and thrills. "Try this and lose weight so you can have more fun or attract more of the opposite sex to you." "See this delicious fast-food hamburger? Doesn't it make your mouth water? Better run out and grab a super-sized." "See this cool, foamy beer with the froth running down the side of the mug? See all the beautiful, smiling young men and women partying as they guzzle? Looks like great fun. Maybe you should go out, have a couple of drinks, and party a little tonight." Advertisers deliberately stimulate the lust of the flesh to promote hedonism, because they want to sell their pleasure-producing products. And it works. We see the commercials and say, "Yeah! I want more of that. Bring it on."

I fully understand why so many hedonists avoid conversations about death. Dying means losing all the pleasures they have crammed into their lives. Late in life, however, when death looms on the horizon, many hedonists finally realize that these thrills and pleasures never brought them the fulfillment or satisfaction they had sought after. They wake up to the hedonistic lie that has entrapped millions upon millions and realize that they have leaned their pleasure ladders against the wrong wall. I want to help you lean your ladder against the right wall. I want to show you how taking on the living words of God can transform you out of hedonistic selfishness into the free and loving person whom God designed you to be.

If I can make this transformation, so can you. I grew up with hedonism running rampant around me, and I indulged my desires for fun and thrills all my life. As early as I can remember, my father spent most of his leisure time fishing and telling exciting tales of his catches when he returned home. The idea sunk in, and most of my life was filled with fun, traveling the world visiting exotic places, and indulging myself in spectacular and exciting activities such as scuba diving, skiing, pampering in beautiful hotels, massages, and music—the list goes on and on, playing in my head like a continuous video. Those mental movies bring up multiple memories of myriad pleasures for more than sixty-five years. No wonder the idea of sacrificial serving was a bit foreign to me in my younger years. The lust of the flesh was a lifelong habit, and it sprang from a childhood belief that life is all about pleasure.

When I found the key to changing that belief, I found several verses showing that the true path to a high-quality life is not in grasping for pleasure, but in yielding to God's Spirit and allowing his blessings to flow through me to others in selfless service. Jesus did not come into the world to find pleasure;

> But God's plan is all about balance, with love having the edge.

he came to serve by laying down his life for you and me. And he urged us to follow his example, saying, "The greatest among you will be your servant" (Matthew 23:11). I really want that kind of greatness, and it can happen only when I become the servant of all. I want to do as Paul instructed the Romans: "Be devoted to one another in brotherly love. Honor one another above yourselves" (Romans 12:10). In later chapters I will give you more verses on overcoming hedonism and serving others. But as we end this section, let's look at the rest of the passage we started with in Galatians. Remember, Paul has warned us about succumbing to the lust of the flesh. Now he says:

> But the fruit of the Spirit is love, joy, peace, patience, kindness, goodness, faithfulness, gentleness, self-control; against such things there is no law. Now those who belong to Christ Jesus have crucified the flesh with its passions and desires. If we live by the Spirit, let us also walk by the Spirit. (Galatians 5:22–25 NASB)

That is the key: walking in the power of God's Spirit, hiding his powerful, living words within our hearts, brings the self-control—the ability that we all desire to crucify our flesh. If we turn our lives over to God, his Spirit and the truth and power of his words will lead us in exercising self-control and overcoming the lust of the flesh.

I know that you want this kind of self-control. No one wants the deadly consequences of lust of the flesh. That's why we call it one of the deadlies. Just one look at those consequences should be enough to scare us into righteousness. Here they are—the gifts the world gives you for following its ways: disharmony, stress, worry, fear, guilt, arguments, addictions, disobedient children, rebellion at home and work, sexual problems (abortions, dysfunctions, diseases), witchcraft and demon influences (hidden anger opens the door to the demonic world), jealousy, envy, workaholism, factions of all types (political, school, church, family), divorce, depression, and despair. The list could be longer, but I think you get the idea.

The way to self-control is to change the beliefs in your heart so that your life is guided by a new standard. And the beliefs you need are readily available to you in the words of God. In the next section of this book, I will show you the four primary beliefs that will rid you of these negative consequences, replacing them with righteousness, peace, and joy in God's Spirit (Romans 14:17–18). I will also show you other scriptures that will help you root out the beliefs of the world. Begin by hiding these scriptures in your heart and watch your beliefs change. Watch as God's Spirit takes control of your life and turns you away from a life dedicated to hedonism toward a life of real pleasure, which is found in loving God and serving others. You'll find that there's nothing in the world like the satisfaction you'll receive when you make love and service to others the new reality in your heart.

Scriptures to Hide in Your Heart

You, my brothers, were called to be free. But do not use your freedom to indulge the sinful nature; rather, serve one another in love. (Galatians 5:13)

Blessed are the poor in spirit,
for theirs is the kingdom of heaven.
Blessed are those who mourn,
for they will be comforted.
Blessed are the meek,
for they will inherit the earth.
Blessed are those who hunger and thirst for righteousness,
for they will be filled.
Blessed are the merciful,
for they will be shown mercy.
Blessed are the pure in heart,
for they will see God.
Blessed are the peacemakers,
for they will be called sons of God.
Blessed are those who are persecuted because of
righteousness,
for theirs is the kingdom of heaven.
Blessed are you when people insult you, persecute you and falsely say all kinds of evil against you because of me. (Matthew 5:3–11)

We all stumble in many ways. If anyone is never at fault in what he says, he is a perfect man, able to keep his whole body in check.

But no man can tame the tongue. It is a restless evil, full of deadly poison.

But he gives us more grace. That is why Scripture says: "God opposes the proud but gives grace to the humble." (James 3:2, 8; 4:6)

These verses tell us that we cannot control our tongues or our lusts. But if we humble ourselves, cry out to God from a position of helplessness, as beggars, God will give us his powerful grace to heal our lustful urges. We therefore can control our words by hiding God's words into our hearts, and then our words become God's words.

Nine
The Deadly Pride of Life

You've seen college football teams running off the field with their index fingers pointed high in the air as they scream out the words, "We are number one! We are number one!" What they're really saying is, "We are the team above all other teams. We are better than all the rest." It's true that they are the champions of that game, that day, that year, but we all know that the feeling of elation that comes from such a victory doesn't keep us happy or satisfied for long.

Yet the clamor for superiority persists. All around the world Americans leave the impression that "we are number one." We project the image that we are somehow better than most other countries. I know that I grew up with that belief buried deep within my heart. The terrorism of 9/11 shocked all of us because we thought, *How dare anyone attack our soil! We'll make them sorry they ever tried that.*

My daughter, Kari, grew up in America, and she, too, took on the typical American pride in how well-off most of us are. But recently she and her family had a dramatic change in their lives. Kari, along with her husband and kids, has decided to adopt a baby girl from a foreign country. This decision came about as a result of a dramatic and life-changing shift within her over the past two years. The change came because she and her family have all been memorizing some key Bible verses and taking each one into their hearts daily. I watched the pride in their all-American lifestyle fade away as they found compassion filling their hearts to reach out in love to an unfortunate victim of poverty. Even I was somewhat taken back by the quick infusion of care that seemed to be filling all of their hearts.

Picture Kari's life and home, and you'll see why it could have easily stayed the same. She's an outstanding elementary school teacher, and her husband, Roger, is one of the most loving men toward his wife and children that I know, and he's a successful businessman. Their thirteen-year-old son is one of my best friends, and their daughter, Hannah, is so cute and friendly that she is my favorite ten-year-old girl on the earth. Kari has it all—a beautiful house, children, friends, a great church, and a successful husband. Why should she change the all-American attitude that so many U.S. citizens have today?

But Kari did change, along with every member of her family. When God's words reach our hearts, we take on the concerns of God. How can anyone see the lives of kids in third-world countries caught up in wars and the AIDS epidemic and not feel compassion for them? When God's words seep into the depth of your heart, your values change and your heart becomes more consistent with the goals of God in loving others. And remember, I don't know of anything more important and satisfying than love. When it takes over your heart, you want to do loving things, and the more you do them, the more you receive. I want to keep feeding the *love machine*.

Kari and her family are so excited about meeting Zoie. Her name means *one who gives life*. I can't wait for the day when she hears what her name means. As I write this, I have yet to meet Zoie. But I love her already because I know she is a creature whom God cherishes deeply, and I am learning to have that kind of love for others in my own heart.

I fear that we Americans tend to have a bad case of the third deadly belief, *the pride of life*. We have been so blessed and we have so much that it's easy to forget God and take credit for getting it all ourselves. We take pride in what we have and attribute it to our own superiority, our own accomplishments. This is what Scripture warns us against as the pride of life.

Without realizing it, even we Christians get caught in the trap our society sets for us. We take on the beliefs of those around us because their lives look so appealing. We see the success of our neighbors—their accomplishments, affluent lifestyles, achievements, and status. What we don't see is what goes on behind their closed doors. All we see are those smiley masks so many people wear to keep up their appearances and their pride. We don't see the emptiness, despair, and insecurity that so often lies buried in their hearts.

Doing It My Way

When we take into our hearts the pride of life, as Paul calls it, we adopt the belief that *it's all about me*. I'm in charge of my life and I get the credit for what I accomplish. This belief is reflected in a classic Frank Sinatra song I remember from the seventies titled "My Way." In this song Ol' Blue Eyes looks back over his life and congratulates himself for his independence. Yes, he's made mistakes and he's been beaten down, but he never gave up his pride. He lived his life exactly as he pleased, and no one was about to tell him what to do.

Of course, Frank Sinatra did not invent the concept of doing it my way. That started long before his time, way back in the primeval forests of Adam and Eve. At the beginning of civilization, Adam and Eve ate the forbidden fruit so they could be free of God and do it their way. They wanted more status and prestige than they had as mere creatures serving under a being bigger than they were. Their move to get out from under God's control was motivated by the pride of life. They wanted to live exactly as they pleased, with no one telling them what to do. In their defense, may I suggest what their reasoning might have been? "Satan told us that if we eat this forbidden fruit, we'll be like God. That means if something goes really wrong, we'll have the power within ourselves to fix things up and start all over again." Is Satan good at motivating people to believe a lie? Yes, very good. Have you ever believed this lie of his? Haven't you ever thought, even once, *Why do I really need God? I can do just fine without him. In fact, I'd like the challenge of figuring out my life and find out just how successful I can be on my own.*

Today, doing it *my way* is thought to be the only way to go. Extreme independence and self-sufficiency are greatly admired, as is a certain bravado and belligerence about it: "I'll plot my own path, and don't you get in my way or suggest that God knows what's best for me or that I should follow his teachings on any level. It's my life, and I'll live it as I please."

As you can see, this belief is very self-centered. It's the me-first belief that we live in a dog-eat-dog world and I intend to be the eater instead of the eaten. I intend to get mine first, and if I have to, I'll run over others to get it. Such self-centered people live as if God does not exist. So they were created by what? The big bang? If they can believe a theory like that, they can easily believe they created themselves and wrote their own rule book on how they should live; and everything is going to be just fine and rosy for them.

Please, look around and open your eyes to what is taking place today. How do we explain the misery, addictions, poverty, emptiness, greediness, and so many criminal elements within our land? Our high level of self-centeredness is eating us alive.

Egoists who hold this belief feel assured that they will get what they want because they believe themselves to be as powerful as their own thoughts. Whatever they put their minds to, they will eventually get. And there is some truth to that, but not in the way many people believe.

I recently read a best-selling book titled *The Secret* by Rhonda Byrne. The main premise of the book is that anyone, simply by the power of his or her mind, can bring into existence whatever he or she can imagine. At one level I appreciate this concept because I've been teaching that what we think about determines our beliefs, which in turn determines our actions. But I have one big problem with the author's use of the premise: even though she acknowledges God, she leaves it up to each individual to determine the kinds of thoughts one will use to create his or her future. This means one's beliefs need not come from God; they are self-determined and may not reflect the best outcome for the person's ultimate well-being. According to Ms. Byrne's philosophy, a person could decide to create a future in which he or she is the most self-centered person on earth with billions of dollars to use solely for pleasure and comfort. That's not exactly a belief that reflects the love and character of God. It's a self-centered concept that says the universe revolves around me, and I can use this technique to get whatever I want—houses, cars, vacations, health, and good relationships. People who create their own beliefs from their own thoughts are likely to center on the pride of life, thinking on what they want, what they want to accomplish, and what makes them look good.

If they do not turn to God as their standard, what grid do they run their thoughts through? How do they determine whether their beliefs are right or true or promote their long-term well-being? If I adopt God's beliefs into my heart, I'm assured that they are right, true, and promote my well-being. God knows me and loves me, and reliance on his words will give me the best possible life. But without God I can imagine almost anything and decide for myself whether it's right or good. Hitler did. Osama bin Laden did. Just think of the hundreds of men and women down through history, and even today, who imagined evil actions that became all-too-real horrors inflicted upon humanity. Simply thinking thoughts that seem to get me what I want for the moment doesn't cut it.

Yes, it's true that what you think about deeply and passionately often becomes reality. That is why I stress so fervently the strong need to think on the right things. Since what you think about will determine the deep beliefs of your heart, it is absolutely essential that you think about the words of God, because those words reveal his character. The more you implant his words in your heart, the better you will come to know and love him, and in knowing and loving him intimately, you will be transformed into his likeness. I choose to let the teachings of Christ rule my mind and think only on those things that are true, honorable, right, pure, lovely, admirable, excellent, and worthy of praise (Philippians 4:8).

The Deadly Effects of Pride

Self-centered egoism or the pride of life can come from one's basic philosophical beliefs. If a person does not believe that God created the world and everything in it, then naturally he will not feel the presence of a guide and protector for his life. This person will naturally turn to himself for guidance, reaching deep within to the "god inside" as the only rule for living. Such people will feel alone in the universe and will naturally run their own lives in their own way.

Self-centered egoism can also arise from the experience of trauma or tragedy. I remember Jeff, one of my close friends in grade school, confiding in me one night while we camped out under the stars. As the night grew colder, he admitted that his dad had threatened him if he didn't swear on his deceased mother's grave that he would never set foot in any church, no matter what. I asked why on earth his father had warned him against a church. He told me that after his mom had attended a church for several years, the choir director seduced her into an affair. When his dad found out and the church fired the man, his mom carried the guilt and shame to an early death. His dad had found her with several bottles of deadly pills next to her lifeless body.

My friend had watched his dad become broken and discouraged as bitterness ate away at his heart. He promised his dad that he would stay away from any kind of Christian place of worship. He hated Christians. I could almost see the venom coming from his mouth in the very way he said it. He tolerated me because at the time I wasn't a believer in God or Christ.

We were very young then, but through the years I watched my friend brand his hatred upon his heart. He married and had a family but eventually lost them through divorce. His former wife told me that she just couldn't live with him any longer because in his bitterness and fear, he never let her into his life.

When deep anger and hatred penetrate the heart as deep beliefs, they tend to shut out everyone, including God (1 John 2:9–11). Long-held anger blinds a person's eyes to the light of God. When my friend turned away from God, he put himself in control of his life and lived it *his* way. His deeply branded belief became the pride of life, and it wrecked his life.

People like this friend who have come through some great pain or loss may think God is not real because he allowed this terrible thing to happen to them. They think over and over again that no one else is looking out for them, so they must look out for themselves. Or instead of dismissing God, they may harbor deep anger at some person who inflicted the tragedy upon them. This leads them into a protective mode in which they mark off self's territory and defend it tooth and nail. The idea that happiness lies in the opposite direction—in loving God and loving even those who misuse and hurt you—seems totally nonsensical to them. They tend to think on what hurt them over and over again until those thoughts become embedded in their hearts as deep beliefs. Deep destructive beliefs. I address the solution to this problem in depth in chapter 12.

I no longer let those who have wronged me get under my skin and damage my heart with resentment. Instead, I eliminate them. Before you gasp in horror, let me explain that I like to eliminate my enemies by forgiving them and turning them into friends. Some of my worst enemies have become my most prized trophies. To gain such trophies involves forgiveness, which can come about only when one gives up the pride of life.

The two deadlies I've already discussed—the lust of the eyes and the lust of the flesh—go hand in hand with the pride of life. People who live for themselves will naturally want to have everything they see that can give pleasure. The pride of life adds to this lust for pleasure the idea of status. Not only do they want all those comforts and goodies for their own use; they want to have more of them than their neighbors. They love it when they see the couple next door peeking out their curtains at their new luxury RV. They want not only the pleasure that they can get from all the stuff they have; they want to feel superior because of how much they are able to accumulate. It gives them a sense of worth and enhances their status in the eyes of others.

Egoism and selfish ambition—the pride of life—is why so many executives scratch, claw, and backstab to get to the top. When they get that top floor corner office complete with private washroom, they have arrived. Not only have they enabled themselves to buy more stuff and indulge in more pleasures, they have achieved a status above that of their fellow employees. They have proved their superiority over others. They're number one.

Seeking a Servant's Heart

Of course, no Christian would ever think this way, right? Oh, how I wish that were true. But I suspect that a lot of Christians have engorged their hearts with this egoistic standard we see all about us. Frankly, when it comes to the pride of life I don't see much difference in many Christians and the rest of the world. How could we see the difference when so many of us have picked up the beliefs that dominate our society? It saddens me when I hear fellow Christians touting that "we are number one" because we should be setting the pace, demonstrating by our example that not self-seeking, but others-seeking, or a servant's heart, leads us to our Creator's choice. We find our status, our recognition, and our security only in God. It's what he thinks of us that counts. Nothing else matters. The only words of praise and commendation I now want to hear is the voice of my beloved Jesus saying, "Well done, good and faithful servant."

I truly want God to be pleased with me. As I hide his words within me, he becomes more pleased with me because he sees more of his reflection in my life. As you join me in memorizing and hiding God's powerful, living words, we'll see more and more of his nature within us and less and less of the self-centered ways of the world.

I am not interested when some book tries to tell me that the secret to life is getting whatever you want. I will turn to my Creator's manual for the best way to live my life. My goal is simply to know him better so I can be more like him. And I find what I need in order to accomplish that everywhere in his book—the Beatitudes, the Ten Commandments, the Lord's Prayer, and the two greatest commandments. Those are the things I choose to think about. If his words tell me that the way to find true happiness and meaning is to love God and others, that's what I find myself wanting to do naturally as more of his words permeate my heart. His truth is what I choose to think about every day.

I now dream every day about helping people in every corner of the world. I crave to know more of God's power so I can use it to serve and pray for a diseased person, to set a man free from lust, to free people from the overwhelming urge to plunge into pornography. I love it when I can help people, like Dave in chapter 6, find this kind of freedom. There are thousands of people out there like Dave who need to experience the love of God. You and I are the ones who are charged to pass on that love.

Several years ago I counseled a Hollywood star who had just won an Academy Award. Naturally, on Oscar night she was on cloud nine. She was at the pinnacle of success and had accomplished the fame, recognition, and status that proclaimed to the world that she was the best. It was heady stuff. Yet, after just six months she was depressed, miserable, and in need of serious counseling. Why? Because she had bought into the belief that getting to the top would mean permanent fulfillment and satisfaction. The great prestige of that award would give her life meaning.

I understood because I had already gone through a similar disappointment. Just a few years before, I had won the highest award for the best TV infomercial. The infomercial had been filmed with Dick Clark, and I thought I had arrived. How pleased I was to watch myself night after night on national TV. But within six months I, too, became discouraged because the glory of my TV life and the ongoing income associated with it seemed empty and unfulfilling. I did what I advised this actress to do: I learned to rejoice again, which means I turned away from false expectations raised by the world's adulation to the one source of true joy—Jesus. *Rejoice* means to keep on returning to the source of your real joy.

As everyone who's been there and done that knows, life doesn't work that way. Getting to the top or getting enormous recognition is as empty as the wind. It's what the wise king Solomon discovered after living a life filled with luxury, women, power, prestige, and entertainment. He had it all, but he learned that all he had was nothing but vanity and vexation of the spirit. The human heart was designed to be filled with God, and to fill it with anything else is like filling the stomach with seawater. It doesn't satisfy, it doesn't nourish, it leaves you craving more, and it will eventually kill you. As Solomon learned, the pride of life is empty and meaningless. Nothing but God himself can satisfy the human heart. As he wrote, "Here is the conclusion of the matter: Fear [remain in awe of] God and keep his commandments [love him and others], for this is the whole duty of man" (Ecclesiastes 12:13).

Not one of the three deadlies will satisfy the human heart. Adam and Eve thought they would. They lusted after the forbidden fruit, decided to do things their way, and by turning from God to themselves, lost their intimacy with the greatest love they had ever known.

Jesus, on the other hand, understood the emptiness of the deadlies when he faced Satan in the desert. Satan did his best to tempt Jesus with the deadlies. After fasting forty days Jesus was famished, and Satan urged him to defy God's order of things by turning stones into bread (the lust of the flesh). After urging Jesus to challenge God by putting him to a test, Satan led him up a high mountain and showed him all the kingdoms of the earth in their splendor. "It can all be yours," Satan told him. He hoped the lust of the eyes and the pride of life would tempt Jesus to turn from God in order to have all the power and glory glittering before his eyes.

But what did Jesus do? He used the words of God hidden in his heart. He shooed Satan away and quoted to him the first commandment: "Worship the Lord your God and serve him only" (Matthew 4:10). And that is the choice we must make when facing the three deadlies. If we succumb to the lust of the eyes, the lust of the flesh, and the pride of life, we serve only ourselves, which means we are following the way of Satan. But if we hide in our hearts the words of God that provide an antidote to the deadlies, we worship God by coming out of our selfishness and serving others.

To begin your victory over the deadlies, I will give you three scriptures to start hiding in your heart. Memorize these verses, chew on them daily, study them, absorb their meaning, emboss them into your heart, and they will do you a world of good in moving you on the continuum from selfishness to service.

Scriptures to Hide in Your Heart

 Without faith it is impossible to please God, because anyone who comes to him must believe that he exists and that he rewards those who earnestly seek him. (Hebrews 11:6)

 And the second is like it: "Love your neighbor as yourself." (Matthew 22:39)

Do nothing out of selfish ambition or vain conceit, but in humility consider others better than yourselves. (Philippians 2:3)

Ten
The High Value of Loving God

I'll never forget being in Ghana, Africa, speaking to a group of ministers and their wives. I had heard from the U.S. State Department that Ghana was a very unsafe place because of the communist leaders and influence. My wife wouldn't come with me because of the official warning. But after a few days, I realized that the people of Ghana exhibited a strange sense of calmness and decorum in spite of the danger. As a result of their demeanor, I felt a sense of safety everywhere I walked. I couldn't figure it out.

The more I became acquainted with these people, the more I fell in love with them. They had a deep passion to love God and to love each other as God loves them, and they always behaved in an uncannily orderly and courteous way. The same was true even of their young people. I actually witnessed more than twenty thousand kids of all ages coming to our general meetings to hear about Jesus. Would you expect this many kids in one place to be orderly, polite, and peaceful? They were.

As you can imagine, as the days went by I became more and more curious as to why the people behaved so well and why we experienced this feeling of safety in a politically unstable land. The answer surprised me. It was rooted in the religious beliefs these people grew up with. A large portion of them believed that their deceased relatives were constantly watching them. When I talked to many of the young people after the meetings, I found out that none of them wanted to do anything disruptive or dishonoring to each other or to the adult leadership because they believed their relatives in heaven would beat the snot out of them eternally when they themselves joined them in heaven. When they goofed up on earth, they had to apologize to their relatives immediately.

These people behaved respectfully out of fear. They had grown up with a theology that said their dead relatives were everywhere, watching them with a judgmental eye. Their heaven was a place where everyone would eventually arrive, but life in that heaven was not good for those who had been bad on earth.

You can see how the deep beliefs in these people's hearts controlled all their actions and words. And you can easily see the superiority of a theology of love over a theology of fear. The people of Ghana believed in a theology of fear, and that came out in their actions because they feared the evil consequences of bad behavior. Pure Christianity, on the other hand, is based on a theology of love. The belief in the Christian's heart affirms a God of deep love who wants to see his beloved children obey him out of love for him because that is the best way for them to find peace, joy, and fulfillment. Huge difference!

The word *theology* scares most Christians. We tend to think of theology as something deep and heavy and, well, pretty dry. But the word *theology* means, simply, "words about God." It has to do with how we describe, think of, and perceive who God is. Nothing deep or heavy about that. Actually, you have a theology yourself. So do I. Everyone alive has a theology of some kind. We have all formed some idea about who God is and what he is like. You may see God as the creator to be surrendered to, or some kind of unknown being, whether a he, a she, or the universal force out there somewhere vaguely influencing life. Pantheists believe that God is in the forces of nature. Hindus have millions of gods. From the nature gods of South Sea islands to the ancestral gods of African tribes, gods of all descriptions abound. Even atheists have a theology. The very word *atheist* means essentially one who has decided against theism or against God.

Not all these gods people believe in are good for your health. Some tribal gods demand human sacrifice. Some tribes will kill you if you don't believe in their official god. In some countries, religious men claim the right to rape and abuse females who worship a different god from the majority. I just read of a "holy" man in a Middle Eastern country who stated that if he found anyone who does not believe in his form of religion, he will cut that person's throat from ear to ear so the people of his faith can remain "moral and pure." I can only imagine what kind of belief he holds in his heart about his god. In our own country's history, women accused of being witches were burned at the stake. Even now there are Satan worshipers who practice animal and human sacrifice. Gods in primitive areas are often seen as agents of terrible punishments to those who fail to toe the line.

As you can see, theology isn't some abstract exercise of the mind with no practical meaning: your theology is crucially important. I assure you that your theology will dictate your behavior, your relationships, your beliefs—really your entire life. So it's essential . . . no, it's absolutely critical that you build your life on an accurate theology. Or, if you prefer, an accurate picture of who God is and what he is like.

But in the do-it-my-way, tolerant, feel-good society of America today, the human tendency is for each person to make God into whatever he or she wants him to be. I'm sure you've heard people say, "I just can't believe in a God who would send anyone to hell," or "I believe in a God of love, who just wants us all to be happy," or "I don't believe in a God who would give us so much pleasure in sex and then expect us not to enjoy it in any way we want." We tend to put self first, deciding how we think the world and our lives should be, and then we create for ourselves a god who approves it all.

You may not trust anyone but yourself. Like Sinatra, you may be determined to do it your way with no one telling you what to do or how to do it. If that's the case, you have made yourself your own god. I've tried this, and let me tell you, I made a lousy god.

As my experience in Ghana illustrates, most of the religions of the world fall into two categories. In the first category, God is distant, and to please him a person must perform certain actions and say certain approved words. People living under these religions fear being punished for any wrong acts or words. There is no personal love relationship between the people and their god. In the second category, God is loving, caring, and forgiving. He designed people to walk with him daily in a love relationship. Only one religion falls into this category, and it happens to be Christianity. A follower of Christ is not in a religion; he's in a loving, caring relationship with Christ.

The God of Christianity—where I find myself worshiping the God of Abraham—sent his only Son to show us how to live on this earth. He came to suffer and die for our sins so that we are forgiven. And now he gives us his very Spirit to empower us to live the loving life he created us to live. God has given me the freedom to love him and others as I want to be loved. Can you imagine living in a community where people are forgiving, gentle, kind, under control, loving, full of peace instead of stress, and more concerned about you than they are themselves? That's true Christianity. In Christianity we find a place where we are loved and cared for by both God and others. That is God's design.

America is in trouble today because people have lost their vision of God. But when God's people, who are called by his name, humble themselves and seek him with all their hearts, he shall save their land (2 Chronicles 7:14). As we hide his commandments of love into our hearts, we will find that we are no longer automatically sinning against him. I so desire this for America and the world. Let the world see the love we have for each other and they will know that our God is real.

I have found that the only God who can do me any good is the God who is real—the Hebrew and Christian God who is introduced to us in the Bible. And it just happens that the God who is real is also the one who loves me dearly and who invites me into a personal relationship with him. When I accepted that invitation and entered into that relationship, I realized how much he loved me, and I willingly made him and his words the guiding principle of my life. God is my boss, my King, and my Lord. I put him in charge. And he rewarded me by transforming my life and giving me more real joy than I ever imagined one human could experience.

Obviously, it doesn't work that way for everyone. Not everyone finds the high value I found in loving God. And there is usually one reason for that: people tend to carry with them mistaken beliefs about what God is really like. Even people who think they believe in the one, true God often see him as someone unlovable and even fearsome. I have found that people can believe anything and everything about God—some of it terribly distorted, and some of it downright false. If you want to change your life, however, it is absolutely necessary that you place your heart in the hands of Abraham's God. And I know that you will be unwilling to do that until you understand his love and his deep care for you. That is why I want you to know the absolute truth about God—who he is, his loving character, and how much he loves you and longs to have a relationship with you. But you may be carrying baggage from the past that keeps you from knowing the truth about God. So let's look at some of this baggage and get it out of the way before I tell you about the true God who loves you and what it can mean for you to love him in return.

Pictures of God I Don't Want in My Heart

A God compared to my earthly father or mother. As much as we would like to think our image of God comes straight from the Bible and the teachings of the church, we sometimes project onto God the unloving characteristics of the people who most strongly influence us. For example, one of the most often-used biblical terms for God is *Father*. God is referred to as Father one hundred eighty-seven times in the four gospels. What does that term call to your mind?

For some fortunate people the idea of God as Father presents a comforting, loving, and protective image that accurately reflects the nature of the true God. But this is not the case for many others. Imagine a little girl of seven who has known only rejection and abuse from her father. What will be her perception of God when her Sunday school teacher tells her that God is like a father? She will likely see God as an unstable, rejecting, abusing person she cannot trust. The term *father* may cause others to see God as distant, impersonal, and uncaring, or like a drill sergeant, demanding and angry, with no tolerance for mistakes. Those who were not blessed with good fathers will need to see past their bad experiences and understand God to be the kind of father they can depend on without reservation.

A Stained-Glass God. Did your church building have beautifully colored glass windows—maybe picturing an ethereal-looking figure of Christ that hardly fit in the real world? Maybe those windows conditioned you to think of God as being separate from everyday life—some holy, spiritual, otherworldly being you could contact only in a religious location, such as a synagogue or a building with a steeple. If you were used to worshiping God in one of those locations, then you may be conditioned to think little about him unless you are in such a building. You may think of God as living in a temple made by human hands and not as living within your heart.

An Absentee God. Many people see God as distant and uninvolved in our lives. Indeed, this is what the deists believe and teach—that God made all things and then left them to run on their own while he turned his attention elsewhere. Many people who are not deists, many Christians in fact, tend to think of God in this way. They feel that he is up there somewhere and even sees us and knows what we're doing. But they have no relationship with him and think it's up to them to pull themselves up and perform well enough to earn his willingness to save them. The idea of a God to relate to personally and intimately seems foreign to anyone with an absentee god.

A Scorekeeper God. People with this kind of god are relentlessly burdened with guilt. He's up there looking down on you with a judgmental eye, ready to pounce the moment you get out of line. He has this great black book where he keeps a detailed record of everything you do, good or bad. When you get to heaven he will tally up both the good column and the bad. If your good deeds outnumber the bad, then he will let you in. But if not, well . . . you're in big trouble.

An Onstar God. This god is not with you every moment of every day in close relationship, but he is on call for the moment you encounter any situation you can't handle yourself. Just push a button and he is there to solve your problem, give you direction, or get you out of a jam. "This is God, what is your emergency?" Prayer is what pushes that button, which means you need not bother to pray until you have a need. In the days before electronics, this god was called the genie-in-a-bottle god or maybe the in-case-of-emergency-break-the-glass god.

A Grandpa God. Ahhh, but isn't this a pleasing picture? Many of us choose to believe in a god who just wants us happy. He never disciplines us, but turns his head when we do something wrong and smiles indulgently and forgives easily when we go astray. He gives us anything we ask for and just wants to be loved and to get along with everyone. He's a relaxed, benign, easy-to-please, available, rocking-chair kind of guy who loves to spoil us by giving us whatever we want. Come to think of it, this sounds likes me with my eight grandkids and two on the way. When eight-year-old Reagan looks at me with those endearing eyes, how can I say no? But her mom or dad can step in and stop my actions: "Dad, don't give her everything she asks for. We have to live with her."

These beliefs about God are quite common. Some of them are pretty fearsome and tend to drive people away from God. No one wants a god like an abusive father, a scorekeeper god, or an absentee god. On the other hand, some of these beliefs are pretty appealing. On the surface, at least. An Onstar god or a grandpa god seem like pretty good gods to have. All the benefits and none of the downside. The problem with these seemingly benevolent beliefs about God are twofold: First, they are not as benevolent as they seem. There is love in God's discipline. Deep down, do we really want to be left alone to make a mess of our lives when the application of discipline would turn us around and lead us to real joy? The second problem with these overly benevolent and self-serving beliefs is simply that they are not true. That is reason enough not to want them in your heart.

Deep down, no one wants to believe a lie, no matter how comforting. No matter how uncomfortable the truth may seem at first, no matter how much I must adjust my beliefs to the truth, I want the beliefs in my heart to be absolutely true. I want them to conform exactly to how God designed me to believe for my good and his glory. And here's the good thing I discovered when I made that decision: the truth only seems to hurt when you look at it from the outside. When you understand the truth from the inside, it's the most comforting, delightful, and loving belief you can have. That's the truth about God that I want to show you next. And in showing you the truth, I will show you the God you can love with your whole heart. "Then you will know the truth, and the truth will set you free" (John 8:32). Just like you, I'm aware that people of most other religions have the same conviction that I have. They, too, believe that their god is the true god. But have they found the same peace, joy, and love I'm finding? And the real question to you is, have you found it yet? Try what I've found, and see for yourself.

The Truth About God

As I looked at the different gods around the globe, I found only one who instills love within our hearts and teaches us how to love others. What Jesus describes as the two greatest commandments solves all of humankind's major interpersonal problems. Actually, if consistently applied, they would solve international problems as well. Those two commandments—to love God and love others—sum up the entire Ten Commandments and all other biblical commands. They give the lives of men and women the greatest possible enrichment. What else would humanity need if we all truly loved God and others?

At this point you may be thinking, *Sure, I would like to believe in a God who could solve all of our problems, but how do I know this God is real? How do I know this is all really true?* To answer that question I could go into all the many rational and evidential proofs showing that God is real and true, but others have already done that quite effectively, and that's not the purpose of this book. You will find excellent and convincing arguments for God by reading authors such as C. S. Lewis, Ravi Zacharias, Lee Strobel, Josh McDowell, or William Lane Craig. I can only give my own story and tell you of the miracles that God has performed in my life.

The best way to know God is real is to try him. Try his ways and see if they work. That's what I did. Why not join me in hiding the Judeo-Christian God's own words in your heart and see for yourself how powerful the changes in your life can be? Submit to his two love laws completely and test them for yourself. See how you will be transformed into a more compassionate person. See for yourself that the peace God will give you is worth more than any amount of money. You'll start enjoying more self-control, more gentleness, more patience, more kindness, and many more expressions of genuine love. All of these qualities come as free gifts from this God I'm telling you about. The best way to learn the high value of loving God is simply to love him and hide his words within your heart so that you won't sin against him.

These words that you hide in your heart are extremely powerful. "For the word of God is living and active. Sharper than any double-edged sword, it penetrates even to dividing soul and spirit, joints and marrow; it judges the thoughts and attitudes of the heart" (Hebrews 4:12). These are the words that will be transforming you into his image by the power of his Spirit.

When I tested God by trying out his words of wisdom and instruction, I came to know that he is real and true. This is the God who set me free from lust, hedonism, materialism, and a host of other bad habits. I think more like him now because I have many of his words embedded within my heart. Those new beliefs that came from God are now a part of me. When you memorize a key verse or section of God's words and then meditate on each verse every day as many times as possible, his will becomes your way of living. The power of God's Holy Spirit enters you and transforms you into a person who reflects more and more of God's loving character.

So if you want to learn the power of the one, true God, what are the primary beliefs about him that you want in your heart? Let's look at a few.

Beliefs About God That I Want in My Heart

What I am about to tell you may seem impossible, but it's absolutely true. It's the miraculous thing God has done in my life.

When I was in my early thirties, I felt strongly about the growing disintegration of families and the relationship problems between husbands and wives. I felt a need to help couples and families address these problems. I sought the counsel of Dr. Henry Brandt, who advised me to do the following: (1) Write a book telling couples and families what God had taught me about being a godly husband and dad. (2) Record tapes on the same subjects and publish them all over the world. (3) Produce movies or videos on these subjects. (4) Ask God to open doors for me to speak at large gatherings to couples and families all over the world. (5) Keep counseling people on a personal basis to avoid becoming "ivory towerish" in my teaching to others. Wow! What a list! From a logical point of view, none of this made sense. It was impossible. I had ADHD, which made me a poor reader; I was terrible at writing because my grammar and spelling were atrocious; I'm dyslexic, and would type twenty-five words per minute with ten mistakes per line. I was far from being a dynamic speaker; I was only an assistant minister in a local church and had no national platform; and I lived in the small city of Waco, Texas, hardly a place to find the resources for such ambitious projects as Dr. Brandt recommended.

Yet I felt the hand of God on me, and I prayed fervently day and night for him to work a miracle and use me mightily to help couples and families. Then in faith I took seriously the scriptures in Luke 11:5–13 and 18:1–8 and set out to prove them true. And they were. Within six months, all five of Dr. Brandt's recommendations were in process, soon to be a major part of my life.

I'll spare you the details of how this miracle came about. The point is that God worked a miracle in my life. You can ask him anything that plugs into his two great commands to love him and love others and watch him open doors for you. Since then I've witnessed God's miracles time and again. He has given me everything that I have prayed for in regard to my service to him and others. Everything. Allow that to sink in for a moment. He has miraculously answered my prayers within two years from the time I prayed them, on the average, and many times within six months.

I still don't understand how God does it any more than I understand what's inside of this computer and how I can send an e-mail to Russia in seconds. But I use my computer anyway. When God says he will be faithful to give his children whatever they ask *in his name*, that's what he means. I just take it as fact and cooperate with my Creator by praying as he tells me to pray.

I want the God of love in my heart. God made you and me so he could love us. And he made us so we could return the same kind of love to him. Had you thought of that? We were created to enjoy a personal, loving relationship with God and to find rich enjoyment in all creation. The Scriptures affirm this idea everywhere: "I have loved you with an everlasting love" (Jeremiah 31:3). "So God created human beings in his own image . . . Then God blessed them and said, 'Be fruitful and multiply. Fill the earth and govern it'" (Genesis 1:27–28 NLT). "God . . . richly provides us with everything for our enjoyment" (1 Timothy 6:17). "Even before the world was made, God had already chosen us to be his through our union with Christ . . . Because of his love God had already decided that through Jesus Christ he would make us his children—this was his pleasure and purpose" (Ephesians 1:4–5 GNT). He designed us to seek him first and love him with our whole heart, soul, mind, and strength. And when we do this, everything we need on this earth will be given to us. That's a powerful promise.

Think about how special we are in God's creation. He made us his deputies to rule the earth, and he intended for us to do it by the power of his Spirit living within us in a close, intimate relationship of love. We alone out of all other creatures are able to receive his love, pass it on to others, and love him in return. That's our purpose for being. The whole idea boggles my mind.

Even more wonderful is the rest of the story. When man rejected God's love and turned away from him, he was heartbroken, so he came after us. He came down and sacrificed himself on a cross to restore the loving relationship we had broken. Now we can reestablish that relationship and again enter into a loving bond with God. When we do this, we come to know and love God fully, and we begin to live in harmony with his purpose for us. Loving God produces the kind of joy he intended for us in the beginning.

Do you see why I want to live under a God like this? Do you see why I love and serve him? I want my tombstone to read like that of an old British cavalier soldier who lost his life in battle for the royalist cause: "He served King Charles with a constant, dangerous, and expensive loyalty."[1] When my stone is engraved, just change "King Charles" to "The King of kings," and you'll have it.

I want in my heart the God who became a man. The first verses of the book of John tell me that Jesus is God incarnate. Jesus is the Word, the essence of God revealed to us in human form. God became a man so that you and I could see in the flesh exactly what he is like. While on this earth, everything Jesus did was exactly what God the Father in heaven directed him to do. The Word became flesh and dwelled among us (John 5:19; 8:28). Is that amazing or what?

We humans simply cannot completely understand the nature of God— how he can have three aspects—Father, Son, and Holy Spirit—and yet be one God. But then, why should we expect to understand him? We are merely his creatures, and it would be strange if we understood everything about our Creator, wouldn't it? In fact, a God you could understand wouldn't be much of a God, because he would have to be small enough to fit inside your mind. But while we can't understand all about God, we can understand what he reveals to us about himself. And he has revealed all we need to know. The late Francis Schaeffer said that we cannot know God fully, but we can know him truly. My Chevy truck helps me to understand God's three-in-one nature. It is one car, but it has three main parts: a chassis, an engine, and a body. God is one with three interconnected parts, which function together to do all that God does. We are told that all three of his aspects were involved in creation. The Spirit of God meditated on the surface of the watery blob that was to be the earth, perhaps planning out the process (Genesis 1:2). The Father spoke the earth into existence (Genesis 1:3–25). And Jesus as the Word that was spoken formed all that exists (John 1:1–3).

Then when his beloved man and woman fell from the perfection he intended for them, God came to earth as a man and saved all of mankind. Why did he do this? Simply because he loved us too much to leave us to die. Just think about how wonderful this love really is. He came to die for us and rescue us from eternal death while we were rejecting him, going our own way, and thumbing our noses at him. He came to give us back the life we had thrown away. Even now he gives us his own Spirit to live in our being and provide the power to conform to his way (Ephesians 3:16–20). That's why I find such high value in loving God. After all he's done for me, I would be a fool not to love him in return.

Just a sidenote about the reality of Scripture. Recently, one of our pastors explained why it's easy for him to believe the Bible's message. There are thirty-five hundred specific prophesies about Jesus Christ and future events from as far back as five thousand years ago. Three thousand of them have happened exactly as prophesized. The probability of those prophesies happening is like throwing a can of ink into a print shop and getting the entire works of Shakespeare in return or like filling up Texas with stacks of quarters as high as the moon, painting one of them red, and finding that red quarter in one try. (This helps me too.)

Loving God means taking his life into me, submitting to him fully, and accepting the tremendous gift of the new life he offers to replace my bumbling efforts to do it my way. When I hide his words in my heart, I no longer have to depend on my own little mind to know the truth about what is best for me. I then have more and more of the mind of Christ (Philippians 2:2–5). Just think of it; I share God's own wisdom. It's like having my computer linked to the Library of Congress, able to download to my own hard disk all the wisdom ever written. I have that kind of access to God's wisdom. And when his words reach my heart, his Holy Spirit empowers me to live his words and become more like him.

I want the God who rules as King in my heart. My wife, Norma, has one requirement when I fly in private planes: there must be two pilots. Her reason is obvious: if one pilot were to get sick or incapacitated, there will be a backup. I've tried to convince her that I should get my pilot's license so that I could take over in any life-threatening situation. But she seems to think that having me at the controls of a plane *is* a life-threatening situation. She suspects that I have not been blessed with the appropriate personality to fly a plane. She wants a professional. She wants me around as long as possible. But I don't think that my ADHD would affect my being a pilot. "Hey, look! There's a chicken over there."

For years I lived my life as if God were *my* backup pilot. I had the stick in my own hand, but I wanted God there just in case. As long as I was flying smoothly and knew where I was, I remained in control. But if things got bad, I wanted God handy so I could turn the controls over to him to land the plane. Now things have changed. When I embed God's words deeply and absorb their message, I step out of the pilot's seat and turn the stick over to him. No longer is he my co-pilot; he is my pilot. I have deposed myself as the king of my life and submitted to the reign of King Jesus. I no longer even sit up in the pilots' area; I stick to the passengers' seats.

Let me just say again that all of Christ's teachings are expressions of his two greatest commandments. I say this because so many people get too nervous about saying, "Christ is my King." They think they have to learn and perfectly obey hundreds of commands. Relax. God will give you the *power* to love him and others and the power to keep any commandment he instructs us to do. It's never a burden, but a delight.

I want in my heart a God who has given me his Spirit. Jesus knew his disciples would be devastated when he left them to return to heaven. So on the night before his crucifixion he promised to send them a Counselor, his own Holy Spirit, to be with them, to comfort them, and to be their constant companion, just as Jesus had been:

> Now I am going to him who sent me. . . . Because I have said these things, you are filled with grief. But I tell you the truth: It is for your good that I am going away. Unless I go away, the Counselor will not come to you; but if I go, I will send him to you. (John 16:5–7)

Ten days after Jesus ascended into heaven, the disciples were together in a room when suddenly, with the sound of rushing wind and the sight of tongues of fire, the Spirit of God came into them. The purpose of the Holy Spirit was to fulfill what author James Packer calls a "floodlight ministry" in relation to Jesus Christ.[2] The Spirit illuminates Christ and makes him real to us. He reveals the truth about Jesus just as the lights on billboards reveal the messages on the signs. The function of the lights is to make the message on the billboard clear to those who pass.

But when he, the Spirit of truth, comes, he will guide you into all truth. He will not speak on his own; he will speak only what he hears, and he will tell you what is yet to come. He will bring glory to me by taking from what is mine and making it known to you. (John 16:13–14)

Jesus introduced us to God by coming to earth as an approachable man, putting human flesh on the Lord of the universe to show us what God is like. Now that he is no longer here in the flesh, the Holy Spirit shows us the ways of Christ by living in us and counseling us just as Jesus did to those twelve companions in Palestine. Just think of it. You and I have the high honor of being the home of God. God will now live in you and me if we will just love him enough to open the door and invite him in.

"But," you may ask, "how can I know whether the Holy Spirit lives in my life?" When God's Spirit lives within you, you have the desire to share with others what God has done for you. You will also reflect more and more of God's loving character. A man I once knew was determined that I should speak in spiritual tongues. God knows I don't want to miss anything he wants me to have, so I tried to be open and listen to the man's reasons for believing I should speak in tongues. But he became so insistent, rude, brash, obnoxious, pushy, and overbearing that I found it difficult to be truly open. And his methods got even worse as he began to accuse me of not being an authentic Christian because I did not speak in tongues. Once he even grabbed my throat and shook me, somehow thinking this would force out of me God's words in a foreign language. As you can imagine, this experience not only frightened me, it turned me off completely.

Finally I asked this man, "If I start speaking in tongues, will I also become more like you?"

For a long moment he gave me that how-dare-you-speak-to-me-that-way? look. But he finally said, "I've been rude and judgmental toward you, haven't I?"

"Yes, you have."

"I'm so sorry," he replied. "I can see why you have resisted my urgings." He prayed for me and walked away, never again to mention that special gift of the Holy Spirit.

God's Spirit will not give us a pushy, divisive, unloving, or obnoxious character. When he enters us we will become more loving, more tolerant, less judgmental and more accepting of each other. When you find your character being transformed into that of Christ's, you know that God's Spirit and his powerful words live in you. If you don't have more of God's loving character, then you should question just what spirit may be directing your actions.

I want a God in my heart who has given me written instructions on how to live my life. Michael Billester, a Bible distributor, visited a small Polish town shortly before World War II. Before he left, Billester gave a Bible to a villager, who was converted by reading it. The villager passed the Book to others who also shared it until two hundred people had become believers through that one Bible. When Billester returned in 1940, this group of Christians invited him to preach. He suggested that several in the audience recite verses of scripture. One man stood and said, "Perhaps we misunderstood. Did you mean verses or chapters?" These villagers had memorized not merely a few select verses of the Bible, but whole chapters and books. Thirteen people knew Matthew, Luke, and half of Genesis. Another had memorized the Psalms. That single copy of the Bible had done its work. Transformed lives bore witness to the power of the Word.[3]

This is the kind of passion for the words of God that I pray you will feel as you delve into the richness of the Bible. It's the kind of passion many writers of the Bible itself have felt for the words of God: "How sweet are your words to my taste, sweeter than honey to my mouth!" (Psalm 119:103). "Happy is the one who reads this book . . . and obey[s] what is written in [it]!" (Revelation 1:3 GNT). "Guard my teachings as your most precious possession . . . Write them deep within your heart" (Proverbs 7:2–3 NLT).

I find the Bible so dear and valuable because it is yet another evidence of how much God loves me. When I read the Bible, I can't help but love God in return. In loving him, I become more like him, which means taking those dear words he has given me and embedding them into my heart until they become a part of who I am.

One Great Obstacle to Belief

One of the biggest obstacles to a belief in God is trying to mix God with hedonism. In a counseling session a woman told me that she didn't believe in God. I asked her one simple question that instantly brought tears spilling down her cheeks: "How many men have you had sex with?"

"Too many to count," she sobbed. "Why in the world did you ask me that?"

"Because when you are sexually active with others who are not your mate, it tends to deaden your soul."

The main reason that immorality dulls sensitivity to God is that we know

God does not approve. Therefore we turn our backs on him in order to get on with what we want to do. As Paul tells us:

> They are darkened in their understanding and separated from the life of God because of the ignorance that is in them due to the hardening of their hearts. Having lost all sensitivity, they have given themselves over to sensuality so as to indulge in every kind of impurity, with a continual lust for more. (Ephesians 4:18–19)

I know this to be true from my own experience. It's clear to me now that my past sexual activities kept me from seeking God. The flesh is opposed to the Spirit. If we feed the flesh, the Spirit withers away. We can't have two gods operating within us at the same time. We will always end up following only one of them, and as long as we entertain our lusts, the one we follow will not be the true God of heaven.

We are often led to believe that well-known atheistic thinkers always support their refusal to believe in God with evolutionary evidence and rational philosophy. But that is not the case. In moments of candor some have admitted to another basis for their disbelief. English novelist Aldous Huxley, the world-famous author of *Brave New World*, chose atheism because it gave him freedom from meaning and morality.

> I had motives for not wanting the world to have meaning, consequently I assumed it had none. For myself, as no doubt for most of my contemporaries, the philosophy of meaninglessness was essentially an instrument of liberation . . . from a certain system of morality. We objected to the morality because it interfered with our sexual freedom.[4]

There you have it. A truth frankly expressed that supports the point I am making. We choose either to pursue our own way—our own wants and desires—or we allow God to direct us in the way we should go, the way to happiness, love, and real joy. When we insist on going our own way, you can be sure that we will ultimately crash. A now-famous and often-used story illustrates why this must be true:

> The captain of a large ship looked out into the darkness and saw faint lights in the distance. Immediately he commanded the signalman to send a message: "Alter your course ten degrees south."

The return message came promptly: "Alter your course ten degrees north."

The captain was not accustomed to having his commands ignored, so he sent a second message: "Alter your course ten degrees south. I am Captain Wilson."

He received a quick reply. "Alter your course ten degrees north. I am seaman third class Jones."

Immediately the now angry Captain Wilson sent a third message, knowing it would strike fear and produce the proper response: "Alter your course ten degrees south. I am a battleship."

The reply came instantly: "Alter your course ten degrees north. I am a lighthouse on a rocky cliff."

That story demonstrates the ultimate folly of our insistence on ignoring God and going our own way. We want *him* to do the moving. But God by nature is solid and dependable. If he simply allowed us to accommodate our whims without warning and instruction to the contrary, he would not be doing us a favor. We would be doomed to crash and shatter our lives.

Now, I would not be doing you a favor if I told you that coming to God, taking his words into your heart, and inviting his Spirit into your life means all your sailing will be smooth, caressing breezes will blow, and you'll never get seasick. No, most of the time we will have the very same pains the world experiences, but the difference is that we'll have God teaching us how to respond. When we adopt God's attitude toward pain, it will not make us miserable, but bring us even closer to him. In chapter 12, I will show you how pain and difficulties actually bring good results to our lives. It's much like the pain we feel when we have a tooth extracted or a boil lanced. The pain is necessary but the results are wonderful. That's the kind of pain God sometimes allows, but it's worth it, as C. S. Lewis points out in this famous passage:

I think that many of us, when Christ has enabled us to overcome one or two sins that were an obvious nuisance, are inclined to feel (though we do not put it into words) that we are now good enough. He has done all we wanted him to do, and we should be obliged if he would leave us alone. But the question is not what we intended ourselves to be, but what he intended us to be when he made us. . . . Imagine yourself as a living house. God comes in to rebuild that house. At first, perhaps, you can understand what he is doing. He is getting the drains right and stopping the leaks in the roof and so on. You knew that those jobs needed doing and so you are not surprised. But presently he starts knocking the house about in a way that hurts abominably and does not seem to make sense. What on earth is he up to? The explanation is that he is building quite a different house from the one you thought of—throwing out a new wing here, putting on an extra floor there, running up towers, making courtyards. You thought you were going to be made into a decent little cottage, but he is building a palace. He intends to come and live in it himself.[5]

That, I believe, summarizes the true value of loving God. When we love him enough to put ourselves in his hands, he remakes us into something more wonderful than we could imagine for ourselves. He remakes us into his idea of what we should be, not our own. He remakes us into his own image. Think of it. Give yourself to God and you can become like God, reflecting his character and his glory.

When you fill your heart with his words, you push out your own self-serving beliefs that keep you bound to your lusts and desires. Instead of filling your heart with self, you fill it with God. He fills that empty space that has ached in the human heart since Adam and Eve kicked him out of their lives. As Pascal put it, it's a "God-shaped vacuum" that exists in every human heart. And it will remain unfilled until we fill it with God.

When we fill our lives with God, we fill our lives with love. That love never ends, but keeps pouring in. We find great joy when we spread that overflow of love into the lives of others. It fulfills our purpose. That's why the two greatest commands are to love God and love each other. That's what we're made for, and when you fulfill the purpose for which you're made, the result is more joy than you ever imagined.

Scriptures to Hide in Your Heart

"The most important one," answered Jesus, "is this: 'Hear, O Israel, the Lord our God, the Lord is one. Love the Lord your God with all your heart and with all your soul and with all your mind and with all your strength.' The second is this: 'Love your neighbor as yourself.' There is no commandment greater than these."

"Well said, teacher," the man replied. "You are right in saying that God is one and there is no other but him." (Mark 12:29–32)

Hear, O Israel: The LORD our God, the LORD is one. Love the LORD your God with all your heart and with all your soul and with all your strength. These commandments that I give you today are to be upon your *hearts*. Impress them on your children. Talk about them when you sit at home and when you walk along the road, when you lie down and when you get up. Tie them as symbols on your hands and bind them on your foreheads. Write them on the doorframes of your houses and on your gates. (Deuteronomy 6:4–9, emphasis mine)

And without faith it is impossible to please God, because anyone who comes to him must believe that he exists and that he rewards those who earnestly seek him. (Hebrews 11:6)

"Whoever has my commands and obeys them, he is the one who loves me. He who loves me will be loved by my Father, and I too will love him and show myself to him."

Jesus replied, "If anyone loves me, he will obey my teaching. My Father will love him, and we will come to him and make our home with him." (John 14:21, 23)

My command is this: Love each other as I have loved you. (John 15:12)

Eleven
The High Value
of Loving Others

World-famous cardiologist Dean Ornish says that if you are loving God and people well, you can eat junk food and still remain healthy. He also tells us that we are 500 percent more likely to contract a major illness when we are isolated from loving people.[1] God designed us to receive and give love. When we don't follow his design, things start going wrong, emotionally, spiritually, and even physically. Life is love, everything else is just details.

When you read the account of creation in Genesis, you can't help but notice the change in the tone of the narrative when it begins to describe how God created man. For six days we see a dazzling display of energy and explosive generation as God speaks and things spring into existence throughout space and over the earth—light, clouds, seas, fish, grass, flowers, shrubbery, trees, bugs, reptiles, birds, and mammals. It's a spectacular and whirlwind account, and on that sixth day the earth teems with vibrant life in forms, colors, textures, and aromas that didn't exist a week before.

But on that sixth day, after the mammals appear and begin grazing and gathering, it's as if a hush settles over all creation. The story slows; the camera zooms in; the music lowers into vibrating chords of anticipation. God is about to do something extremely important, extremely special. For the first time, God doesn't merely speak a new creature into existence; this time the act of creation is hands-on and personal. "The LORD God formed the man from the dust of the ground and breathed into his nostrils the breath of life, and the man became a living being" (Genesis 2:7).

Clearly, in all God's creation there is something special about man and woman. Genesis tells us explicitly just what it is: they were created in God's own image (Genesis 1:27), and God gave them the entire planet and all its creatures to rule and care for. Furthermore, God breathed into them his own Spirit, giving them an intimate connection with God that no other creature had. The man and woman were the only beings in all creation designed to carry the very life of God inside him. In other words, they were God's deputies, his agents, his representatives to all the rest of the creatures on the earth.

And God's attention to our creation didn't end on that sixth day. The psalmist David expresses his great awe and wonder at the detailed and careful attention God gives each of us as he lovingly forms us within the womb:

> For you created my inmost being;
>> you knit me together in my mother's womb.
> I praise you because I am fearfully and wonderfully made;
>> your works are wonderful,
>> I know that full well.
> My frame was not hidden from you
>> when I was made in the secret place.
> (Psalm 139:13–15)

Obviously our creation was a giant labor of love on God's part.

Why did God create man and woman on just this one celestial planet and none other? That alone gives me goose bumps. And why give man and woman a luscious home in a world of pristine beauty created just for their nourishment and enjoyment? Because he wanted creatures to love who would willingly love him in return. The very thought is staggering: he created me just so he could love me. And love me he does, with a tenacious, never-ending, sacrificial kind of love that refuses to let me go, even when I wander away from the good he offers. There is nothing good you can do to make him love you more. There is nothing bad you can do to make him love you less. There is nothing you can do to add value to your life or to take value away. You cannot escape his love. You cannot sin your way out of it. You cannot do anything that will keep him from loving you. You are extremely valuable simply because the God of the universe places such high value on you.[2]

If we have any doubts about the high value God places on us or how much he loves us, the incarnation and crucifixion of Jesus lay them to rest. When man turned his back on God's love and plunged into the deadlies, God was heartbroken. He couldn't stand to lose us. So he left all the comfort and riches of heaven and came down to the sweltering, trouble-ridden earth to suffer a humiliating and painful death in order to reconcile his precious humans to himself.[3] When the God of heaven and earth leaves his glory to come and die for you, how can you doubt his great love and your great value?

In the previous section, we discussed the three deadlies: the lust of the flesh, the lust of the eyes, and the pride of life. We looked at what happens when we become obsessed with pleasure, possessions, and position. One reason people strive for these deadlies is to fill their empty lives. They somehow think their value or self-worth is determined by how much fun they can have, how much stuff they own, or what title is written on their office door. But none of these things affects their value in the eyes of God. The janitor has the same worth as the CEO. The busboy has the same worth as the restaurant owner. The checker at Wal-Mart has the same worth as the president of Wal-Mart. And that value resides in the fact that we are created and beloved by the supreme Master and Controller of the universe.

Loving What God Loves

In the greatest sermon ever preached, the one Jesus delivered to a crowd gathered on the side of a Judean mountain, he said, "In everything, do to others what you would have them do to you, for this sums up the Law and the Prophets."[4] This idea of loving others is a theme throughout the entire New Testament—and really throughout the entire Bible.

For a picture of just how strongly God feels about our need to love others, look at his famous parable about the sheep and the goats. When Christ returns, he will judge all people, dividing them on his right and left as a shepherd divides his sheep from goats. He will send the goats on his left into eternal punishment. But those on the right will be given eternal life. What was the basis for his approval? Here's how Jesus explained it:

> For I was hungry and you gave me something to eat, I was thirsty and you gave me something to drink, I was a stranger and you invited me in, I needed clothes and you clothed me, I was sick and you looked after me, I was in prison and you came to visit me. (Matthew 25:35–36)

The ones on his right were happy but surprised. They didn't remember ever seeing Jesus hungry or thirsty, needing clothing, sick, needing shelter, or in prison. So Jesus explained further: "I tell you the truth, whatever you did for one of the least of these brothers of mine, you did for me" (Matthew 25:40).

Do you get the picture? Every time we show love to another person, we show love to God himself. He loves all of us so much and identifies with our needs so much that he makes no distinction between loving our fellow humans and loving him. And according to this parable, loving others is so important to God that he makes it the primary criteria for judgment. It's not your correct theology that earns God's approval. It's not attending the right church. It's not performing all the right rituals in just the right way. The big thing in God's eyes is how much you love and serve your fellow humans.

The great disciple of love, John, amplifies this idea in his first letter: "If anyone says, 'I love God,' yet hates his brother, he is a liar. For anyone who does not love his brother, whom he has seen, cannot love God, whom he has not seen" (1 John 4:20).

In the previous chapter, we discussed why it is important to love God. He is worthy of love and service because of all he does for us. But why is it so important for us to love other people? What can they do for us? In fact, it often seems that other people are not doing things *for* us so much as doing things *to* us. What's the point of loving them? Well, it's really quite simple: if we are to be like God, we must love like God. That means loving what he loves. Sometimes after introducing one of my friends to another friend, the first thing I hear is, "Any friend of Gary's is a friend of mine." That gets to the heart of why we should love other people. Any beloved of God's should be a beloved of ours. That means we must place the high value on all humans that he places on them. And we must love them as he does. And the great part of this is that God gives us his love so that we can love others!

C. S. Lewis understood the high value of loving others and the value God places on them. He reminded us of the potential for eternal glory in heaven that each person bears when he wrote:

There are no ordinary people. You have never talked with a mere mortal. Nations, cultures, arts, civilizations—these are mortal, and their life is to ours as the life of a gnat. But it is immortals whom we joke with, work with, marry, snub, and exploit—immortal horrors or everlasting splendors . . . Next to the Blessed Sacrament itself, your neighbor is the holiest object presented to your senses.[5]

This gives us a picture of how valuable we are to God and thus how valuable we will be to each other as God's words and Holy Spirit control us. God made us to be like him and to live with him forever in eternal joy and happiness. That is huge! That alone shows the immense value of each person. We are created to be immortal.

Do I Have to Love *Everyone?*

No doubt you have encountered a number of people that "even a mother can't love"—difficult people you deal with on your job, in business relationships, in your church, in your immediate social circle, or even in your own family. No doubt you have been hurt by mean or uncaring people, people who deliberately cheated you, lied to you, undermined your projects, stood in the way of some cherished goal, or even caused injury or death to someone dear to you. Does God really expect me to love a person like that? Do I really have to love people who do bad things and hurt other people?

I have to tell you that the answer is *yes*. But the great news is, don't try loving others with your human, measly love, but cry out to God and ask him for his powerful love. Then you can start loving anyone, even yourself, the way God designed us to be loved. One of the major reasons God crashed into humanity some two thousand years ago is he knew we *can't* love others in the way they need without reestablishing a connection with God through his Son, Jesus Christ. And this is where life has become so exciting for me. I get his love when I see and admit to God that I am a bankrupt beggar, a helpless person bringing nothing of eternal value to him. Then I can use God's love with both myself and others. James 4:6 tells us that God gives his grace to the humble but resists the proud. How blessed is the person who is poor in spirit (a humble beggar) because he receives "the kingdom of God . . . righteousness, peace and joy in the Holy Spirit" (Romans 14:17). For the past several months, I have been thrilled to fall before God each day and admit how much of a beggar I am. I do realize that I can't love as God, so I don't try to anymore. I do my part of humbling myself before him, and he does his part by granting me his powerful love.

Most humans have enough love for at least one unlovable person whose life is filled with terrible deeds, attitudes, thoughts, and flaws that would make an angel blush. Who is that person? It's the one whose face you adore every morning in the mirror. As Paul said, "After all, no one ever hated his own body, but he feeds and cares for it, just as Christ does the church—for we are members of his body" (Ephesians 5:29–30). We all love ourselves. Even suicidal people love themselves. Many take their own lives because they love themselves so much that they take that extreme measure to rid themselves of pain.

So admit it: you do love at least one imperfect person. In fact, loving yourself seems to be a logical necessity if we are to love others as we love ourselves. And the way you love yourself provides the key to the way you should love others. So let's look for a moment at just what it means to love yourself.

I'm sure that all your life you've heard the phrase "hate the sin but love the sinner." That's the way you love yourself. You certainly don't like everything you do. You don't like the mistakes you've made, the habits you can't get rid of, your failure to control your lust, your temper, or your powerlessness against addictions. Yet in spite of these flaws and sins, you still want the best for yourself. In fact, the reason you hate these sins and weaknesses is that you know they are not good for you. They keep you from living the kind of life you want to live and being the kind of person you want to be. When you look at your own life, you understand your weaknesses and your desire to be better. You may not justify these weaknesses and sins, but you understand your struggle against them, and therefore you forgive yourself for them. You care for yourself in spite of your flaws. In other words, in this one particular case at least, you hate the sin and love the sinner.

This is exactly the way God wants us to love others—as we love ourselves. That is, we hate the sins and weaknesses that cause them to act obnoxiously or cheat or steal or harm, but when we have God's love, we want the best for them. We will want them to be rid of the motivations and deadly desires lodged in their hearts that make them act the way they do. We'll want them to have the peace and happiness they want as much as you want peace and happiness for yourself.

I think one reason we have trouble loving those who hurt us is that we think of love as a warm, fuzzy feeling. We think that loving people means we have to like them. Again, think of the way you treat yourself. I certainly haven't always liked myself. For example, not too long ago I was in Springfield, Missouri, and had time to kill. Norma and I had talked a little about buying a motor home, and I just happened to wander by a business that sold them. On the lot stood a fine-looking used motor home. It was a 1991 model, but the salesman explained that it had a brand-new engine. The guy took me step-by-step through all the remodeling, repair, and upgrades they had done to this vehicle. I loved it. It even smelled great. And to top it off, he gave me an awesome price. I plopped down the money and drove happily away, thinking what a nice surprise I had for my wife.

I almost didn't make it home. The engine began to make strange noises, so I drove to a mechanic who agreed that the engine wasn't running right, but he couldn't identify the problem. What was worse, Norma didn't like the motor home. I thought Missouri had a "lemon law" that allowed buyers to return purchases for refund within three days. But the seller gleefully told me that Missouri had no such law and refused to undo the deal.

I tried to sell the thing but got no takers. So I loaned it to my son Michael to drive to his next seminar in Houston. It broke down on the way. While it was being repaired, he had to rent a car, drive to Houston, and pick up the motor home on his return trip. It broke down again in Springfield. He called friends to pick him up there and drive him home to Branson. I had the motor home repaired at considerable cost, and it finally ran great.

One day soon afterward, my daughter, Kari, called. "Dad, I heard you got the camper fixed," she said. "May we use it?"

I agreed, and she and her family packed it up and headed out for vacation. It wasn't long before she called me on her cell phone. "Dad, I'm at the three-way intersection in the middle of traffic, and this camper of yours has broken down."

"Just push it out of the way," I wisely advised.

"Dad, the brakes lock automatically when the engine is off. It won't move."

I had the thing towed and told the mechanic to go over the whole vehicle with a magnifying glass and fix everything that even looked like it might be thinking about not working. It took him three days and a small fortune, but it then ran like a finely tuned Rolls Royce. No more problems.

I offered it to my son Greg for his upcoming speaking trip. "It's running great now," I assured him. No more problems."

"No thanks, Dad. I think I'll pass."

Michael had another seminar. I offered it to him with the same assurance. He didn't want any part of it. Kari's family had another trip coming up, and I offered it to her. She wouldn't touch it with a ten-foot pole. I offered it to several friends, but they all said, "Thanks, but no thanks." Their minds had already been poisoned by rumors. My wife refused to step inside the thing even when it was idle.

So I lowered the price to a ridiculous figure and sold the monster. I thought of going into business. I would buy used motor homes, spend a fortune fixing them up, and sell them for less than I paid for them. What a great way to love others.

During that entire fiasco, my stomach churned with tension and anxiety. I began to doubt my good sense and competence and started running myself down. *Smalley, what in thunder is wrong with you? You're such an idiot. Can't you do anything right? Why didn't you think this thing through at the beginning? Why didn't you try out that camper before you bought it? Why didn't you show it to your wife first? You dummy!* I don't like to be belittled, but there I was, belittling myself through the whole episode. I didn't like myself at the time.

I don't run myself down like that anymore. I remember that even though I am a fallen creature filled with sins and weaknesses, I am created in the image of God, and I have the glorious capacity to become like him. Now when I face a weakness or a problem in my life, I think, *Oh, there's another weakness. I'm not only weak, I'm bankrupt. The Holy Spirit is going to move right into that spot, and that's the very place where the image of God will be perfected in me. Thank you, God, for this weakness, because that's where you will become visible in my life.* In doing this I simply follow the model of Paul, who had a bothersome weakness that he prayed for God to remove. And then Paul writes, "But he said to me, 'My grace is sufficient for you, for my power is made perfect in weakness'" (2 Corinthians 12:9).

So you see, I no longer dislike myself because of my weaknesses. They are part of the human condition as fallen creatures, and God's love for us is so strong that he willingly moves into our lives and fills those weaknesses with himself. The weaker I admit I am, the stronger his love within me. If God can love me in spite of those bothersome flaws, I can love myself as God's dear creature in spite of them.

We are called simply to apply to other people that same principle we apply to ourselves. We don't have to like people with an obnoxious or hurtful sin. We don't have to feel lovey-dovey affection for them. What God requires is for us to will good things for them as he empowers us. Pray that they will find power in the words of God and instill them into their hearts so that God will enter their lives and fill those weak spots with himself. Don't try to pretend that the terrible things others do are not really bad. It's not loving to trivialize sin or dismiss it as unimportant. Keep on disliking their greed, their abuse, or their untruthfulness. Don't gloss over these terrible things. But want for them the same thing you want for yourself: to bring God into their hearts so they can be free of the deadlies and have a life filled with the great love God designed for us.

Loving Your Enemies

I love what Mark Twain said about difficulties in the Bible: "It ain't the parts of the Bible that I don't understand that bother me, it is the parts that I *do* understand." I suppose the following words of Jesus must be among the most difficult passages of the Bible—not because they are hard to understand, but because they are hard to obey:

> But I tell you who hear me: Love your enemies, do good to those who hate you, bless those who curse you, pray for those who mistreat you. (Luke 6:27–28)

What? Love your *enemies*? You may be thinking, *surely this doesn't really mean exactly what it says.* You may understand that you are to love others as yourself, and that you must learn to love the obnoxious and bothersome people in your life. (He gives us that type of love because that's his type of love.) But must you love real enemies? People who have done terrible things to you or others? Do I have to love Osama bin Laden or Hitler? Does a mother have to love the killer pedophile who raped and killed her seven-year-old daughter? Did Corrie ten Boom have to love the Nazi officer who tortured and killed her sister? Did Elizabeth Elliot have to love the South American Indians who killed her missionary husband? Surely Jesus is not insisting that we must go that far.

Elizabeth Elliot did indeed think Jesus meant to go that far. A few years after her husband was killed, she returned to South America with another family of missionaries and witnessed the conversion of her husband's very killers to Christ. Christ himself set the example while he was on the cross. He looked out over those gloating Jewish leaders who had trumped up charges and hired false witnesses to get him killed, and those brutal Romans who had flogged and mocked him and nailed him to the cross, and he said, "Father, forgive them, for they do not know what they are doing" (Luke 23:34). In fact, the very reason he was on the cross was so he could forgive not only them but also all of us who have sinned against God and thus become his enemies (Romans 5:9–11).

Let me tell you how I have learned to love my enemies. I force myself to think not of what my enemy has done to me but rather to think of what he is created to be. He is created with what Lewis called a tremendous "weight of glory" as a being made in the image of God and capable of becoming like him. I realize that whatever my enemy did to me was caused by some wrong belief that somehow got into his heart—some deadly thought that may have been passed on to him by his parents or that he absorbed from his friends and coworkers or that he fell into through lust, materialism, hedonism, or pride. I remind myself that he—the essential person that he was created to be—is dearly loved by God, and God grieves because of the sin in his life. If I am to reflect God, I must do the same. And when I can't, which is all of the time, I cry out to God for his gift of love. God is love, and again he gives it only to the humble, the beggars who realize they are in love bankruptcy.

Can you imagine being a relative of one of the murdered victims of David Berkowitz, also known as "Son of Sam"? How hard would it be for you to forgive him? Few humans could muster up the love to do it. Yet when David got down on his knees and asked for forgiveness, God gave it to him. He has been transformed by God and his words. (You can read his testimony by typing his name in on Google.) It's the same kind of love and forgiveness God gave to you and me, who crucified him with our sins. If we are to love as God loves, we must pass along the forgiveness he offers us and forgive those who have hurt us badly. And that means even people like Son of Sam.

It's true that some people are really hard to love. They don't want to be that way; everyone needs love and desires it whether they know it or not. They are hard to love because one or more of the deadlies has lodged in their hearts and pulls the strings of their life. They are trapped. A deadly has taken over and controls all their attitudes and actions. People caught in this way should not be objects of scorn, but rather objects of compassion, concern, pity, sympathy, help, and most of all, love.

Do you know people who are hard to love because of their evil, wicked behavior? Think of them as being trapped by one of the deadly beliefs. Realizing how the curse of the deadlies can ruin people's lives, I find it easier to love those people when I think of them as being caught in the grip of the evil that has lodged in their heart.

I found another key to loving my enemies in the second phrase of that troublesome verse in Luke. Jesus said not only to love your enemies but also to "do good to those who hate you." Bummer. At first glance it seems that this already difficult verse gets even more difficult. Can I get by with loving my enemies as a mental or spiritual exercise solely within my own heart? No, apparently I am to put my thoughts into action and actually do something good for that enemy of mine. I am to walk across the room and forgive the Nazi who killed my sister, as Corrie ten Boom did. I am to go back to that hostile tribe and convert the killers of my husband, as Elizabeth Elliot did.

I actually had the privilege of doing that with a person who had done terrible damage to my emotional life. He over-controlled all my activities and time, wounding my family and me by overworking me to the point that I watched my own kids tear up each time I left home. But when I learned that his tyrannical behavior stemmed from many tormenting experiences early in his own life, I was filled with compassion for this man. I understood that people tend to give out the same abuse they have experienced themselves. Almost 100 percent of child molesters, for example, were abused as children. When I learned of this man's pain, I released the hate and enmity I had felt over the years and freely forgave him. I can tell you that I could never have done that on my own. That kind of love and forgiveness had to be given to me by God himself. But the important thing to note here is that the power to forgive came to me only after I felt his pain. I got inside his heart and understood him. I grew to love him as my understanding of his own pain increased.

What such actions do is show your enemies the heart of God. After doing something bad to you, the last thing they expect is for you to turn around and love them, forgive them, or do something good for them. In their minds, the world just doesn't work that way. Believe me, it will make a huge impression on them. They will not understand and will likely be puzzled. It's not unusual for people who have good returned for their evil to be melted by the action and open themselves to hearing how you were able to repay evil with good.

When you repay evil with good, you are exposing your enemy to the love of God, which can have a positive effect on his or her life—possibly even a heart-changing effect—either immediately or in time. He or she may not react well at first, but over time I've seen many of my enemies return love to me after seeing me live what I preach.

In the last segment of the passage about loving our enemies, Jesus says that you should "bless those who curse you, pray for those who mistreat you." When I bless my enemies, I will that they should have God's goodness placed into their lives. I want the best kind of beliefs to come into their hearts so that they can come under the lordship of Christ. When I pray for anyone who has mistreated me, I simply follow the example of Christ who prayed for his conniving persecutors and brutal Romans who, to say the least, mistreated him. How can I refuse to do that for anyone when Christ did it for these people who had treated him so horribly? And I must always remember he did it for me as well.

Learning to Love by Serving

As I said earlier, we get confused about the meaning of love because we tend to want to connect the word with feeling affection or liking another person. When we like someone or have genuine affection for him or her, we have no trouble having loving thoughts about that person. But when affection is not involved, we may be uncertain about how to love that person. How do I know

I'm loving people for whom I have no liking or affection? For an answer, let's turn once more to C. S. Lewis, who wrote so eloquently on the subject:

> Do not waste time bothering whether you "love" your neighbour; act as if you did. As soon as we do this, we find one of the great secrets. When you are behaving as if you loved someone, you will presently come to love him. If you injure someone you dislike, you will find yourself disliking him more. If you do him a good turn, you will find yourself disliking him less.[6]

Lewis shows us a great principle: it's hard to dislike someone when you do something good for him. The good deed is somewhat like an investment. When you expend time and energy on anything, you invest yourself in it, which increases its values in your eyes. Therefore, when you spend time and energy on behalf of another person, your estimation of the worth of that person increases. It follows that if that person is your enemy, your bad feelings toward him are likely to change to good feelings because you have invested something of yourself in him.

That may be one reason God encourages us to serve others rather than to serve ourselves. But there is also another reason: when we serve others, we are serving God, as Jesus told us in his parable of the sheep and goats (Matthew 25:31–46). That is why we can willingly serve a hard, cold, tyrannical boss or a spouse who is closed off from us. We are serving God. Ephesians 5:21 says, "Submit to one another out of reverence for Christ." When we submit to God, we serve God. When we submit to one another, we also serve God. A young person can serve a domineering parent because her service is rooted in her reverence for Christ. Serving God and serving each other is rooted in our gratitude and thankfulness for what God has done for us. This is why Scripture says that we love because he first loved us.

The one scripture that motivates me the most to serve others is Galatians 5:13, which I've already quoted many times: "You, my brothers, were called to be free. But do not use your freedom to indulge the sinful nature; rather, serve one another in love." Today I no longer use the freedom that Christ has given me to serve my own lustful or sinful pleasures. Instead, I use my freedom to love others by serving them. And I willingly do this because this verse has already reached my heart, and I review it each and every day. I absolutely love watching God's words changing me more into his image day after day. His words are really true: when I hide them in my heart, I don't continue to sin against him.

When we understand this deep reason behind our willingness to show love by serving, it makes loving others, even our enemies, much easier. We think of God as our Lord or boss or King. We are his servants. In the Old Testament, a servant could love his master so much that he would make a commitment to serve him for the rest of his life. To ratify that decision the master would drive an awl (an instrument something like an ice pick) through the earlobe of the servant. From that moment on, the bondservant surrendered himself totally to his master in the confidence that his master would treat him well.

If you are willing to become a bondservant of God, you can willingly serve others no matter what their return gesture may be. People can be frustrating and cruel, but when your allegiance is to God you can love them anyway. You can love them without any thought of what you might get back in return because you know that God fills you up with all the fullness of himself. When you try to help others, they may judge your motives. Help them anyway. If you succeed in life, you will win false friends and even enemies. Succeed anyway. Your good deeds of yesterday are already forgotten. Keep doing good anyway. As you help and serve others, they will often bite you and hurt you. Serve anyway. What they do and think does not matter. By serving them you are serving your God and showing to them his loving nature. Just remember that it's God who rewards you and keeps you in his arms all the days of your life.

Hiding Words of Love and Service in Your Heart

Why do so many people who claim to follow Christ do terrible things to others? Many Christians mistreat their spouses and children, cheat on their taxes, rip off their customers, betray their families, and do all the unloving things that you might expect an unbeliever to do. Here is my answer: We humans can have any number of beliefs stored in our hearts. We can even have contradictory beliefs functioning simultaneously. That is why it is extremely important to take note of your behavior all the time. Your behavior is an extension of your beliefs, a way of gauging your progress toward conforming to the image of God.

What kind of example do you display to your family, friends, strangers, to a rude driver who cuts you off in traffic, or to a sales clerk who cheated you at a store? How do you respond to people who offend you? As you carefully monitor how you act in these various situations, you'll see the patterns and habits that reflect the beliefs in your heart. Like me, you may have a belief in Jesus and even have memorized the great commandments of loving God and others. Yet you may still notice character qualities in your actions that do not reflect loving God and others on a consistent basis. Why? It's possible that you still have a portion of the deadly beliefs still growing within your heart, even though you have planted the belief of loving God and loving others.

We all have the seeds of the deadlies smuggled into our hearts by God's enemy. But we don't have to let them sprout and take root in our lives. I like the St. Augustine grass that grows so lushly on lawns in the south. When you set out that *carpet grass*, as it is called, it will take over your yard if you water it regularly and feed it the right nutrients. Soon it will choke out all the dandelions and crabgrass. God's words are like that. Plant them in your heart and nurture them with the nutrients of daily meditation and study, and those seeds will grow each day within your heart and choke out the sprouts of the deadlies.

The seeds that grow in your heart—the deadlies or the words of God—will depend upon which ones you water and nurture the most. If you feed the please-yourself side of your nature, the three deadlies will take root, sprout, and choke out everything else. But if you feed the love-God-and-others seeds, your heart will soon be filled with the healthy growth of your character, conforming more and more into the image of God.

Maybe you have been feeding your deadly beliefs for so long that they have grown deep roots and tall branches. The good news is that you can start choking off any beliefs you want by beginning to meditate on better beliefs that will lead you to become more caring and loving. The words of God in the Bible are alive and powerful. They can change your beliefs. Think regularly on the love passages of the Bible and the seed will continue to grow deeper roots and larger branches until it becomes like a tree planted by the rivers of water, and the leaves never wither again. When that tree becomes firmly rooted in your heart, you will come to love naturally and automatically because whatever strong beliefs you plant in your heart determine what you think, say, do, and feel.

As you continue into the next pages, you'll discover one of my very favorite pastimes: finding *gold* in every trial or difficulty I face. As my wife says daily, "There are pearls in every pile of poop that others throw at us." Let's see how we can locate those pearls every time.

Scriptures to Hide in Your Heart

You, my brothers [and sisters] were called to be free. But do not use your freedom to indulge the sinful nature; rather, serve one another in love. (Galatians 5:13)

If I speak in the tongues of men and of angels, but have not love, I am only a resounding gong or a clanging cymbal. If I have the gift of prophecy and can fathom all mysteries and all knowledge, and if I have a faith that can move mountains, but have not love, I am nothing. If I give all I possess to the poor and surrender my body to the flames, but have not love, I gain nothing.

Love is patient, love is kind. It does not envy, it does not boast, it is not proud. It is not rude, it is not self-seeking, it is not easily angered, it keeps no record of wrongs. Love does not delight in evil but rejoices with the truth. It always protects, always trusts, always hopes, always perseveres.

Love never fails. But where there are prophecies, they will cease; where there are tongues, they will be stilled; where there is knowledge, it will pass away. For we know in part and we prophesy in part, but when perfection comes, the imperfect disappears. When I was a child, I talked like a child, I thought like a child, I reasoned like a child. When I became a man, I put childish ways behind me. Now we see but a poor reflection as in a mirror; then we shall see face to face. Now I know in part; then I shall know fully, even as I am fully known.

And now these three remain: faith, hope and love. But the greatest of these is love. (1 Corinthians 13: 1–13)

Twelve
The High Value of Trials

A medical research group in California has found that an attitude of gratefulness is extremely beneficial to human health. With every thought of gratitude and thankfulness, healthy chemicals are released into the body. On the other hand, with each negative, critical, or worrying thought, the body is flooded with harmful chemicals that can damage one's emotional and physical health.[1] This study bears out the premise of this entire book. If you change the belief in your heart from worry-producing, negative thoughts to positive, grateful thoughts, it will improve your mental and physical health. It will improve your life.

For the most part, the stressful, traumatic, and trying events that happen to us produce these negative thoughts, which can result in resentment and worry. Wouldn't you love to find a way to rid yourself of such thoughts? Wouldn't you love to change the beliefs in your heart so that instead of feeling anger, resentment, or stress because of your trials, you experience more love and joy because of your difficulties? It's possible, believe it or not. And this is not just my idea: I learned it from the apostle Paul. He told us to stop worrying and find peace.[2] But how?

Just recently I had another chance to learn this principle. I face just as many frustrating experiences as you, but over the past couple of years I have finally come to the place where my trials do not do me in. I have replaced resentment and worry with gratefulness. In fact, amazing as it seems, I now find joy in my trials. Impossible? Not at all. Here's how you can do it as well.

High-Rise Anxiety

Just a few months ago the owner of the land next to my house decided to build two huge high-rise condos consisting of forty-three units. I was beside myself. I could not stand the idea. Buildings like that would look horrible and terribly out of place in a residential neighborhood. The other neighbors and I objected, but he plowed ahead with his dream.

I had no trouble understanding the man's reasons. Condos would generate much more income than selling the land to build three or four houses. But at the same time, these monster buildings would hurt my neighbors and me, not only financially—our property value would drop drastically—but in other ways as well. The project would increase traffic on our street, and noisy kids would disrupt the quiet. The thought of it all made me sick at my stomach.

One morning as I lay awake and worried about all this, a passage of scripture popped into my mind that I had been hiding within my heart:

> We also rejoice in our sufferings, because we know that suffering produces perseverance; perseverance, character; and character, hope. And hope does not disappoint us, because God has poured out his love into our hearts by the Holy Spirit, whom he has given us. (Romans 5:3–5)

Suddenly I visualized a trophy sitting on the bed stand next to my head. It was huge. I started to smile as I realized that these condos would win me a grand prize. They would win me greater transformation into the character of God as I endured the pain, financial loss, and disappointment they would cause. I realized that the passage in Romans applies in all circumstances, even to ugly condos next to one's house. Within seconds I was giving thanks to God. And I actually fell back to sleep. That was certainly different for me.

You may think I had gone utterly daffy. Why would anyone ever give thanks to God for a thing like this? But before you send the white coats after me, look closely at what Paul was telling us in this passage. Our trials—the difficult situations we face in life—can produce character traits that every Christian needs in order to conform to the image of God. And usually we don't bother to make such changes unless we are compelled by circumstances. Trouble is about the best change agent there is. And if I'm to be salt and light to a hurting world, I want my life to show it so that those wanting to know God can see what will happen to them by looking at me.

That is why I thanked God that morning. I was thanking him for the opportunity he had placed before me to build a more godlike character. No doubt he knows I need all such opportunities I can get. Using those condos as exercise equipment, I could see my spiritual muscles of perseverance, character, and hope growing bigger and firmer. That was why I imagined a trophy. I felt that I had won something valuable. I had just received a free ticket to God's workout gymnasium, reading, "You have just won two huge condo units." I knew that trophy for achieving more loving godlikeness would soon be mine.

Now don't get me wrong; I still didn't want those buildings next to me, devaluing my property and messing up our peaceful neighborhood. We are not required to want bad things to happen to us. It's perfectly acceptable to try to prevent them. After I got up that morning Norma asked, "What are you going to do about those buildings?" I responded, "Oh, I'll oppose them at the hearings with all of the other neighbors." Yet if those buildings had to be there, I would no longer worry about it because I knew I would benefit. I would accept them thankfully and praise God. I would have two monster trophy buildings reminding me each day that God would use them in my life to bring me more endurance, more of his loving character, and more hope. And hope would never be disappointed because God's Holy Spirit would pour his love endlessly into my heart. This would more than make up for the losses caused by those buildings. I was actually secretly excited inside because I knew that I would win, no matter what the outcome.

As the building hearings were in progress, I got down on my knees and prayed every day. "God, Norma and I don't want these buildings next to us, but we will submit to whatever you allow. I know that you will work out everything for our good because we both want to do what you called us to do: love you and love others. If you allow these buildings to go up, just between you and me, I'll give you thanks just for the privilege of allowing me to accept this difficulty in my life and learning to live happily in your presence. I promise to praise you every time I drive into my garage and see those buildings standing there."

In the previous chapter, I spoke of loving our enemies. In a sense, this developer was my enemy. I don't mean I hated him or wanted to do him in; yet he was an adversary whose intentions would do me considerable harm. Therefore I found it extremely important not to hold a grudge against this man or resent him for what he was doing to me. So I added him to my prayers and asked God to bless him and do good to him. I even decided that when the building began, I would go over and make friends with him. I might even suggest a few ideas that could improve his project. I'm sure he would appreciate that.

It excites me to see all the areas of life in which love provides the answers. If you apply the principle of love even when dealing with trials or difficulties, the problem turns into a blessing. First, I love God. I trust him to bring good out of every trial when I open myself to the blessings that come from enduring with patience and hope. Second, I love my neighbor or enemy whose actions could do me harm. Suddenly my trials are no longer trials. They are character-strengthening exercises that make me more into the glorious creature that God intends me to be.

If you thought *I* might be daffy, I used to wonder about the apostle Paul. How could that man possibly be so happy with all the terrible troubles he went through? From the moment he became a Christian, trouble dogged him like a hive of mad hornets. He was distrusted, people tried to kill him, the Romans beat him several times, he was stoned, run out of town, and often put in prison, and he survived shipwrecks and a venomous snakebite. And on top of all that, he endured some kind of health problem that often hampered his work. Yet you could never find a more upbeat, joyful, and utterly dedicated man. This guy was sold out to the Lord, and he seemed to love every minute of it. Not only did he rejoice in his suffering, he rejoiced just for the love of his Lord: "Rejoice in the Lord always," he wrote. "I will say it again: Rejoice!" (Philippians 4:4). *Rejoice* means to return to the source of your joy. And that word keeps popping up in all of Paul's writings. The man was irrepressible. And right after telling us to rejoice he wrote, "Give thanks in all circumstances, for this is God's will for you in Christ Jesus" (1 Thessalonians 5:16–18). Did you pause on the words "thanks in *all* circumstances"?

But I don't wonder about Paul anymore. Now I understand. When I grow up I want to be like Paul. He knew that his trials were the hammer and chisel of the master sculptor, chipping away at him and forming him into a copy of the One he loved more than anything in the world. Every trial, every difficulty, every bad time, every experience of being cheated, ripped off, put down, or beat up gives you another opportunity to win that trophy. Accept those difficulties joyfully and with thanksgiving and they will open your heart to receive more of God's character—his patience, his compassion for others, his strength in your weak places, and his great and mighty love.

When you think of trials as blessings (James 1:2–5), your attitude toward them turns completely on its head. With that trophy waiting to be awarded, how can children of God remain upset when trials start hitting them? I understand that now. But if trials hit you and your heart is not prepared with the right beliefs about them, you will not see them as blessings. You will see them as burdens, as blights on your life, and they will wear you down. So it is essential that you prepare your heart by embedding beliefs that trials are sure to come, and when they do they can be tremendous blessings.[3] If you are thus prepared, your trials will not devastate you; they will strengthen you instead. And, like Paul, they will give you reason to rejoice. At the end of this chapter I will give you several key passages to hide in your heart that will help prepare you for trials. And if you want, you can go to our Web page—GarySmalley.com—as well as to appendix 5 to find my current top Bible verses to memorize and hide within your heart.

Treasure Hunting in Your Trials

I love what writer and speaker Barbara Johnson used to say: "Pain is inevitable, but misery is optional." And Barbara wasn't just spouting off; she knew what it meant to face trouble. She lost two sons, another son was estranged for several years, she lost her husband, and she suffered from a debilitating brain tumor. Yet her hilarious books and bright, bubbly speeches brought joy into women's lives for many years. Her primary message was this: you can't avoid having difficulties hit your life, but you can avoid the misery they can inflict. World-famous psychiatrist M. Scott Peck penned these words about accepting trials as natural occurrences that come to everyone's life:

> Life is difficult. This is a great truth, one of the greatest truths. It is a great truth because once we truly see this truth, we transcend it. Once we truly know that life is difficult—once we truly understand and accept it—then life is no longer difficult. Because once it is accepted, the fact that life is difficult no longer matters.[4]

I've not only accepted the reality that many and varying trials will hit me throughout my life, but I've been learning with great delight that every trial has a treasure hidden within it. The trick to keeping your trial from causing you misery is to find that treasure. I call this *treasure hunting*. I begin with the idea that within the difficulty is a diamond or a gold nugget. And the principle works. Each time I look for the treasure within the trial, I always find it. Every negative thing that has come my way—bad times, difficult relationships, hardships, pain, discomfort, disappointments, discouragements, irritations, and all other unpleasant happenings have turned out to be camouflages for great gifts. Those gifts simply needed to be uncovered.

Since I learned this principle, I have been constantly on a treasure-hunting expedition. Life for me is an adventure, and I've found that I live it to the fullest by finding the positive within each negative. I'm not saying that the very moment a negative experience hits me I immediately see the gem within it and welcome it with open arms. I'm not perfect yet (surprise, surprise!). But since I put into my heart the scriptural principles of rejoicing in trials, I realize that every trial is an exercise machine to produce stronger character. Because of that knowledge, no woe-is-me anguish lasts long in my life. I'm now able to manage the negative emotions with the belief that "in all things God works for the good of those who love him, who have been called according to his purpose" (Romans 8:28). And what is his purpose for me? To love him and love others. Now every blow that hits me increases my love for him and others. And whatever negative emotions I have at first are eventually transformed into joy. I have never experienced an exception.

You may think you have experienced exceptions. You may have suffered devastating, soul-wrenching blows that you are convinced could not possibly have any positive value. You may even feel insulted by the suggestion that it could. "How dare you think I could possibly rejoice in the death of my son!" Don't misunderstand me; I'm not claiming that every experience is good. Death is horrible. It is an insult to God's creation, and he hates it so much he died to kill it. Yet even from such a terrible experience, great good can come although the good may not be immediately apparent.

No one can be expected to immediately find a blessing in the death of a loved one. Death inflicts a major wound that will take time to heal before you find the pearl that can grow from the pain. Yet let me assure you that every trial—from minor irritations such as a cold, bad weather, problems with your house or with your job, and illnesses all the way to the loss of a loved one or your own impending death—has within it a gem just waiting to be found.

Here is the downside when you don't seek the gem within each trial: you must deal with the trial on its own terms, which means you must see it only as a problem and possibly an insurmountable one. Mind you, I'm not saying you shouldn't deal with the problem. You must seek a cure for your health issue. You will have to repair the roof after the tree fell on it. You will have to come to terms with the loss of your loved one. Finding the gem within trouble does not eliminate the trouble itself. But what it does is give you a positive outcome from the negative experience. This can make a huge difference. It's often the difference between hope and despair, love and loneliness, peace and anguish. If you see nothing in the trial but the difficulty, the pain, or the tragedy, you have no way to look up. You are stuck inside the problem with no windows to let in sunlight.

But when you seek the gem within the trial, which, of course, is the ability to use the trial to build your character into a robust image of God, you don't have to let the difficulty grind you down or sink you into despair. In fact, when you gradually develop your own deep belief from Bible verses such as 2 Corinthians 12:6–10, you'll begin quickly to see your troubles as blessings in disguise, and you can greatly diminish or even eliminate the following common conditions that often accompany trials:

Depression. Depression is the loss of hope. All thoughts center on the idea that things are either going to stay in their present gloomy state or get worse. Seeing the blessing in trials can lift your depression. I'm not speaking here of deep, clinical or chemical depression, of course. When you have this kind of depression, you must not just sit there and do nothing. Treat it like a squeaky door and put some oil on it. Go to an expert and find out what is at the heart of your depression and take the necessary steps to find a cure. But when you realize that the difficulty you are going through has the great and highly desirable side benefit of forming godly character, hope appears and depression can disappear.

Discouragement. The difficulty seems so deep, or it keeps repeating itself, or each time you think you've conquered it, it comes back. If you can adopt the beliefs of Paul, you will eventually let go of your expectations that everything should go right and accept what comes with grace and thankfulness because it will help you to become more like God. Discouragement can morph into hope and holiness, even when things keep going badly.

Anxiety. You have a nagging awareness that you must somehow deal with a stressful situation. You have fears that it may not be resolved well, and you play it over in your mind repeatedly and worry about whether you can solve the problem. Just knowing that all trials contain pearls relaxes my own heart and I can go through the pain of any trial while letting God handle it. You turn things over to him and trust him with the outcome. You trust him to give you what wisdom and ability you need to apply to the situation, and then you do your best without further worry. You are prepared in advance for the possibility that the outcome will not be ideal, and you accept that fact, knowing that even then God's grace is sufficient for you. Whatever happens, your character will gain strength and your dependence on God will grow. This is one of the best things that can happen when you are weakened by painful trials: trust God and you gain more of his power to manage your life.[5] By taking this approach—thanking God for trials and using them to help your spiritual formation—you may not change the circumstance, but you will certainly change your outlook toward it. No longer must you bemoan your bad luck; you can rejoice, as Paul did, that your trials shape you into the image of God. I now realize that *bad luck* is no longer a part of my vocabulary.

A Guide to Treasure Hunting

When trials hit us, we don't have to grope blindly to locate the treasure within it. I have discovered two specific steps we can take to locate the gem pretty quickly. Let's look briefly at those steps.

As soon as the trial hits, start giving thanks for the pain.

Whether your trial involves mental stress or physical pain, it's the emotional pain that actually does the work toward remolding you into the image of God. The essence of his image is love, so start looking for the different expressions of love that are moving into your life while the pain lasts.

When my previous book was published, plans were in place for me to partner with one of the world's most popular pastors in getting out the message of that book. But the pastor changed the course of his ministry, and the partnering deal fell through. It was a major blow—painful, disappointing, embarrassing, humbling, and a bag full of other negative feelings. But instantly I began to thank God for my suffering, long before actually seeing any character benefits or increased power from him. I knew it was coming. I'm still not sure just what God has in mind for that book, but it continues to sell, so I presume he has plans for it. I never give up on a dream that God gives me. I thank him instantly for the trial of every disappointment and then wait in faith for him to give the positive results.

I think that is why James tells us,

> Consider it pure joy [deposit joy into your heart's bank before you actually reap the benefit], my brothers, whenever you face trials of many kinds, because you know that the testing of your faith develops perseverance. Perseverance must finish its work so that you may be mature and complete, not lacking anything. (James 1:2–4)

James is telling us to let the pain continue until it makes us "mature and complete." When you are complete, you have all of the love you can gain from the pain of the current trial. When you reach this completeness, the pain

Don't seek God—For his Rewards—But too seek Him.

will stop. This means as long as the pain continues, you must keep searching for the results.

When I was suffering emotional pain and anguish over my heart attack, my kidney transplant, and the continued stress that brought on these conditions, I kept thanking God for the pain and crying out to him to open my heart and let me learn what I needed to know about his love. I wanted the pain to end, and I begged him to end it and calm my hurting heart. He finally did—after I came to realize that I had been seeking his rewards more than I was actually seeking him. When this fact hit me, I increased my desire for him, craving him day and night. My emotional pain began to diminish until it was gone. Then he started rewarding me again with wisdom, financial gain, and great new ministry opportunities. It was only eight days after the kidney transplant that God began to reopen my heart to him, and I've been running toward him ever since. But I would still praise him even if he hadn't started rewarding me again. The insights he gave me far outweigh any difficulty I suffered during both my heart attack and kidney transplant.

As you can see, when I began to seek the gem in the pain by thanking God for what I knew he would give me, he came through. He gave me more faith, a new dream, goals, a vision of telling the church throughout the world about hiding his truths within our hearts, and seeking a new revival within the church. That's where I am today, watching him open door after door for me to bring the message of this book to more and more people.

Look deeply for the love gold *to be found within your difficulty.*

Four years ago while I was vacationing and speaking on a cruise with my wife, I kept scratching at an itch on the side of my hip. One night in the shower I noticed red marks and blister-type sores in the area I had scratched. Norma thought it was poison ivy, and that made sense because just before the trip I had been in the woods near my house, where I could have contacted the insidious weed.

Not wanting to dampen our vacation, I said no more about it. That was a huge mistake. When we returned home I went to my doctor, who told me instantly that I had a really bad case of shingles. With an earlier diagnosis, he could have given me something to nip the disease in the bud, but it was now too late. He warned me that even after the sores cleared up, I might have to live with awful pain for the rest of my life. It all depended on what type of shingles I had.

That doctor knew what he was talking about. It hurt like fire day and night. And the affected area kept growing, covering the front and back of the right side of my hip. I tried every pain medicine in the drugstore, but nothing helped. The only time I got any relief was when bathing or swimming. After about six months, the blisters began to diminish, and the pain started to ease. I could actually sleep on my side for a few seconds each night.

I still have the shingles, but now the only pain I feel is my clothing scraping my skin like sandpaper. Throughout this ordeal, I treasure-hunted for the blessing to be found within it. And what I found is the gold of God's love showing in the following ways:

Empathy. My painful experience has given me a much deeper sensitivity to the pains of others. Now I don't have to imagine how people feel when they experience some kind of chronic pain; I *know* how they feel. This experiential knowledge allows me to understand how to minister to them and help them through their experience. I am now much more effective in this kind of ministry because I have been there and done that.

Compassion. Now I can feel real love and compassion for hurts of all kinds in other people, especially those who cannot find relief for their pain. My heart reaches out to them in a genuine way, and I want to find some real way of helping them either out of their pain or to cope with it. No more be-warmed-and-filled type of meaningless well-wishing. My new sense of compassion makes me reach out with real love and a deep desire to ease the pains of others. I find myself hugging people more easily today compared to the stuffy interactions of a few years ago.

Sensitivity. After experiencing my own bout with pain, I find that I can sense more acutely when a hurting person needs a word of encouragement or a helping hand. Until you've felt it yourself, your sensitivity is bound to be somewhat dull. You may want to help, but you haven't the experience to know what kind of help to give. Knowing pain enables one to sense the real needs pain brings. This is almost exactly what Paul told us: "Praise be to the God and Father of our Lord Jesus Christ, the Father of compassion and the God of all comfort, who comforts us in all our troubles so that we can comfort those in any trouble with the comfort we ourselves have received from God" (2 Corinthians 1:3–4).

Humility. When you have been through continuous pain, you understand the helplessness one feels when facing a difficulty that has no solution. That's when we learn humility—we understand that we are helpless without God. When we are in pain we know we need him, as a beggar, desperately every hour. When that lesson sinks in, we realize that the need for God continues past the pain. We need him all the time, whether in pain or not.

The apostle Paul prayed for his affliction to be removed, but God apparently knew that this greatly talented apostle needed a weakness to remind him of his dependence on God. Therefore, instead of removing the affliction, God told his beloved servant that his grace was sufficient to deal with the difficulty. From this Paul learned that it was in his weakest places that he was the strongest, because those were the places where God himself filled in. That gave him humility, for he realized that his greatest strength was not his own, but God's strength working in him.

Since I crave God in my life and desire above all else to have a real and loving relationship with him, I am honored to use my shingles pain to remind myself all day long how much I need God. I am so thankful to God for the pain of my shingles, for that has shown me my own weakness and God's loving strength. And that's all I need to get through the day.

Trauma and the Limbic System

According to neural scientist Dr. Daniel G. Amen, memories of serious traumatic experiences such as a debilitating disease or accident, a home break-in, robbery, rape, or beatings lodge deeply in the brain's limbic system. This gland is about the size of a walnut located in the center of the brain. The limbic system is also the part of the brain that controls relational bonding and mood.

Naturally, when the memory of some terrible experience invades this part of the brain, moods and emotions are deeply affected. Brain scans show a measurable physical effect on the limbic area in traumatized people. It actually heats up. When this occurs, the person tends to become cynical, gloomy, complaining, judgmental, and blaming. He tends to be more pessimistic, moody, irritable, or even clinically depressed. He has increased negative thinking, a negative perception of events, decreased motivation, and a flood of negative emotions. He will experience appetite and sleep problems, decreased sexual responsiveness, and a tendency to be more socially isolated.

Now here is the interesting part: Dr. Amen says that with the right kind of thinking you can actually soothe, calm, or cool off the limbic part of your brain. (Hmm. Does that remind you of anything we've been discussing in this book? I love it when I find confirmation of God's ways in the discoveries of science and medicine.)

If we do not learn to think ourselves out of our tragedies, the memory locked in the limbic area can disrupt our behavior to where we remain in a negative emotional state. Left to itself, the limbic area remembers traumatic experiences and replays them over and over again. This generates heat in the limbic area and produces one negative thought after another. When traumatized people look at the past, they feel regret. When they look at the future, they feel anxiety and pessimism. In the present moment, they are certain to find something unsatisfactory. "I am not going to be successful. Every time I start to get ahead, I get knocked back. No one ever listens to me. No one likes me. I don't fit in. I know something bad is going to happen. I am a failure." The lens through which they see themselves, others, and the world has a dim grayness that darkens all thoughts, attitudes, and activities.

According to Dr. Amen, the person thus afflicted is suffering from Automatic Negative Thoughts, which he identifies by the acronym ANTs. He says that heated limbic areas are infested with these ANTs. The affected person must imagine that these are venomous red ants and learn to stomp those ANTs into the ground. Here are three steps—or stomps—that show how it can be done.

First, you must realize that it's no longer the negative event that's keeping you down. No matter how devastating, that event is in the past; it's over and gone. Now it's your *thoughts about the event* that give you trouble. Your negative feelings no longer come from external events; they're all inside yourself. Think of ANTs as an infestation in your brain, contaminating both your mental and physical well-being. Think of the damaging chemicals released into your body by negative thoughts as ANTs crawling about inside you. It's true that ANTs are nothing more than negative thoughts, but thoughts are real and they can hurt you. So you must deal with them.

Second, understand that these ANTs don't always tell the truth. Are you really sure that nobody likes you? Is it really true that nobody ever listens to you? Do you really always fail at everything you do? Analyze these thoughts objectively and you will see that they are almost always gross exaggerations or even outright lies you tell yourself.

Third, seek to bond with positive people who can lift your spirits. In doing this you might say you are momentarily *borrowing* their uninfected limbic system to help you cure your own. When we are bonded with positive people, we feel better about ourselves and our lives. This capacity to bond plays a significant role in the tone and quality of our moods. As we feel more love, our moods become more positive. So here again we see the importance of loving others. Mutual bonds of love between people who love God provide healing for emotions all around, and do much to stomp out your ANTs.[6]

If you have children, increase bonding by doing special events with them, taking them to interesting places, finding activities you enjoy together, spending time talking with them with no agenda. Build your relationship with your husband or wife, your parents, or your friends. Recognize the importance of physical contact: holding hands and hugging. Sexual activity with your mate is one of the best things you can enjoy as a great bonding tool.

Finally, kill those ANTs by smothering them with new positive thoughts. This leads us back to the major theme of this book. You can change your life by changing your heart, and you change your heart by replacing the Automatic Negative Thoughts with positive, life-giving ones. The most significant life-giving thoughts all come straight from God, given to us through his words in the Bible. I have found that one of the best ways to take control of your thoughts and root out the negative ones is to use Philippians 4:6–9 as your measure for what kind of things you will allow yourself to think about. That passage gives you eight good standards for evaluating your thoughts: whatever is true, noble, right, pure, lovely, admirable, excellent, or praiseworthy. If a thought doesn't fit those standards, it can be an ANT, and it must be stomped out.

All pure thoughts

Changing Your Heart

As my barber, Gary Larman, cut my hair recently, he began to explain to me why he never gets depressed anymore and rarely even gets discouraged. Instantly my ears perked up (possibly putting them in danger from his clippers) because I was right in the middle of writing this book and on the hunt for good material. He told me that about once or twice every year or two, a funky discouragement may start to come over him and cause him to feel a little worthless. Then he dropped the great gem of wisdom we often get from our barbers. He said he never allows negative thoughts to stay inside his mind. "As soon as I feel those feelings coming, I start thinking of everything and anything God has done for me and every blessing he has given me. I think about my family, my job, owning a styling company, my friends, my church, and any other blessing I can throw in. Then in about an hour or so, voilà! Those feelings turn tail and run. After another year or two they grow bold enough to try sneaking in again, but now I know how to root them out. And it always works."[7]

I have found that the best way to deal with negative thoughts left from traumatic events is to do the very thing that I've been harping on throughout this chapter: rethink the result of the event. It may have been devastating. It may have done you permanent, irreparable damage. Still, within that event is a blessing, and you can extract it with the right kind of thinking. Let's revisit

Romans 5:3–5, which tells you how to think in order to reframe the terrible thing that happened to you and heated up your limbic system:

> We also rejoice in our sufferings [they are like trophies], because we know that suffering produces perseverance; perseverance, character; and character, hope. And hope does not disappoint us, because God has poured out his love into our hearts by the Holy Spirit, whom he has given us.

Is that good or what? As every trial hits a person who is thanking God, God pours his love into his or her heart through his Holy Spirit. When this truth reaches your heart as a new belief, you'll never again look at trials in the same way.

You can't undo the traumatic event. You can't bring back what you lost. But you can replace the belief that this event has ruined your happiness with a belief that allows you to step again into joy. You can believe that because of this event, you can now experience the love of God in a way that may have been impossible before it happened. God can use your pain to reshape your life, giving you patience, understanding, hope, assurance, and love. Of course, you can *Bad* never be thankful for the loss. The tragedy was real, and it would be false to *things* pretend that somehow it was good within itself. But you can be thankful for the benefits you will reap for having endured it. That's what it means to thank God for your trials. And that is what I now do every day, in every event that threatens to topple my emotional equilibrium. And it always works.

This chapter has been all about finding a *grateful heart* and the next one is about the awesome power and value of developing a *forgiving heart*.

Scriptures to Hide in Your Heart

And we know that in all things God works *for the good* of those who love him, who have been called according to his purpose [which is loving others]. (Romans 8:28, emphasis mine)

Be joyful always; pray continually; give thanks *in all* circumstances, for this is God's will for you in Christ Jesus. (1 Thessalonians 5:16–18, emphasis mine)

Consider it pure joy, my brothers, whenever you face trials of many kinds, because you know that the testing of your faith develops perseverance. Perseverance must finish its work so that you may be mature and complete, not lacking anything. (James 1:2–4)

Not only so, but we also rejoice in our sufferings, because we know that suffering produces perseverance; perseverance, character; and character, hope. And hope does not disappoint us, because God has poured out his love into our hearts by the Holy Spirit, whom he has given us. (Romans 5:3–5)

But [the Lord] said to me, "My grace is sufficient for you, for my power is made perfect in weakness." Therefore I will boast all the more gladly about my weaknesses, so that Christ's power may rest on me. That is why, for Christ's sake, I delight in weaknesses, in insults, in hardships, in persecutions, in difficulties. For when I am weak, then I am strong. (2 Corinthians 12:9–10) (Is this verse not the best?)

Thirteen
The High Value of Forgiveness

My grandson Michael, an eleven-year-old in the fifth grade at a public school, was having a problem. The trouble was with a boy—we'll call him Sam—who was in the *in-group* of fifth- and sixth-grade boys. You know the kind: usually the bigger, stronger boys—the jocks who are good at sports and hang around together, buttressing their egos by showing their disdain for little kids who lack their size and athletic ability. Michael had not developed physically as fast as Sam and his friends, so Sam targeted him for abuse, both physically and verbally. He said things to Michael such as, "I'm going to take you down, you little punk!" or "You'd better watch your back, kid. I'm gonna hurt you one of these days." He called Michael every name in the book and even lied to other kids about things Michael did. As far as Michael could tell, he had done nothing to provoke such aggressive behavior.

The abuse had its effect on Michael. The other boys in class began to shun him, not wanting to get on the bad side of the jocks. He began to feel lonely because it seemed that no one in the class liked him. My daughter, Kari, Michael's mom, began to do all she could to ease Michael's pain. She backed away only after Michael begged her to not interfere.

Michael was raised to take his Christian commitment seriously. He knows that with Christ he has a light in him and that he must let that light shine to others. Therefore, he did not retaliate against Sam's abuse. He took it gracefully, repaid Sam's evil with kindness, never retaliated, and never seemed to let it get him down. This doesn't mean he didn't struggle privately. He didn't like

147

the abuse, of course. He didn't like the feeling of isolation from other kids. Yet he knows that when he follows Christ, sometimes the world is going to hate him. So he stuck by the principles he had placed in his heart. He said to himself, *I have to remember that I have a choice. I can be resentful and fight back, or I can accept this difficulty as a blessing and grow from it.*

So Michael chose to forgive Sam for all the abuse. He prayed to God not only for Sam's forgiveness but also that the boy would be blessed, and he went on about his business at school.

Shortly after Michael made this decision, Sam called him and left a message. He wanted Michael to call him back. Michael was absolutely flabbergasted. "Why is he calling me?" he wondered. He was so nervous about it that he didn't want to return the call. His mom and dad encouraged him to do it, however, and he finally worked up the nerve. So he called Sam, and to Michael's great surprise, the boy asked him to come over and play on Saturday. Michael didn't know what to do but accept the invitation, but after he hung up he was terrified. "I don't understand why he's inviting me over," he said. "What if it's some kind of ambush or trick? Maybe this is a setup to embarrass me or hurt me in some way." I told him there was only one way to find out. We prayed about it, and he said, "God, you're gonna have to help me on this. I really need your courage." He also relied on the Bible verses he had memorized, especially Proverbs 16:7: "When a man's ways are pleasing to the LORD, he makes even his enemies live at peace with him."

On Saturday morning, Kari dropped Michael off at Sam's door. That evening he called me all excited and said, "Granddad, guess what; I have made a new friend." He recounted to me all the fun he had in the several hours he'd spent at Sam's house. As it turned out, Michael's anxiety was for nothing.

Later we learned "the rest of the story," as Paul Harvey would say. In a Sunday school class at his church, Sam had taken notice when the teacher said that every young person who is serious about being a Christian needs good, strong Christian friends in his life. For some reason, Sam's heart was open to this message, and he could think of no boy who acted more like a Christian than Michael. So he called up Michael.

Since then, Michael has spent the night at Sam's house, and Sam has spent the night with Michael. He has gone to church with him on Sunday. But perhaps the coolest evidence of the reality of the new friendship occurred the week after Michael had first spent the night with Sam. Michael came home from school beside himself with excitement. "Mom, you're not gonna believe this," he said. "Sam saved me a seat at the jock table. He told everyone, 'You can't sit here; this chair is for Michael.'" Only a few weeks later, Sam's deep commitment to Christ was capped by asking Michael to be his "Timothy" as the two of them began praying for a revival at their school.

The tremendous power of God's words in the heart is proven once again. When we love God and forgive those who wrong us, God can cause even our enemies to be at peace with us. Better yet, he can destroy enemies by turning them into friends.

In reflecting on this incident later, Michael told me that this was when he started becoming an adult. (I'm amazed that a thirteen-year-old can learn this concept.) He said that children tend to blame others and circumstances for their problems and feelings. But adults take responsibility for how they feel, because how they feel is based not on what others do to them, but on what they think and believe. An adult realizes that one's feelings are based not on what actually happens to a person on the outside, but on what the person believes on the inside. Children don't realize this and allow their thoughts to be negative, resentful, angry, and vengeful when people do bad things to them. Those thoughts cause negative beliefs, and those beliefs can produce sad emotions that stick in the heart and mess it up for years. Michael said to me, "I decided to take control of my thoughts and thereby manage my feelings because what I think about all day long eventually becomes my deepest beliefs, and my beliefs control my thoughts and actions. I know now that I can have a higher quality of life if I choose the thoughts I want. All I have to do is put the right beliefs into my heart." He's put this same story in his own kid's book that will be coming out soon.[1] Not that I favor my own kin, of course, but do I have an amazing grandkid or what!

Anger and Forgiveness

Michael assumed it was "adult" not to blame others for his unhappiness, but to forgive, and to store beliefs in his heart that cause him to think and act in a godlike manner. Actually, I wonder if he might not be overestimating the maturity of most adults. I regret to say that I've seen all too many adults in my life (including me, at times) who never seem to reach this kind of maturity. One of the surest evidences of this is in their anger. I am convinced that anger stands in the way of forgiveness more than any other emotion. Let me explain.

Let's go back to the three deadlies: the lust of the eyes, the lust of the flesh, and the pride of life. When these deadly beliefs lodge in your heart, they set you up for anger. These beliefs create expectations that your satisfaction in life comes from getting a fair share of material goods, pleasures, and recognition. Since these things do not actually satisfy the human heart, the desperate quest for satisfaction usually accelerates into an increased appetite for more and more of them. "I'm not satisfied yet. I must need even more things, more pleasure, and more status." Satisfaction always remains just out of reach, which means disappointment is inevitable when you feel you're not getting your fair share of what you need for happiness.

You see, the quest for satisfaction in pursuit of the three deadlies always puts the focus on me, me, me. More comfort, ease, and accumulation for self. More fun, pleasure, and entertainment for self. More notice for "what I have done" so people will recognize my accomplishments and status. So when the expected satisfaction doesn't come, I get angry. And who do I get angry with? Well, I'm certainly not about to blame myself! No sir. This would not make me feel good. But not to worry; there are plenty of people in my life to lay the blame on. I will get angry at them. They didn't see to my needs. They treated me unfairly. They stole recognition that I deserved. They denied me a pleasure that would really have made me happy. I get angry with them for what they've done to me.

Most anger boils up because the self feels violated. Someone has stepped over the boundaries we place around ourselves to protect our rights, our property, our desires, our feelings, and our perceived value. Cross that line and anger rises to self's defense. The self lashes out with, "No one can treat me that way and get away with it."

Of course, not all anger is provoked by the self's failure to get what it wants. People often suffer real evil at the hands of others, including theft, personal injury, untrue gossip, cheating, lying, and even the inflicting of injury or death to a loved one. These are not merely perceived offenses against a violated self; they are truly evils that can happen to godly people who are not infected with the deadlies. But it remains true even in such cases that when we react with long-lasting, harbored resentment and anger, it will cause certain damage to our hearts.

The danger of anger, justified or not, is that it's corrosive. Hold on to it and, like a deadly acid, it will eat away at the heart, destroying compassion, empathy, and love, while building tough scar tissue that is difficult to penetrate. Many people who live by the three deadlies cannot let go of resentment, and they harbor anger for years. Yet anger can also damage the lives of people who do not live by the three deadlies. When anger lodges in our hearts, we can become cynical, bitter, distrustful, and uncaring about the feelings and well-being of others.

Thus anger destroys relationships, the very thing we need in our lives to become more like God. Destroyed relationships close us off from love. And when we don't love others, we fool ourselves if we think we love God. As the apostle John said, "If anyone says, 'I love God,' yet hates his brother, he is a liar. For anyone who does not love his brother, whom he has seen, cannot love God, whom he has not seen" (1 John 4:20).

Harboring continued anger destroys happiness, yet those who feel they've been severely hurt or wronged often have trouble getting rid of it. Can such people ever learn to be happy again? Not until they change the beliefs in their hearts. And the first step toward making this change is to forgive. That is the key to cleaning out the heart and getting rid of anger. As the apostle Paul said, "Bear with each other and forgive whatever grievances you may have against one another. Forgive as the Lord forgave you. And over all these virtues put on love, which binds them all together in perfect unity" (Colossians 3:13–14). We are to forgive and replace our anger and bitterness with love, which brings us back into relationship not only with each other but also, as Paul points out, with God.

Unthinkable Forgiveness

As you read a passage like that one from Colossians, you may shake your head and think the Lord sometimes asks the impossible. He just does not understand the terrible thing you have endured. "What? Me? Forgive that man after what he's done to me?" Yes. Anything anyone does to you can be forgiven. *Anything.*

Several years ago a church leader did severe damage to my reputation by lying about me to a number of leaders of other churches. As a result, I was flooded with cancellations of seminars all over the country. This damaged much more than my reputation; I was depending on the fees from those seminars to cover my expenses and staff salaries. I was devastated. Lower than a snake's belly. I was upset, angry, resentful, and anxious. I couldn't shake it out of my mind. "How dare that man steal my career from me!" I fumed as I cried out to God.

After a few days of waiting on God, 2 Corinthians 12:9–10 came rushing into my mind, where God tells us his grace is sufficient for us and that we should delight in insults, hardships, persecutions, and difficulties. "No, God," I said, "I don't want to remember this scripture right now. How can I delight in this insult, in this difficulty?" I wanted to be angry. I wanted to fume and rant. I didn't want to give up my resentment toward this man. One day I got alone for hours to pray and think this thing through. Why was I so upset with this man? Why did I have so much trouble forgiving him? Then it was as if God said, "Why not couple this passage with Matthew 7:1–4?" So I read the passage:

Do not judge, or you too will be judged. For in the same way you judge others, you will be judged, and with the measure you use, it will be measured to you. Why do you look at the speck of sawdust in your brother's eye and pay no attention to the plank in your own eye? How can you say to your brother, "Let me take the speck out of your eye,'" when all the time there is a plank in your own eye?

What was God trying to tell me here? Was I as guilty as this man I was accusing? No, that can't be! But as I pondered this scripture, a sick feeling began to come over me. Yes, I have done the same thing as this man. I have been guilty of hurting someone's reputation. In fact, I remembered a specific incident very vividly. Years back I had shared hurtful information about another Christian leader, and I had never confessed to him or sought his forgiveness. Before the night was over, I wrote a letter to the man I had wronged, confessed my sin, and begged his forgiveness. A few weeks later he wrote this note to me:

Dear Gary:

Greetings in the name of our Lord Jesus. It was so good to hear from you. I would be delighted to talk with you about whatever you desire, but I believe I know what you are referring to in your letter. I have long ago forgiven you, and God has used that experience in my own life to convict me of my own actions toward a few dear people in my past. God seems to be using your actions toward me to cleanse both of us.

Do call when you can because I would love the fellowship we could have around our precious Savior.

In His Name,

God used this man who had defamed me to show me an ugly fact. I had many of the same flaws as the man who had defamed and angered me. He did an evil thing; I sometimes do evil things. He was rude; I am sometimes rude. He was dishonest; I am sometimes dishonest. I am so thankful that God in his loving mercy chose to use this man to show me the depth of my own sins. And I am grateful for the cleansing of my heart that came through forgiveness. Where would we be without forgiveness?

Today, years after that incident, I delight in remembering 1 John 2:9, 11:

"Anyone who claims to be in the light but hates his brother is still in the darkness . . . he does not know where he is going, because the darkness has blinded him." That passage convicted me then, but it brings me joy today. I realized that I had become dead toward God and others, and it was because of my deep anger. When I fell to my knees in repentance and accepted the responsibility of forgiveness, I forgave the man who had defamed me, and all of my ministry in the 1980s and '90s flourished. It has since become easier for me to forgive because I have experienced the freedom and blessings that can come from it. Today I have no anger or bitterness in my heart toward anyone, which means I can live my golden years as a free man.

We often hear of burying anger deep within the heart. But it does not just lie there quietly in some little corner grave where it's dead and forgotten. Anger does not remain dormant; it always grows deadly tentacles that wrap around our hearts and choke off the light of God. That's what happened to me. When I saw myself for who I really was and realized that I was just as guilty of hurting others as the man in the story above had been with me, I fell to my knees in repentance before God and sought his forgiveness. Forgiveness cleaned my heart and made me receptive to relationship again—with God and with others whom I had wronged or who had wronged me.

Whatever has been done to you, you can forgive it. I don't claim it will be easy, but with God's power, you can do it. He is our ultimate model. As I've already pointed out, after all the rejection, pain, brutality, hate, false accusations, torture, and death he endured, he looked out over those who had inflicted all this outrage upon him and forgave them. He calls us to be like him. That means we get to forgive as he did. He even gave us a sample prayer of forgiveness in Matthew 6:12: "Forgive us our debts [our sins], as we also have forgiven our debtors [those who sin against us]."

A Compelling Reason to Forgive

Often we are reluctant to forgive because it galls us to see the person who did us wrong going scot-free while we suffer the consequences of their wrongdoing. It violates our ingrained sense of fairness, even of justice. But God tells us we need not worry about that. Justice and vengeance are in his domain, and he will take care of what needs to be done in that realm. "Do not take revenge, my friends, but leave room for God's wrath, for it is written: 'It is mine to avenge; I will repay,' says the Lord" (Romans 12:19).

Still, we seem to want the satisfaction of seeing him do it. We want to see the lightning bolt and delight in the horrified expression on our enemies' faces when they get their well-deserved zapping. But God works in his own good time and in his own good way. That may even mean your enemy will not receive the punishment you want to see. He or she may receive mercy instead.

That's what really bugged Jonah. He hated his enemies, the Ninevites, and when they responded to his preaching, repented, and turned to the Lord, he didn't rejoice or pat himself on the back for his highly effective sermons. No, he went off to himself, crawled under the weeds, and sulked. He had so much hate in his heart that he couldn't stand to see his enemies receive God's forgiveness and grace.

Often we don't see either God's grace or his punishment inflicted on our enemies. We simply see them going about their daily business with impunity as if they hadn't a care in the world—as if they were completely unaware and unrepentant of the terrible pain they inflicted on us. This makes our anger burn all the hotter and makes forgiveness that much harder. But if we truly trust God, we will rest in the assurance that he will do what is best for everyone involved in every situation. If punishment is needed, he will administer it. If grace is sufficient without punishment, he will take that route. We don't need to know; we need to trust. God will do what is right. That's what he does. It's the business he's in, and he knows how to run it. We've got to leave the fate of our enemies in his hands. Each of us is individually responsible to God, and we have no need to know how God is dealing with another person. As the great Lion Aslan often says in the Narnia stories, "I tell no one any story but his own."

But think about it: Do you really want justice done all the time? Now, that's a trick question, so think carefully before your answer. How about to yourself? Do you want God's justice done to you, or would you rather have his mercy? It doesn't take me long to answer that. It's a no-brainer. I may look about at all the wrongs done to me and say I want God to bring my enemies to justice, but when it comes to me—no sir! I don't want justice at all. I want mercy heaped high and running over. I want the forgiveness that comes with God's loving grace. Without that I'm doomed, and so are you.

So if we don't want justice for ourselves, why are we so eager to see it done to our enemies? That attitude really doesn't make sense, especially when you realize that God wants us to be like him. That means he wants us to give out mercy and forgiveness to our enemies instead of justice, just as he is ready to do. In fact, he feels so strongly about this that he makes it a condition for receiving his forgiveness. This principle is so important that he included it in what we call the Lord's Prayer, which I quoted above: "Forgive us our debts, as

concern whether she does what she should or not. You are not responsible for what she does; you are responsible only for what you do. You control *you*, not the other person. So whether you are the offender or the offended, as long as an offense stands between you and a fellow human, you must make the move to reconcile, whether that means forgiving or seeking forgiveness.

In his book *Waking the Dead*, John Eldredge writes about how important it is for us to dredge our past to see whether we have deep bitterness or anger toward family members, particularly your father or mother. Did they put you down or say things to you that closed your heart? Were you rejected or told that you were no good and would never amount to anything?[3] As I read this book I wondered what hurtful things I might have said to my sons and daughter as they were growing up. I started thinking about Michael. I remembered how much that kid used to irritate me. I wondered what I said to him, if my irritation showed, if he felt pushed away, unwanted, or even unloved because of my attitude.

I thought of Matthew 5:23–24, and it occurred to me that I should call Michael and ask him if I said things that hurt him or closed his heart. Were there things we needed to talk about to clear away any resentment or anger between us?

I'm glad I called. Soon afterward he and his family were staying at my house, and his wife, Amy, came to me early one morning and asked, "Dad, can we talk?" We all know that a question like that means something's up. Sure enough, it was. She was brilliant in explaining to me how I had offended Michael in a major way about three years earlier and it was still an issue with both of them. I listened carefully to understand her as she explained the offense. Then, later that day when Michael and I were alone, I told him of Amy's fine explanation and told him that he had married way over his head. Smiling, he agreed. Then, I looked him in his eyes and asked if he could forgive me for missing so many opportunities to affirm him and for not blessing him in ways that he needed my blessing. I never even noticed his need of me. The truth is I have felt for years that he is a better speaker than I am, far above me in writing skills, and brilliant with electronic equipment such as computers. Why would he ever need my blessings? But my son still needed his dad, and I loved that. I don't really know when a son or daughter no longer needs our love and blessings. As we hugged each other, he forgave me.

I sat down at my computer after my meeting with Michael and made a long list of all his great qualities. I repeated everything I had just told him and added that he is funnier as a speaker than I am and more practical. He responded not only with appreciation but with a suggestion for a new ministry we could do together. That told me beyond doubt that everything was forgiven and cleared between us.

Because we are all sinners, we must be alert to offenses against others all our lives and always be ready to confess wrongs and forgive. Forgiveness will keep our lives in harmony with each other and God. It's always the responsibility of both parties.

Forgiveness Cleans Your Heart

Forgiveness heals the wounded heart. Both hearts, actually—that of the forgiver and the forgiven. Forgiveness is a valve that lets off bitterness, anger, and resentment—acids that can eat away at the heart, leaving scar tissue that hardens the heart to the love of God. And God will not violate your free will by entering a heart that will not allow him inside. That's why it's so important that we keep our hearts soft and open. We want to be open to God's voice as he speaks to us through his Word. We want our hearts open and receptive to everything he wants us to have that will bring us closer to him. And we also want the hearts of those we offend to remain open to God and others.

If your heart is closed and hardened because of things that people have done to you, you desperately need to learn the great value of forgiveness. You need that cleansing, that emptying of the pride of life, that forgiveness brings so that you can again receive the love of God and pass it on to others.

If people have done hurtful things to you, that does not make you unique. There's not a person on this planet who has not suffered in some way from the hand of others. I can bring up plenty of such hurts from my past at the drop of a hat—the events with publishers, the man who defamed me, and the author I mentioned in this chapter; the builder of the condos next to my house; my high school girlfriend who "done me wrong"; my father who said hurtful things to me; the girl in my childhood who led me into sexual hedonism—I could clutter my heart with all kinds of anger, bitterness, and resentment against people who have brought pain into my life.

But why clutter up my heart with all that useless junk? The past is gone; why allow it to continue messing up my heart and ruining the present? With forgiveness I can clean all that stuff out so that my heart becomes an orderly, clean, organized room where God and I can sit comfortably and enjoy a loving relationship. That, my friend, is the high value of forgiveness.

At the end of this chapter, you will find a few of the most powerful verses from God's words that you can use when you face a need to forgive. These verses will give you the reason for forgiveness and the power to carry it through. I pray that you will use them well.

Next, I will show you the huge differences that hiding God's words make if you have any addictions or habits you want to break. Take eating too much, for instance. There is a love bucket in everyone, and if someone's bucket remains low for a period of time, it's easy to try to fill it with any number of substitutes. And parents, wait until you see how helping kids hide God's words will make them change in front of your eyes. Then read what happens when both husband and wife join with me in this new adventure. The results are wonderful.

Scriptures to Hide in Your Heart

Be kind to one another, tender-hearted, *forgiving* each other, just as God in Christ also has *forgiven* you. (Ephesians 4:32 NASB, emphasis mine)

Then Peter came to Jesus and asked, "Lord, how many times shall I forgive my brother when he sins against me? Up to seven times?" Jesus answered, "I tell you, not seven times, but seventy-seven times." (Matthew 18:21–22)

Anyone who claims to be in the light but hates his brother is still in the darkness. Whoever loves his brother lives in the light, and there is nothing in him to make him stumble. But whoever hates his brother is in the darkness and walks around in the darkness; he does not know where he is going, because the darkness has blinded him. (1 John 2:9–11)

Bear with each other and forgive whatever grievances you may have against one another. Forgive as the Lord forgave you. And over all these virtues put on love, which binds them all together in perfect unity. (Colossians 3:13–14)

Fourteen
How Your Beliefs Affect Your Eating Habits and Addictions

Okay, I admit it. My wife and I had what millions of Americans and others around the world have: a mild food addiction. We both tried every diet known to mankind. Nothing ever worked for us. Then shortly after hiding just a couple of scripture verses in my heart, I began to see changes in my eating habits and improvement in my weight. Anytime I discover something new that works for me, I want my wife to join me in it. That's my lifetime pattern. I became like a pleading puppy, begging her to join me in eating better and exercising regularly and getting on her case for not taking care of her health.

She reacted with the same kind of resistance she had given me for more than thirty-eight years of dogging her to exercise and eat better. My new twist on it—"Let's hide God's Word in our hearts together"—seemed to her just one more example of my unremitting pleading for her to try my new fads, which irritated her like a dripping faucet. She resisted my attempts to be her food and exercise coach, and my relentless pleas often resulted in confrontation and arguments.

A normal person would have given up, but not me. I admit it; when I get excited about something that helps me and could help others, I keep on it. I just turned up the leaky faucet until it became a running stream. Big mistake.

What I didn't know then was that if you want to help a person who has a habit she can't control, the worse thing you can do is confront her critically

161

about it. Why? Because most uncontrolled habits are, on some level, addictions. And addictions are fed by weak relationships. No doubt my wife interpreted my criticism of her as a breach in our relationship, which would only increase the power of the addiction. The more love a person feels and the stronger the relationship becomes, the more inner power the addicted person has to deal with and manage his or her addictions.

Psychiatrist Gerald May has written that all addictions are medication for the pain of weak relationships.[1] Alcoholics Anonymous has found that repairing and rebuilding broken relationships is the key to overcoming alcoholism. So if you are married to someone who is afflicted with one or more of more than three hundred possible addictions, you can help your spouse, not by riding him or her to do better, but simply by increasing your love. If you are the addicted person, the best thing you can do is rebuild more love in all of your relationships.

The main reason I wrote the book *I Promise* was to give couples ways to rebuild a loving and secure marriage. Feeling secure or safe within a marriage is the key to love and the key to gaining the power to overcome addictions.

I finally did give up trying to change my wife after my son Greg shared with me his current marriage research showing that you can never change another person. You can only change yourself. If you try to change your mate so that you will be happier, you actually weaken your marriage by making the marriage relationship more unsafe for your mate. So finally I gave up working on my wife and started working only on myself. When I turned off the dripping faucet and got completely off of her case, I witnessed a miracle. Here's how it happened.

I invited Norma to dinner to explain how I intended to treat her for the rest of our lives together. As we sat at the restaurant table, I reached over and took her hand and asked her to forgive me for all the times I had tried to change her in so many ways. I told her how wrong I had been in trying to teach her, blame her, criticize her, or judge her. Such actions had been detrimental to our marriage and our love for each other. I told her that from this day forward, I would never again try to change her or even criticize her unless she begged for it. I would never blame her for upsetting me or making me unhappy. If she needed to change something in her life, that would be between her and God, not me.

She whispered that she would forgive me, but I could tell that she was wary. Past experience with me had taught her to be cautious. She didn't know what I was up to.

Since that night I haven't tried to change Norma in any way. Instead I have done everything I could to affirm that I love her. I have praised her just for being who she is. I have thanked her many times for warning me in the past of some of my goofy decisions and admitted how much better off I would be if I had listened to her in many situations. I have shown her the high value I have for her and how much it means to have her in my life. In short, I have poured out love on her.

And now, four years later, can you guess what she does almost every day? She exercises. She eats better, carefully choosing the best foods for her health. She is even in charge of our staff's "Eat Healthy" plan.

I was walking with her recently, and she winced a little and began to limp. I asked if her knee was hurting and should we stop? Her answer stunned me. "Yes, my knee is really hurting today, but yesterday during my walk, I told my knee, 'You can hurt me as much as you want, but I will still walk, even if I have to drag you down the street with me.'" Now that's motivation! I've seen more changes in her in these past four years than I had seen in the previous twenty. As I have gotten off of her case in all areas, she has become who she really is and wants to be—and I love it.

Do you see the power of belief in making a radical change in one's life? No amount of reasoning, nagging, or pleading helped Norma change at all. My efforts to change her were futile because they were external and did not reach her heart. In fact, they had the opposite effect, causing her to feel insecure because I was fostering in her heart the belief that my love for her was conditional. And as Dr. May says, insecurity fosters overeating. I caused her to believe I would love her more if she changed her eating and exercise habits to make me happy. That was another way of saying, "I will love you if you do what pleases me." Naturally, when I put a belief like that in her heart, she would not be able to find the motivation to change.

But when I loved her unconditionally, as God loves me, the belief in my wife's heart changed. She knew my love was real and would be there regardless of what she did. With that kind of belief and security in her heart, her dependence on food diminished. And when the belief in her heart changed, so did her eating and exercise habits.

Why Do We Overeat?

Why do we eat? You may think that's a silly question. We eat because we get hungry, of course. We eat because food is fuel for our bodies, and we can't live without it. But really, we eat for more reasons than that. We eat because of the pleasure it brings. God has blessed us with a sense of taste, which means many foods bring great delight to the tongue and palate. In fact, eating is one of our greatest sources of pleasure.

We also eat for social reasons. Mealtimes are times for food and fellowship among families and in organizations and churches. Many business meetings are held over lunches or dinners. Who knows how often a well-cooked filet mignon or boiled lobster has clinched a sale or consummated a massive corporate merger? I signed my first book contract thirty-five years ago at a boardroom lunch. I was terribly embarrassed when I spilled hot coffee on the corporate president, but he still signed.

We eat for fuel, pleasure, and social interaction, but why do we overeat? Most animals in their natural habitats eat only what they need. Why are we humans different? In general, we overeat because we are caught up in at least two of the three deadlies—the lust of the eyes and the lust of the flesh. Food looks good so we desire it. Just seeing good food can turn on our gastric juices and saliva glands, and the anticipated pleasure of eating what we see can overpower the will. Food also tastes good, so those caught up in the hedonistic belief that life is one long pursuit of pleasure give themselves over to their appetites. They overindulge, seeking the richest, best tasting foods that do the most to satisfy their palates, but not the best for the health of their bodies.

The Empty Love Bucket

Psychological factors can also cause overeating. Most commonly, food can provide a way of compensating for a lack of something else. For example, as we noted above, many people feel unloved. The lack of love is a serious deficiency because love is a vital component for life and health. The limbic area of the brain hungers for love from the day we are born to the day we die. In fact, studies have shown that the brain cannot even stay organized without a steady inflow of love. So a person who lacks love may try to fill this gnawing sense of emptiness by stuffing his stomach with food.

According to health and dietary expert Dr. Dean Ornish, if you want to control your weight, reverse heart disease, and increase your overall health, you must take four actions every day:

1. Love God
2. Love others

3. Exercise regularly

4. Eat healthfully[2]

The reason Dr. Ornish tells us to love is that love is reciprocal. It is the primary mode of interplay between humans. Love is generally a mutually participatory activity, which means that when we give love, we also receive it. And our need for love is extremely powerful, every bit as important to our health as our need for food.

I picture this need as an empty bucket; let's call it your *love bucket*. Perhaps your love bucket is low, a result of either your growing-up years or your present relationships. Perhaps your mom and dad didn't know how to give love because they received so little of it when they were kids. Perhaps your spouse doesn't have a clue as to how to give the life-enriching love you need in your bucket.

So it's no big surprise that within the complexities of the human machine, wires can get crossed and switches muddled so that there is a psychological mixing of the limbic area's need for love and the stomach's need for food. When one lacks love, he feels an emptiness, and the stomach is very compassionate and comes to the rescue. "Bless your poor little heart," says stomach. "I can see that you feel empty. I can't stand to see you that way. I'll be glad to let you fill up that empty bucket by stuffing food into me." Good ol' stomach; he's all heart (or at least, he thinks he is). So why not take him up on his offer? Love, after all, seems awfully hard to come by, and food is just a few steps away in the refrigerator or a few blocks away at McDonald's. And away you go.

Well, lo and behold, that Big Mac and fries were really good. You do feel better. You feel full. But, alas, in just a little while the food digests, the emptiness returns, and the cycle starts all over again. That's how having an empty love bucket can lead to food addictions that destroy health.

How Do Beliefs Affect Your Eating Habits?

Many people remain in their addictions simply because of a wrong belief: they think they can't do anything about their compulsive appetites. They feel powerless to overcome their addiction largely because a pervasive attitude has overtaken our culture that believes we are all victims of our appetites. According to naturalistic philosophy, which now dominates the worldview of the Western world, humans are nothing more than highly developed animals. Nature programmed into us certain internal urges, and those urges lead us around by the nose because they are part of our nature and we can't do anything about them.

That's why you see abstinence education scorned by schools and *safe sex* along with condom use and distribution taught instead. They are bowing to the belief that we have overpowering urges and simply cannot manage them, so let's do the next-best thing and protect ourselves from the damage these urges can cause.

That belief is totally wrong. We, unlike animals, are created in God's own image, and he gave us a will that helps us make decisions as to which urges to obey and which to control. Now, don't get me wrong; I'm not saying it's always easy to make those decisions to thwart those urges. In fact, I am fully aware that when we fall into addictions, willpower alone is not enough to pull us out. The will of an addicted person has come largely under the control of the appetite. I know that you cannot overcome addictions by yourself. But what I am saying is this: you are not powerless to change. You are more than an animal, more than a hapless victim of circumstance, and you can make decisions, take steps, and find the help to overcome any addiction and put yourself back on the track to health and happiness. But it means you must first change some beliefs.

Beliefs That Can Set You Free

What new beliefs can break your struggle with food problems or addictions? Here are my top five:

Believe a Foodaholics Anonymous group can help you.

Foodaholics Anonymous, or FA, is a group with chapters in several parts of the nation designed to help those who struggle with overeating problems. The concept is simple: you meet regularly with others who have the same problem to discuss effective controls and gain support and encouragement. These groups are formed under the auspices of local churches and focus on the love-bucket problem by providing a sympathetic, understanding group of people who obey that greatest commandment of loving God and loving each other.

If your church does not have an FA group, you can create one. You can get information on how to do it at Celebrate Recovery at www.PurposeDriven.com. As members strengthen their own relationship with God and their caring relationships with each other, love flows among the group, and the love buckets begin to fill from real people and from the real God.

Sarah had struggled with food addictions for more than ten years. She grew up receiving little expression of love or affection from her dad. He had been molested as a young teen, which affected his ability to love his three children.

One of the girls seemed to make it through with her mom's love and the love of her friends. But Sarah didn't get her bucket filled; she turned to food as a substitute and soon found herself enslaved by the twin monsters of bulimia and anorexia. In desperation, she joined an FA group at the church of a friend, and with their help got firmly on the road to recovery.

An FA group can mentor you as well. It can help you in loving your mate, your children, or anyone in your life where relationship help is needed. You feel safe in a genuine, loving, small group that understands how to accept you just the way you are and nurtures you toward freedom by first building up your relationship with God to find his enabling power living in you.

The bottom line is this: God can give you all of the love you'll ever need, and it can overflow in your life like nothing you've ever felt. That's how big our God is. When that belief reaches your heart, watch how the power for self-control seeps into your daily life.

Believe that God loves you.

When the mirror shows all those pounds building up on your hips, thighs, or belly because of your hunger for love, it helps to realize just how dearly you are loved by the most powerful being in all the universe. Some people find that it helps to visualize God's love by putting their arms around themselves, imagining that God himself is hugging them, expressing his compassion for the pain they have felt and for the hurtful words people have said to them about their weight.

Try it. Say to yourself the words that express God's love and understanding. The words might be something like this: "Bless your dear heart, you've had to put up with a lot of junk from people, haven't you? You are very special to me. Your body is important to me—I made it, you know—and it hurts me to see you so distressed about it. I know you don't want to be this way. I know you don't want to overeat as you do. But if you will depend on me and be open to my guidance, I will lead you to help in overcoming your problem. And if you just ask me and follow my leading, I'll fill you up with my love to overflowing and give you my own strength. Please 'cry' out to me daily and I guarantee you that I'll come to you and fill you up to all of the fullness of myself."

In doing this, it's important that you don't tell yourself the kinds of lies many people fall into when they reach a state of despair about their overeating. Don't tell yourself that you are a bad person or a loser. On the other extreme, don't tell yourself that your weight and overeating are not really a problem or that this is just the way you are. If you tell yourself lies, the truth can never set you free. What you think, even if it's untrue, will lodge in your heart as beliefs. And wrong beliefs can drag you down.

Does having an out-of-control habit reflect God's best for you? Is it his will? No. He designed you to take in both his spirit and his words to enable you to live a free and blessed life. Don't gloss over your bad habit. It keeps you from being the healthy person God wants you to be.

It's important to recognize that your out-of-control lifestyle is not you; it's something that you can get rid of, that you can detach from to free yourself to be the glorious being whom God made you to be. Remember that when God created man and woman, he called his creation *good*. It's a sin for you to contradict that pronouncement by calling yourself *bad*. God loves every person he created as if each were an only son or daughter. You are infinitely dear to him. Here's a quote from Max Lucado that expresses this truth:

> If God had a refrigerator, your picture would be on it. If he had a wallet, your photo would be in it. He sends you flowers every spring and a sunrise every morning . . . Face it, friend. He is crazy about you![3]

Believe in caring for yourself.

Not everything about changing your beliefs is lofty and theological. At some point you must face the nitty-gritty of actually doing the practical things that must be done to care for your health. This means doing what you've heard a thousand times before: eat right and exercise. One purpose of the two preceding beliefs is to set the stage for this one. You believe in the power of joining or forming an FA group, you believe in the value that God places on you, so now you will begin to do the practical things that must be done to care for yourself. The support of the group and awareness of the overwhelming love of God can give you the discipline to get serious about regular exercise and the study of the kinds and amounts of foods you should eat to keep that body God created in a healthy condition.

When I struggled with my own problem of overeating, I knew that exercise was important, but I hated it. I tried all sorts of exercises, and all of them were sheer drudgery and boredom. But I finally found what worked for me, and I've been doing it for more than thirty years. I can't exercise without doing something else to take my mind off of the work of exercising, so I found that I could tolerate jogging if I would pray the entire time. I have had my best times talking to God as I ran slowly up and down residential streets. God gave me ideas for most of my ministry opportunities while I was jogging.

When I switched to a treadmill, I rigged up a stand that would hold my computer, and for years I've walked up to two hours at a time while finishing my e-mails and even some of my books. I've also pedaled stationary bikes while reading or watching TV or the kids playing. If you have trouble exercising, you might try this. Find something that can hold your attention and focus on it while you exercise.

One happy result of taking these steps of discipline to care for yourself is that self-discipline will eventually result in freedom. I know it sounds contradictory, but according to Dr. Ornish, the more that love for yourself grows within you, the less you will be dependent on food to fill that empty love bucket.

Think of it. God's will for us is to love others in the way we love ourselves. It's painfully obvious that many people don't give a rip about themselves, because it shows in their lack of self-care. The more you find love from God, others, and yourself, the more willing and able you will be to eat the right kinds of food and do the exercise required to keep your body healthy. With your love bucket full, you will not feel impelled to eat all the extra food you have stuffed into your body in the past to fill that void caused by the lack of the real thing God designed you to have—his love and the love from others. Little by little you'll find a new freedom to eat just about whatever you like. People who learn not to eat too much can eat pretty much whatever they want.

Wouldn't you love to find that kind of freedom? You can have it if you put your appetites under God's control. As Paul said, "You, my brothers, were called to be free. But do not use your freedom to indulge the sinful nature; rather, serve one another in love" (Galatians 5:13).

Believe in listening to your feelings.

I don't want you to misunderstand what I mean here. I did not say, "Believe everything your feelings tell you" because your feelings don't always tell you the truth. In fact, unless the deepest beliefs of your heart are fully aligned with God, your feelings will seldom tell you the truth. That is what's so insidious about the saying, "If it feels good, do it." Any philosophy that tells you simply to follow your feelings can lead you straight into hedonism.

My point is not that you should *follow* your feelings but that you should *listen* to them because they are windows to your deepest beliefs. They are data that you can analyze to know what kinds of beliefs you harbor in your heart. If a hot fudge sundae after a meal of chicken fried steak and fries always makes you feel good, you can bet that feeling might not tell the whole truth about your well-being. What that feeling does tell you is that you have a wrong belief in your heart. You may believe that food can fill the emptiness of your life or that more pleasure is what makes life worthwhile and eating all that stuff gives you great pleasure.

So while your feelings may not tell you the truth about your well-being, they can tell you the truth about your beliefs. So learn to listen to your feelings critically, honestly, and analytically. Use your feelings wisely to reveal to you the truth about your inner beliefs.

As I write this, a twenty-eight-year-old young woman with a food addiction is spending several hours doing just this. She is listening to her feelings, trying to understand why she had been so needy for love from the wrong kind of men. I asked her to listen for what her feelings were telling her about her husband. She was really upset with him—*bitter* would be the better word—for his lack of affection to her except when he wants sex. Clearly this girl's eating problem is a substitute for the lack of love she feels in her life. As hard as it is to do, when you want to conquer an eating disorder, ask God to show you what you need to know about yourself. What lies inside your heart that you need to see so that you can love God and others more and, thus, feel his love for you (Matthew 7:1–5 and James 1:5–6)?

Believe in surrendering yourself to God.

Earlier in this chapter I said that in spite of what the culture seems to believe, we humans are more than just highly developed animals. As creatures that reflect God's image, we have the power to decide whether to give free rein to our impulses and appetites. We are not bound by instinct to pursue every want that titillates our senses. At the same time, I realize that when addictions grip us, our wills are taken captive and we do become, in one sense, helpless.

When we feel helpless, stuck, out of control, or weak, we are in a perfect spot with God. We are inches away from his perfect will, because he only gives his grace (power) to the weak, to beggars, or to the humble. It's his will for us to humble ourselves daily to receive his power for living. He gives his love to the humble, enabling them to fulfill both of his highest commands: loving him and loving others. Isn't it great to know that when we feel weak and defeated, we are actually most receptive to receiving his love and power, enabling us to do his will?

We cannot overcome our addictions alone, yet we are not truly helpless. We still have the ability to make a decision to call for help from our higher power. To put it another way, we can admit our helplessness and call for God's strength to supply the power we lack in ourselves. As James tells us, when we turn to God . . .

He gives us more grace. That is why Scripture says: "God opposes the proud but gives grace to the humble." Submit yourselves, then, to God. Resist the devil, and he will flee from you. Come near to God and he will come near to you. . . . Humble yourselves before the Lord, and he will lift you up. (James 4:6–8, 10)

Admitting helplessness is not in fashion these days. We live in a world where the pride of life tells us that the individual is supreme and the self should always be in control. That is a deadly belief. It will kill you if you hold to it, especially when you are in the grip of any uncontrollable appetite. The only way out is to freely admit to God, "I can't do this on my own. I am helpless to overcome this problem." Throw yourself on his mercy, put yourself in his hands, and let his will replace your own. Then in your weakness you will become strong.

Here's what I do every day of my life. I see myself flat on the floor with my head down and my hands spread out in front of me, palms up. I'm talking to God in this position. I say to him, "Oh, God of Abraham, I am helpless. I don't bring you anything in myself, but as a beggar I cry out to you today for your mercy and power. Thank you that you are giving me the kingdom of heaven."

That's right. When you humble yourself to God, he promises to give you the very kingdom of heaven. "What is that?" you may ask. He gives you peace, joy, power in the Holy Spirit, and all of the other attributes of God while you remain humble before him (Romans 14:17 and Matthew 5:3).

Choosing Your God

When you turn to God for strength to overcome your eating problems, you are, in effect, switching gods. When you try to fill the empty bucket in your life with food, it shows you that your belly is really your god. But your belly did not design you (Philippians 3:19). It did not breathe God's life into you, and it has no business telling you how you should fill your life.

God designed you and created you to be filled with love from him and love for him. He intended to fill you with so much of his love that it would overflow into love for others and abound in reciprocal relationships resulting in a life utterly swimming in oceans of love.

To fill yourself in any other way is to live by a belief that is a deadly lie—a lie that can ruin your health and kill you. No one but God can fill you with God's type of love, which is the way you were designed to be filled. That is why your deepest belief must be centered on the two greatest commandments: to love God, your King (Lord), with all of your heart, soul, mind, and strength, and secondly, to love others in the same way that you want to be loved.

You actually need to fill yourself with three types of love: God's love, love from others, and your own love for yourself—in that order. It's like a circle of love. God fills you first; you use his love to care for others; and then you use the overflow to care for yourself. That will fill your love tank for sure.

If we walk away from that belief into the deadly belief that self can find its own ways to fill its empty bucket, then we will suffer the negative consequence of addictions. That's the choice: either surrender to him and his will of love, or pay the price in bad health and a life moving toward emptiness.

If we surrender to his will of love, we gain freedom from addictions and enter the joyful life God promises.

Concluding this chapter are verses from God's words that you can place in your heart to help you find God's strength in overcoming eating problems. These verses will help you connect to God's love and find the love that will fill your empty bucket. Most of us have a job that also will help fill up our love bucket. You may work too many hours climbing the success ladder and after many years, like many of us, you find out your ladder is leaning against the wrong wall. You'll read how beliefs have a major effect on the type of job you have, how much you earn, how successful you'll be, and many other direct connections between your current beliefs and how your job is affected by them. That's coming up next. (By the way, I wrote an entire book, *Healthy Eating*, which shows you the four main foods that keep people overweight and presents my own weight-reduction plan that explains how to put calories and exercising together for the easiest way of losing weight.)

Scriptures to Hide in Your Heart

You, my brothers [and sisters], were called to be free. But do not use your freedom to indulge the sinful nature; rather, serve one another in love. (Galatians 5:13)

"Have faith in God," Jesus answered. "I tell you the truth, if anyone says to this mountain, 'Go, throw yourself into the sea,' and does not doubt in his heart but believes that what he says will happen, it will be done for him. Therefore I tell you, whatever you ask for in prayer, believe that you have received it, and it will be yours." [If you ask for anything that he has already stated is his will, he'll give it to you when your prayer reaches your heart as a belief.] (Mark 11:22–24)

If you keep My commandments, you will abide in My love; just as I have kept My Father's commandments and abide in His love. [His commandments: love him and others.] These things I have spoken to you so that My joy may be in you, and that your joy may be made full. This is My commandment, that you love one another, just as I have loved you. (John 15:10–12 NASB)

Blessed are the poor in spirit, [a beggar, helpless, bankrupt] for theirs is the kingdom of heaven. (Matthew 5:3)

Fifteen
How Your Beliefs Affect Your Vocation

I vividly remember as a young kid believing that I was stupid. I couldn't spell, I couldn't write, and I couldn't speak in front of people. I assumed that I would grow up and get a normal, average-paying job similar to that of my wage-earner father. It ran in the family, after all. My brothers, all our kinfolks, and almost everyone I knew took very important jobs so necessary to our country: in factories or public service, or they worked as waitresses and carpenters, or they took much lower-paying, dead-end jobs, as my father did. No one in my circle had any higher expectations.

Even when my parents opened their own restaurant, it was a greasy spoon type of place, catering to the average Joe in a small town. The eating area was no larger than fifteen by twenty feet, furnished with used tables and chairs, set on cracked and stained floors. The restaurant was an exact picture of what my parents believed about themselves. It was below average because they believed themselves to be below average.

I went straight from high school to a mailroom job at Hughes Aircraft in Southern California. For some reason, the foreman of the electrical drafting department took a liking to me. He urged me to get out of that factory and go to college. No one in my family had ever gone to college, so it never occurred to me to consider it. I didn't believe I had the brains for it and I told him so. But the man kept nagging at me until finally he said if I would enroll in college, he would pay for all my first year's expenses—thirty dollars a semester, plus all my books and supplies. (This was many years ago!) If after a year I didn't want to stay in school, he would give me back my factory job with all the raises I had missed while away.

I had no driving ambition to achieve an education, but what did I have to lose? I accepted his offer and gave college a whirl.

I enrolled and began classes but had no idea how to study. After the first year, my grade point average was 1.6. It didn't really disturb me; I figured that was about right for a dumb kid like me. My grade fit my beliefs about who I was. Since I passed my first year, I decided to try another. After completing my third semester, I received a letter from the college. If I didn't raise my grade point average to at least 2.0, they would force me to drop out.

I worked hard at raising my grades, asking every friend I had to help me study and spent a lot of time reading, working problems, and preparing for tests. When the announcement of my semester grade arrived in the mail, I hardly dared to open it. My stomach tightened and my palms got sweaty. My entire future was sealed inside that envelope. Finally I ripped it open and looked: my average for the semester was exactly 2.0. I screamed and jumped about like a frog on a hotplate. I made it! Just barely, but I made it. I stayed in school and finally graduated, cramming four years of college work into five years.

After college, someone gave me the book *Think and Grow Rich* by Napoleon Hill. That little book really opened my eyes to the power of belief—the power of the mind to affect one's well-being and success. The author had studied more than five hundred successful men and found that every one of them had a deep passion, a conviction, a belief that if they focused on what they wanted in life, nothing could stop them from achieving it. The power was not in one's intelligence or in one's financial backing. It was in the deep-seated belief that you can achieve what your mind can conceive if you pursue it with energy and single-minded passion.

I wished I had known of this concept before I enrolled in college. My negative beliefs had kept me from achieving. I believed I was just naturally stupid; therefore, my grades were those of a stupid person. Now I know the truth. I am a person of immensely high value because the Master of the universe created me as a little copy of himself. Now I know that I can do all things through Christ, who gives me strength (Philippians 4:13).

Equipped with this new belief about myself, by God's grace I eventually went back to school, earned a masters degree and eventually two honorary doctorates for my marriage research. I interviewed more than sixty thousand women around the world and found out that they all have a built-in marriage manual. The more I learned about the amazing female, the more I wanted to tell the world what they taught me. So that's where my heart went, establishing a career in speaking, writing, and counseling. I am still the same old me who never expected to have more than a blue-collar job. The only difference is in what I learned to believe.

So do your beliefs affect your vocation—your job or career? You bet they do. Thomas Edison believed he could find a solution to any electrical or mechanical problem. As a result of that belief, we have electric lighting, motion pictures, recorded sound, and electrical generators providing power to entire cities. Henry Ford believed he could make automobiles affordable to the average family. As a result of his manufacturing methods, more than 90 percent of American families now own automobiles.

Yet while many people buy into the power of belief, they also hold erroneous ideas about how to put those beliefs into action when it comes to vocation. Before we go further, let's consider three of the worst beliefs and how they can hold you back.

Bad Belief Number One:
You Are What You Do

When asked about our jobs, we tend to say, "I'm a doctor," I'm a fireman," "I'm a teacher," or "I'm a stay-at-home mom." Of course, these answers are not literally true. You were not manufactured and programmed to be a doctor. You chose to do the work of a doctor. What you are is a human being made in the image of God who has found his or her calling in caring for the health of others.

In our hearts we understand this principle. Most of the time we understand the difference between what we do and who we are. But not always. Do you remember the character Bubba Blue in the movie *Forrest Gump*? Bubba was Forrest Gump's Vietnam army buddy, and he had a one-track mind. He was a shrimper, and he was obsessed with shrimping. He could neither think nor talk of anything else. It was shrimping, shrimping, shrimping every day from the moment he awoke in the morning to the moment he fell asleep at night. In his mind, he was a shrimper. He thought that what he did defined who he was.

No doubt you know people who throw themselves so totally into their work they seem to become what they do. They may come home to the family, go through the motions of eating and relating to the wife and kids, but clearly their minds are still at the office. The moment the meal is over, they grab their briefcase, pull out a stack of papers and a laptop, and it's back to work for the rest of the evening.

They may not have to work. They may not be behind at all; there may be no big meeting in the morning to prepare for, no contract that must be drawn up. They work because it's what they do. They don't feel alive or that they have purpose unless they are plunged into their work. They think their work gives their lives meaning and worth. They think they are what they do.

I know a man who had been a pastor all his life. In his late forties, he became a victim of a power struggle at his church, which resulted in his getting fired. He could not find another pastorate, and he had to take a job in the business arena as a hardware salesman. The poor man was devastated. He had dreamed of being a pastor from childhood. Because being a pastor was all he had ever done, he expected to die in the pulpit or retire at a ripe old age. For more than a year he struggled with his self-worth, his self-image, and his sense of identity. In his mind *he was a pastor*, and now that he did not fill a pastor's role, he didn't know who he was.

Statistics show that a high percentage of retiring corporate executives and highly motivated businessmen will die within just a few short years of retirement. The reason: without their vocation they can no longer find a sense of meaning and purpose. They have made the mistake of defining themselves by their work, and the loss of that definition leaves them anchorless and empty.

This is why Bob Buford, who retired from a highly successful career as owner and developer of a huge chain of cable companies, has written books urging businessmen not simply to retire, but rather to retire *to* something meaningful.[1] Buford, a strong Christian, understands clearly that a person must not define himself by what he does. What he does must flow out of who he is. Who he is must be well established in relationship to God. A person must find his identity in following God's will for his life, and his vocation must conform to that inner sense of identity, that calling to be an instrument in God's hands.

If we place ourselves first in God's hands, we will be willing to be remolded into a different form when God deems it's time for us to make a change in our vocation. We must always be ready to submit willingly to such a change. If our identity is secure in him, a change in vocation is merely an outward adjustment. It has nothing to do with the meaning and purpose of the person you are at the core of your being.

Bad Belief Number Two:
You Must Climb the Ladder of Success

My dear friend Ron spent forty-two years in his chosen career as an electrical engineer. Ron was good at what he did, and his skills earned him a comfortable salary on which he easily supported his wife and family. He worked his entire career for one large company, and time and again management offered him lucrative promotions that his peers would have died for. But Ron turned them all down, and his friends could not understand why. They thought he was crazy to turn his back on bigger salaries, bigger offices, better titles, more travel, and all the company perks that come with being a top executive.

But Ron saw it differently. He saw midnight hours at the office, headaches in dealing with employees, departmental budgets, boring meetings, continuous moves, a neglected family, and difficult family adjustment to frequent moves. Furthermore, promotions would take him away from doing what he really loved—hands-on involvement in the creative processes of engineering.

Ron's friends believed that a man's worth was measured by his position and paycheck. Ron believed that his worth was defined by the values God endorsed, which were to love and serve others. He loved God and chose to live by those values. He loved his family and chose to let his vocation serve their needs rather than use his career as an ego trip to show the world what an important person he could become.

You have known plenty of men and women who are opposite from Ron. In fact, they are the most common types in the workplace. From the moment they are hired and assigned their first cubicle in that vast maze of worker-ant compartments, they have their eyes on the president's office, secretly saying, "My name will be on that door someday." From that moment forward they scramble, claw, bite, trample, and do whatever it takes to reach the next level, and the next, and the next. In their bloody wake they leave a neglected family, neglected health, unnurtured friendships, smoldering enemies they have trampled, peace of mind, and virtually everything that makes life truly worth living.

Usually when such people get to the top, they find the victory empty. They have sacrificed everything that makes life worthwhile, so they feel alone and unloved. I've heard many deathbed regrets from men who said they would trade all their great wealth just to have back those moments they lost playing ball with their sons, attending their daughter's concerts, taking their kids fishing, getting them through their first dates, and spending time alone on the beach with their wives. How sad to realize too late that one has chased the soap bubble of success and lost a treasure that can never be recovered.

Ron was a happy man in his forty-two years as an electrical engineer. Why? Because he saw himself as serving a different boss from that of his coworkers. His boss was God himself, who told him that his main job was to love God and love others. So loving others was Ron's true career. Electrical engineering was just one way to make it happen. And it was a career that he found deeply satisfying.

What better boss can one have than the creator of humans who wrote the manual on how to operate the human machine? To me it seems a no-brainer. This is a boss we can trust. Each day, whatever job we drive to, whether it's manning a station on the assembly line or leading a multimillion-dollar corporation, we should rise in the morning, salute the God of the universe, and say, "Reporting for service, sir. Point the way and I'm ready to go. Just let me know what you have for me to do today."

That is the path to true career satisfaction. Kick the ladder aside and follow the leader to true satisfying holiness. Happiness is a by-product of loving God and serving others.

Bad Belief Number Three: Work Your Fingers to the Bone

One reason my friend Ron did not want to move up the corporate ladder was that he knew the company philosophy about hard work and success. The higher in management one got, the more time one was expected to put in. Ron had watched those who moved up, first into departmental supervision, then into middle management, and finally into executive positions. At each level their responsibilities increased, and the company expected them to meet those responsibilities by simply working harder. And since they had achieved their promotions by working hard already, working harder simply meant working longer. It was not unusual for vice presidents to put in sixty to seventy hours a week.

Few people in America have been as successful in business as Lee Iacocca, former head of the Chrysler Corporation. But he was wiser than many executives. He knew the value of balance, not making work one's only focus in life. He wrote:

I'm constantly amazed by the number of people who can't seem to control their own schedules. Over the years, I've had many executives come to me and say with pride: "Boy, last year I worked so hard that I didn't take any vacation." It's nothing to be proud of. I always feel like responding: "You dummy. You mean to tell me that you can take responsibility for an $80 million project and you can't plan two weeks out of the year to go off with your family and have some fun?"[2]

Solomon was the king of Israel when that nation was at the height of its glory. Solomon had wealth; stables filled with the finest horses; a state-of-the-art equipped army; interests in philosophy, history, theology, and poetry; not to mention his three hundred wives and seven hundred concubines. This man's schedule could have been as full as he wanted to make it. He could have spent all his time presiding over his empire, dabbling in his hobbies, managing his household, and saying, "Yes, dear" to his wives. Yet in his God-given wisdom, he understood the value of balancing work and life. He wrote:

> Better one handful with tranquility
> than two handfuls with toil and chasing after the wind . . .
> There was a man all alone;
> he had neither son nor brother.
> There was no end to his toil,
> yet his eyes were not content with his wealth.
> "For whom am I toiling," he asked,
> "and why am I depriving myself of enjoyment?"
> This too is meaningless—
> a miserable business! (Ecclesiastes 4:6, 8)

Five Key Beliefs to Build a Great Vocation

It's not uncommon for young people (and sometimes older people as well) to be uncertain about choosing their vocations. Usually when you ask a small child, "What do you want to be when you grow up?" you will get varied answers based on what he or she has been exposed to. The answers can range from policeman, baseball player, cowboy, mommy, singer, to airplane pilot, astronaut, or whatever happens to be the occupation of Mommy or Daddy. Usually by the sophomore year in high school, we hope a young person's direction will start firming up toward a focused goal.

But it often doesn't happen. Many kids graduate still not knowing what they want to do when they grow up. It's an important decision. After all, you will spend probably tens of thousands of dollars educating your children in their career choices. The decision needs to be right. But how do you make such a decision with any degree of certainty?

Here are five basic principles that can serve as guidelines. I learned them from my pastor, Harold Carlson, while I was attending college. He called them *the five* Ms. They have guided me for almost fifty years.

Master. Your first step in approaching your life's vocation is to decide who is to be your master. It's a well-known biblical principle that man cannot serve two masters. His true allegiance will always be to one, and the other will get whatever is left over.

In order for you to find true fulfillment in life, your master must be Christ, and your service to your job, your family, and others must be an extension of your primary service to him. I see many well-meaning Christians make that commitment, but I'm afraid that in reality the commitment is not always genuine. Often one's commitment to his or her career soon competes with the commitment to Christ. When this happens, dutiful Christians often try to balance the competing claims, giving as much time and attention as possible to both. This may mean doing more volunteer church work out of guilt or a mistaken concept of what it means to serve Christ. You don't serve him by doing a lot of extra religious stuff; you serve him by submitting your life to his direction. More often than not, the attempt to "do more for Christ" leads to exhaustion, and soon it becomes apparent that the real master is the career.

The solution is not to balance the demands of your career against the claims of Christ, but rather to keep the career claims subject to Christ. This means making him totally the Master—the boss, as I have said before—of your entire life. Then he is in charge not only of you, but of your career as well. You don't serve him by doing extra religious work, but rather by being his person in whatever environment you are placed. This means that whatever job site you've been hired to work on, you are really Christ's employee. You are working ultimately for him. You obey your manager or your foreman because your big boss, Christ, tells you to. You serve your true Master, Christ, when you serve your supervisor on your job. You serve Christ by demonstrating his likeness, his ethics, his care, his diligence, and his love in everything you do.

The bottom line is this: our King, Christ, calls us to love him and others. Those are his orders. When we crave to know him, serve him, have him as our deep personal friend, where we share everything with him, then we are deciding to believe that he is everything, and serving him is the most important thing for us to do on earth. From the Ten Commandments: he is our God, and he alone do we serve! We have not other gods, and we don't worship anyone or anything but him. And his words are true, leading us to freedom.

Our boss is God, and his orders are to love others. That leads to our mission.

Mission. What is Christ's will for your life? When you determine this you will find your mission. Already you know the overarching answer to this question; we've hit on it many times in this book. The underlying mission of every child of God is to love others. This means following the example of Christ and finding a career that provides the best way your particular talents can be employed in the service of others.

Actually, this principle doesn't narrow down the field much, because all jobs are ultimately service jobs. No matter what you choose to do for a living, it will in some way involve serving others. Whether you are Bill Gates or a checker at the local grocery store, you earn your living by serving others. The checker serves by being an important link in providing households with food. Bill Gates serves by providing software that enables us to use our computers in productive ways. The president of Honda serves by providing affordable, reliable automobiles for people worldwide to get from here to there, or more importantly, get to where your loved ones are.

Your basic mission is already decided for you. You are going to serve people. It is important that you hold this fact firmly in your mind, because many people lose sight of it. They forget that the purpose of working is to serve others, and they begin to think of their careers as serving themselves— their own bank accounts, their own egos, to finance their own indulgence in the pleasures of the three deadlies.

If you choose your career and enter it with the true desire to bless other people with a needed service, that fact alone will do much to inform your choice of a vocation. From there your primary task will be to determine just how your own talents, abilities, opportunities, and interests can best be utilized in service. When you determine that, you will determine your mission.

Method. Let's say, using the criteria we've listed above, you have decided that your mission is to eliminate pain within others. You are a sensitive person who hates to see people suffering, and you always wish you could do something about it. You feel so strongly about this that you decide the best way you can serve Christ by serving others is to do what you can to alleviate pain. Even as a kid, you were always helping little animals when you saw them hurt.

Very well, then what is the best method of eliminating pain? You can eliminate physical pain through medicine, surgery, physical therapy, dentistry, pharmacy, or a hundred other methods. You can alleviate emotional pain through psychiatry, counseling, or ministry. Which of these fields do your talents or interests fit best? Are you deft with your hands and gifted with great patience and above-average intelligence? You might consider becoming a surgeon. Do people tend to come to you with their problems because you are a sympathetic listener? That might indicate your aptitude for counseling. Are you physically active and enjoy exercise and sports? Perhaps you would make a good physical therapist. Do you have a sadistic side? Then consider dentistry. (Okay, that's a joke. I still remember Steve Martin as the sadistic dentist in *The Little Shop of Horrors*. The truth is, there is virtually no pain involved in modern dentistry.) The point is, your talents and interests were given to you by God himself to enable you to serve your mission in a particular way. By doing an inventory of those talents and interests, you may find the right method to accomplish your mission.

Dream up an idea for a wonderful serving job that you would love to get up every morning and do—even if you didn't get paid. Now go out and train for that job, and people will actually pay you to do it when you get really good at it.

Maintain. The fourth M is to maintain what is working and what God is blessing. When you choose a method of serving that fits your talents and interests, you must then make decisions that will move you toward your goal. This often means finding resources to support those decisions. You will need money to go to school. You will need to gain admission to the right university that offers your field of study. All the pieces are seldom in place as you look down these unknown paths.

If you pray to God as you make these decisions, you can depend on him to provide insight and open the right doors. Or sometimes he closes the wrong doors. Your task is not always to understand; it's not always possible to see the way clearly much further than the next step. God holds your future. It's your task to trust him as the boss and venture forward in sheer faith that he will make a way for you. Put your staff in the water. If the sea parts before you, start walking.

Stay alert as you walk the path. Note where doors open and where they close. Take those that open; forget the others. God is directing your path, so you need not worry about the future. Your task as you prepare for your vocation is simply to maintain what works and get rid of what doesn't. Or make what isn't working work. But stop riding a three-legged horse. One of my lost opportunities was when Oprah called me to do an entire show with her on her stage. I turned her down because I was too busy and asked her producer if I could come at a later date. He assured me that it would happen. It never did. But I went on rejoicing as God opened up many more doors, and I remained grateful. But be careful to look deeply into all *open doors*. Some, as you consider them, may be taking you down a road that can make it difficult to continue serving others.

Mate. The last M is your mate. If you are married, you have a valuable partner to help you as you move toward fulfilling your God-given vocation. As you follow God through the doors he opens for you, it is vital that you stay in harmony with your husband or wife. Whatever God calls you to do, it will always involve love. That's just God's way. It's what he is about.

When love is present, the two of you serve God in tandem, walking the path together side-by-side. Since your goals are the same—to serve God in a way that fulfills your mission, serves others, and serves your home—your mate provides a valuable alternate viewpoint that will give you more insights into your path than you would have alone. Your husband or wife can often see the other side of the dilemma and provide input that you would have overlooked if left to your own thinking. Of all my marriage books, *I Promise* is my favorite because it will give you very specific ways to disagree with your mate and come out of your arguments more in love and feeling like a winner.

Your mate also provides a focal point for keeping you centered. His or her presence in your life can be a continuous reminder that you work to serve others. She will be the primary "other" that a husband serves. He will be the presence in the home that reminds her that she doesn't live to work; she works to live.

In my own home, I lived every day to serve first my own wife and kids and when they were filled up with my love, they released me to love other people's kids and partners in life. It was a wonderful life to have my children in harmony with me and walking hand in hand as I served others. They not only "sent" me out into the world to change it, but prayed for a blessing from God for me. Now I get to see them doing the same thing with their mate and kids. Just last week, my three older grandkids came to me and asked if they could take over my ministry someday. They each wanted different positions. Taylor wanted to be the psychiatrist; Michael and Cole wanted to be psychologists. All want to write and speak and help families and couples with their relationships with God and each other.

Serving Others: The Real Key to Vocation

Some of the happiest days of my life were when Norma and I were in our early years of ministry back in Waco, Texas. We had three children, and I was working as a youth minister making twenty thousand dollars a year. That was more in those days than now, of course, but it wasn't a huge salary even then. I specifically remember telling God I didn't need money. I just wanted to love people and minister to them. I started every day with a morning jog, taking time to thank God for Christ in my life, for my family, for my vocation, and for all the many ways he had blessed me. I felt healthy, successful, and excited about life in general.

But in time things changed. I grew successful. Through a series of God-given circumstances, my work expanded over the next two decades into a worldwide ministry of counseling, writing books, TV infomercials, films, videos, and public-speaking engagements. You would think with all that my gratitude and happiness would only increase. But it didn't. It all went south instead. I made tons of money, and I began to be concerned about managing and spending it, as well as anxious to push for ways to earn more. I began to spend all my time and energy on the rewards God gave me for serving him, and in the process I didn't have much time left to serve my "rewarder." I began, out of necessity, to serve another master: myself. I became focused on the gifts and forgot the giver. It was such a slow process that I didn't see myself leaving God out.

I've told the rest of the story before. I ruined my health, ending up with a major heart attack and kidney failure requiring a transplant. That's what happens when you forget to serve God and others and focus on your vocation as a way of managing yourself and your money. I learned my lesson. I shoved management of my assets off the table and let others take it over. I returned to my first love—my love for my God and others. And today I'm happy to say that I feel as if I'm in heaven already, serving people with my God-given vocation and thanking God every day for another day in which I get to serve him as my King. And my biggest dream is to help churches all over the world provide the opportunity for their members to hide God's words within their hearts.

Probably what I'm most excited about with the whole concept of hiding God's words is helping parents learn how to instill this habit within their children. Can you only imagine what our world will look like when kids brand his words within their hearts? Let's do all we can to turn this world around with kids empowered by the words of God and transforming those kids into reflections of God's love. Is there anything more important? That's the next chapter.

Scriptures to Hide in Your Heart

Work willingly at whatever you do, as though you were working for the Lord rather than for people. (Colossians 3:23 NLT)

You may say to yourself, "My power and the strength of my hands have produced this wealth for me." But remember the LORD your God, for it is he who gives you the ability to produce wealth, and so confirms his covenant, which he swore to your forefathers, as it is today. (Deuteronomy 8:17–18)

So I say to you: Ask and it will be given to you; seek and you will find; knock and the door will be opened to you. For everyone who asks receives; he who seeks finds; and to him who knocks, the door will be opened. (Luke 11:9–10)

Sixteen
How Your Beliefs
Affect Your Children

I t's a running joke among psychiatrists and counselors that every time a patient lies on their couch, the first question should always be, "Tell me about your father." The stereotypical assumption among counseling profession-als is that every problem anyone has in life can stem from one's relationship with his or her parents. Whether it's heredity or environment, the general assumption seems to be that who we are and what we do are determined largely by our par-ents. The question pertinent to us as it relates to the theme of this book is "What role did your mother and father play in developing the beliefs you hold today?"

It's almost certain that your parents did play such a role. According to my own research and observations for almost fifty years, if your children are in harmony with you, love you, and feel loved by you, they will almost certainly take on many of your values. Most Republicans had Republican parents. If your parents loved JFK, then you probably do as well. If your dad disliked Ronald Reagan because of his policy with the unions, then you may dislike him too. Statistically, you are likely to be a member of the same denomina-tion as your parents. Political, religious, and marital beliefs are deeply rooted in what your parents believe.

The corollary to that statement is also true: if your children are not in har-mony with you, if they don't love you or feel loved by you, they will likely reject many of your values. The inescapable fact is that you will influence them in one way or the other, either positively or negatively. Your relationship with your children will inevitably shape their lives and their beliefs.

I followed two primary parenting rules in raising our kids: honor them every day, and repair any relationship damage on the day it happened. Norma and I never let the sun go down on our kids' angry hearts toward us or any family member.

You may be surprised to learn that one of our rules was to honor our kids. You know all about honoring one's parents; that's one of the Ten Commandments. But honoring one's *kids*? Love, discipline, teaching, and correcting you can understand, but is it the parents' place to honor their kids? Yes. When I say we honored our kids, I don't mean we set them on a pedestal and bowed down to them in any sense. We did not have ceremonies or issue proclamations or have an "Honor Your Offspring" day with cake, greeting cards, and a party. To honor your kids means that you treat them as highly valued individuals created in the image of God. It means you don't treat them as your possessions or extensions of yourself. Yes, you are responsible for their education, to influence their character development and growth in maturity, and to expose them to your love for the Lord and his words. But this gives you no right to ignore their fundamental uniqueness and need for basic consideration as human beings.

Honoring your kids means when they're old enough, they have their own territory and possessions, and you respect their space, their privacy. You don't go into their room without knocking, and you don't open their mail or the drawers in their rooms. You allow them their opinions and the honest expression of them. When those opinions need correcting, you do it with reason and love, not in anger and recrimination.

Another way to honor your children is to "train a child in the way he should go, and when he is old he will not turn from it" (Proverbs 22:6). This passage is often misinterpreted as meaning that if you teach your child about God, religion, and right from wrong, he will stay on the straight and narrow path the rest of his life. Actually, it means to be sensitive to your child's God-given talents, skills, interests, and passions. These elements will reveal to you "the way he or she should go" or the way each one is *bent*. Does your child show skill and interest in art, writing, math, making things, playing with dolls, or cooking? Watch these tendencies, test them, and encourage those where interest is maintained. When you see a clear tendency, work with your child to develop it into a marketable skill.

All too many parents decide from the start that their child will go into the family business or follow in one of the parents' footsteps. The child may show no aptitude or interest in it, but the parent decided at the child's birth that he or she would carry on the family tradition. That is not training a child in the way he or she should go. Your child was not created to be an extension of your ambitions.

It often happens, however, that children do follow in their parents' vocational footsteps. Both of my sons freely chose to go into marriage-and-family fields closely related to mine. I know of a pastor whose four sons all became pastors as well. I know of a stay-at-home mother who raised three daughters who also felt that being full-time moms was the greatest vocation they could possibly choose.

When this happens, you can be sure that love and respect exists between the parents and the children. Love and respect are the channels through which values and beliefs pass from one generation to the next. So if you want your beliefs *to take* in your kids, if you want them to believe in the high value of loving God and loving others, you must model those values to them. They must see you loving God, and they must see you in action loving others. They especially must not see your love only as it applies to others; they must feel it in their own lives. They must be the happy recipients of it. This flow of love will implant those beliefs and values in their own lives.

Norma and I knew that if we loved, taught, and respected our kids, they would grow up feeling highly valued. If they knew they were loved, they would keep an open heart to us and to God, and whatever God called them to do, they could do it with the knowledge and skills we encouraged them to develop. We told them again and again how much we loved them and how we would support them in anything they chose to do in life. We also told them that there was nothing they could do to keep us from loving them. Even if they turned bad and committed crimes or lived lives in opposition to God's will and ended up in prison or worse, we would still love them. We wanted them to know that we loved them as God loves us. No matter what they did, it would not separate them from our love. We hoped that with this kind of love flowing between us, they would be receptive to the teaching and values we instilled into their lives. We also hoped that with this awareness of our love and God's love in their hearts, they would have the confidence and security to do whatever God called them to do.

Early in our children's lives, we planted three basic beliefs into their hearts. In order to reinforce these beliefs and to be sure they understood how important they were, I must have asked them ten thousand times, "What is the greatest thing in life?"

"We know, Dad; don't keep asking us."

"But I want to know you know," I responded. "What are those values?"

"We must honor God, honor others, and honor God's creation."

When we stayed at any motel, it was inevitable that one of our kids would start jumping from one bed to the other. Soon the others would join in. Always, I would stop them and say, "Who owns that bed?"

"I don't know," they replied.

"Do you own it?"

"No," they said. "It's not ours."

"Very well, then," I responded. "If you go to the motel manager and ask for permission to jump on his bed, then you can jump."

I loved watching them walk away to the front office to ask. Every time, they came running back into the room flying toward the bed. "He said yes!"

What I was trying to teach my kids is that we honor God by honoring others. And we honor others by valuing what's important to them—which includes their possessions.

Those three basic beliefs—honor others, honor God, and honor God's creation—held our children's hearts toward God, and now that they are well into adulthood, we are blessed that this has not changed one iota. They are now actively passing on those beliefs to their own children.

When our kids were growing up, we even memorized a few passages of scripture together. But at the time, the principle of hiding God's words in the heart had not dawned on me, so we did not know just how important scripture could be to our beliefs. But now we know that it is vitally important. So let's get right into it. I want to give you three simple but important steps to start you and your kids on the exciting journey of hiding God's words within your hearts.

Leading Your Children by Changing Your Own Heart

Most adults who want to follow God know of at least two or three areas in their lives that sorely need to be changed. I've already told you about my own problem with lust. You may suffer from the same problem or from something altogether different. Perhaps you realize that you are too materialistic. Your lifestyle is too grand, you're caught up in consumerism, and you depend on your possessions for status and security. Using a good concordance, find scriptures that show you God's view of this subject. You might find scriptures such as 1 John 2:15: "Do not love the world or anything in the world. If anyone loves the world, the love of the Father is not in him."

Or maybe your problem is that you are a consistent complainer. You cannot accept adversity, always thinking your life is less than it should be because you encounter difficulties. You might choose to absorb and chew on Romans 5:3–5: "But we also rejoice in our sufferings, because we know that suffering produces perseverance; perseverance, character; and character, hope. And hope does not disappoint us, because God has poured out his love into our hearts by the Holy Spirit, whom he has given us."

When such a scripture changes you, and your children witness the change, they cannot help but wonder how it came about. "Mom always used to complain every time any little thing went wrong, like the time when she burned the cake when the pastor came for dinner, and she moaned and groaned as if the world had come to an end. But look at what just happened: The school just fired her from teaching seventh-grade English because she mentioned Christ to a troubled girl while counseling her after hours. And I could see God's smile on her face through her pain, and she said, 'The Holy Spirit is pouring a lot of love into my heart because of the deep pain I felt at what happened to me today.' What in the world has come over her?" When the kids see such a change in you, you can explain to them how it came about. They will see the power of God's Holy Spirit working in your life, and it will impress them enough to try it for themselves. They'll have a model to see how it is done when they face whatever character flaws they have in the future.

When the Holy Spirit changes you through the power of his words, as he changed me, you become a living, walking example for others. It's the most effective way to lead people to become more like Christ. It's not what you say, but the evidence of your life modeling God's love that influences the people you love.

Leading is much better than telling. You can explain to your children the principle of hiding God's words in your heart, and that's a good thing to do. But the principle takes on new power when they see you not merely telling, but doing it. They see the principle in action. They see it as a tangible reality instead of an abstract teaching concept.

Never Force Your Children to Join You

Kids are kids. They are not as mature as some adults, and at young ages they have little or no interest in scripture memorization. Naturally, you would like to change that. You want them to become interested in the Scriptures. You want them to hide certain basic passages in their hearts to give them beliefs that will guide their decisions and actions in life. And so, in your zeal to do your best for them, you decide to have your nine-year-old and eleven-year-old memorize a short list of pertinent scriptures. You drill them every night and insist that they meet certain memorization goals you set for them. And you are diligent in modeling the principle to them, memorizing scripture right along with them.

But soon you may see that it's not working. Clearly they hate the memorization sessions. They dread the evening when they must meet with you and go through another round of memorization drudgery. The verses are not sticking in their minds, and their hearts are not into the process. What should you do? You dearly want them to have deep-seated, godly beliefs in their hearts. Should you force them to continue, saying, "This is for your own good, and though you hate it now, you'll thank me for it someday"?

No. If you force your kids to memorize against their will, criticizing them for their lack of interest in "spiritual things" and disciplining them for their attitude, you will achieve the opposite of what you want. You may close your children's hearts to you. They will feel that you are overly controlling. If they sense any unloving condemnation or criticism from you, they will feel unsafe and insecure. Their hearts will be wounded, resentment can set in, and they may reject the values you are trying to instill into their lives.

I know one father who forced his kids to memorize scriptures. He was strict and overbearing in the process, and punished the kids severely when they failed. And what are the words those kids hide in their hearts now? "I hate my dad." They hated those scripture memorizing evenings in their home so much that the hatred focused on their father and settled into their hearts as beliefs. None of those kids want to be like their father when they have kids of their own. And that is a tragedy because deeply seated anger toward a father places a person's heart in darkness (1 John 2:8–11).

Imagine a son growing up and marrying while his heart is filled with resentment and hatred toward his father. Dr. Scott Stanley, a leading marriage and family expert, once told me that hidden anger toward parents is a leading contributor in divorce. It stands to reason. Relationships modeled at home are going to affect children's relationships when they leave home.

The truly effective way to instill beliefs and values in your kids is through relationship. God created us for relationship; first, for relationship to him and second, for relationship to one another. The first time it's recorded that God ever called anything "not good" was before he created Eve. He saw that "it is not good for the man to be alone" (Genesis 2:18). Human beings need relationship. Because we are created for relationship, we long to feel safe, secure, and loved in the presence of another person. When we are in good relationships, love opens the heart to the other person. When the heart is open and love flows, then beliefs and values easily float along the stream of love, passing from one heart to another. When the relationship between parent and child is right, this transfer of beliefs and values happens naturally, by the process of osmosis, with love as the catalyst. In Deuteronomy 6 we have this principle outlined:

> Love [crave after, to know deeply] the LORD [your King] your God with all your heart and with all your soul and with all your strength. These commandments that I give you today are *to be upon your hearts.* Impress them on your children. Talk about them when you sit at home and when you walk along the road, when you lie down and when you get up. (vv. 5–7, emphasis mine)

Here we see values and beliefs transferred from one generation to the next by relationship. The picture we get as we read this passage is one of a father who is so heartily into loving God and his words that he enthusiastically talks of them all the time with his children—when he sits down at home, when he walks along the road, when he lies down at night, and when he gets up in the morning. This father lives and breathes God's love, and he expresses it in every action and word. And since he is with his children at every opportunity, they are sure to absorb his values—not merely because they have been formally taught but rather because the whole aura of the parent penetrates the children all the time. This father's values are sure to reach the deepest levels of his children's young and tender hearts.

I watch myself loving God all day long. I find numerous times during the day to review my most important Bible verses. My grandson, Michael, seems to love doing this with me whenever we are together. But his ten-year-old sister is not quite into it yet. The other day she looked at me during a short trip to a restaurant and said, "Grampa, no preaching or scripture for today. I only want to hear about it while you're preaching at a church. I want a grampa, not a preacher all of the time. Save it for then." I nodded. My first thought was to smile because she is always so cute, but then I started thinking about what it would take to find her interest points and see what might increase her desire to hear God's words at any time. I didn't know what all of her natural interest bents were, but before long, I saw one. She loves to sing and dance. I saw the gleam in her eyes when her friend Emily taught her a little Bible verse song and dance routine. Hannah had the verse memorized in ten minutes. *Aha!* I thought. *There's the key. Tie the verses to a song or dance, and she'll love memorizing them.* She has already learned the Ten Commandments, and I'm watching her move them into her heart.

Be attentive and you can find ways to interest your kids in scripture. You might want to check out the organization called Awana, which now exists in thousands of churches. It was created to help kids memorize at least one thousand Bible verses by the time they finish high school.

You can make the Deuteronomy 6 thing work in your family's life. When you love your children enough to maintain a continuing relationship with them, and when you develop real enthusiasm for God, your kids are sure to catch your fired-up attitude. And when they see you memorizing scripture and making its principles work in your life, they may be inspired to join you in the process.

You might even try a little reverse psychology. Tell your kids that you have been wondering if they are old enough to start memorizing. It's an exercise for kids who are, well, exceptionally smart children. You may have to wait a little longer before they are ready. Before they are ready they will have to take a test, which you will give them at the proper time. Of course, they will insist that they take the test now. Give them three or four questions, not too simple, yet simple enough that you know for sure that they can answer at least three of them. Then when they pass the test, admit that they are indeed ready and give each a verse to memorize.

The point here is to avoid dragging your children into memorizing scripture against their will. You don't want them to think of it as an unpleasant drudgery. Let them see the importance of it by the changes in your own life, your own enthusiasm for God and his words, your overwhelming love for them, and your obvious interest in their ultimate welfare.

Mix Memorization with Love and Fun

This last point is quite simple, and it's a way to integrate the previous points we've made in this chapter. Let's say you and your family are taking an automobile trip. The kids are antsy and tired of riding. They're picking at each other in the back seat and asking, "Are we there yet?" at the rate of about 2.5 times per mile. Give them a Bible verse to memorize, and as a prize offer to let them choose one activity they love while you are on your trip, whether it's canoeing or rafting, a water park or miniature golf. Or, if such activities don't fit the scope of your trip, let the prize be to stop at the restaurant of the child's choice. As soon as they finish memorizing the verse, they get their choice.

You can offer similar incentives at home. Whoever memorizes this verse first gets to pick the family movie rental for Friday night. And whoever memorizes the most verses by the end of the month gets to spend the day with Mom or Dad at the office or something they have expressed a lot of interest in doing.

Notice that I don't suggest offering money prizes. In fact, notice that all the prizes I mentioned involve relationship—an activity together, a meal together, a movie together, a one-on-one day with a parent. But I've noticed that money is certainly something that does turn on most of my grandkids. Some of them more than others, but they've memorized a lot of money from me.

By being creative and coming up with similar rewards, you accomplish several things at once. You create relationships with your kids; you achieve scripture memorization; you expose your children to your life and how God works in you; and you make learning God's words a meaningful yet painless and enjoyable activity. When I give money to each of my grandkids, it's always in the context of relating with them. It's always tied to shopping at their favorite store with me or with members of their family. They know ahead of time that we'll spend quite a bit of time going over the meaning of each verse. I like that time the most.

You *Will* Affect Your Children's Beliefs

I remember reading years ago a statement by the strident feminist writer Gloria Steinham dismissing the value of raising children. She said that "children grow up, brought or not." In other words, child rearing is overvalued. It doesn't matter whether parents bring up their kids attentively or leave them on their own to fend for themselves. They grow up anyway.

Yes, but how do they grow up? What are their values? What are their beliefs? How do they fit in as responsible, productive members of society? How do they learn to love God and others? Unless these values are taught and demonstrated in action, it's unlikely that children will ever plant them deeply in their hearts as guiding beliefs. That is the tremendous responsibility of parents. If you read William Golding's chilling novel *Lord of the Flies* in high school, you remember how in that story a group of boys left on their own developed terribly evil and destructive beliefs. This classic tale illustrates what happens to kids left to grow up without loving parents attentively modeling God's words of life and love to them.

The sad truth is that values can be lost in just one generation, never to be fully recovered. Passing along values is like passing along raw eggs. If you hand the egg on carefully, it can make it to the end of the line. But once you fumble it, it is shattered and lost beyond recovery. Once godly values are fumbled in the transfer from one generation to the next, the love and unselfishness that holds society together can be shattered. Individuals can become hedonistic seekers of their own pleasure, responsibility to others can cease, and it's just a matter of time before the nation crumbles into individualistic anarchy.

As a parent, you hold the future in the lives of your children. You will make the next generation into a godly, believing one or a godless, hedonistic one. The very survival of our nation is at stake. It all depends on how successfully you transfer your beliefs to your children. So I urge you to take God's words seriously. Hide them in your heart. Inspire your children to adopt them as beliefs. You will certainly save your family, and you may actually save an entire nation.

Since I'm known as the marriage guy, no book of mine would ever be complete without sharing how your new "heart-branded" beliefs can enrich your marriage. There is one belief in particular that is the all-time, most important one that no successful marriage can live without: safety. In the next chapter, I'll explain how you can add this key belief to your marriage.

Scriptures to Hide in Your Heart

"Love the LORD your God with all your heart and with all your soul and with all your strength. These commandments that I give you today are to be upon your hearts. Impress them on your children. Talk about them when you sit at home and when you walk along the road, when you lie down and when you get up." (Deuteronomy 6:5–7)

"Train a child in the way he should go, and when he is old he will not turn from it." (Proverbs 22:6)

Fathers, do not exasperate your children; instead, bring them up in the training and instruction of the Lord. [Love them and train them to know Christ and his teachings.] (Ephesians 6:4)

Seventeen
How One Key Belief Can Keep Your Marriage Thriving

If I had understood the message of my book *I Promise* forty years earlier, my own marriage would have been 90 percent more loving and caring from the very beginning. In that book I first introduced the concept of changing your life by changing your beliefs. When we work on ourselves to change our own beliefs and quit trying to change our mates, we produce a new safety that allows our marriage to bloom far beyond our wildest dreams.

Before I wrote *I Promise*, I had the stupid belief that if I could change Norma's annoying habits and "resistant" personality, I could increase my own happiness. I've already addressed this myth, but it's such an important concept that I want to bring it up again and, in this last chapter, discuss how beliefs such as this and others affect your marriage.

My present beliefs about marriage are 180 degrees from those I held when my wife and I wed. As a result, both she and I are much closer, more in love, and much dearer friends than we have ever been. You'll notice that all of my key marriage beliefs today lead toward what I have come to understand is the single greatest relationship belief: safety. When each mate feels safe with the other, they'll naturally pull closer, and the best friendship just happens naturally. You need only this one belief of building a safe or secure marriage and your dream marriage will be yours. These four beliefs will lead you closer to that safe relationship:

1. My mate is not the cause of any of my unhappiness; it's my beliefs that determine whether I'm happy or not.

2. I cannot change my mate, and if I try, I create an unsafe place for him or her and we drift further apart. My spouse is safer because I'm not on his or her case to become a better person in order for me to be happier.

3. I am dependent upon God to supply me with his love, and he gives it only to the humble—to those who come to him helpless as beggars (James 4:6).

4. God's love makes my home the safest place on earth. Peaceful, forgiving, merciful, gracious, compassionate, tender, and all the attributes listed in 1 Corinthians 13.

Let's briefly explore the meaning of each of these beliefs and show how they can improve your marriage.

Right Belief Number 1:
My Mate Does Not Cause My Unhappiness

One of my favorite stories of how Norma and I were before we discovered the belief of safety is the morning I decided to wash my own clothes in preparation for a trip. I wandered down to our laundry room and was about to throw my stuff into the washer when I noticed her lacy white lingerie, along with a few sweaters and blouses, still in the washer. They had just finished washing.

I know the rule: place everything on the top of the dryer, and never, ever attempt to dry her nice things. But I had a thought, and that was my undoing. *Maybe I could do an additional little happy for her. I'll put these dainty things in the dryer for just five minutes.* I had seen her do this, taking them out while they were still wet and hanging them on these little circular clothespin hooks she has in the washroom. *That's a no-brainer,* I thought. *Anyone can handle a job like this.* So I did.

I fully intended to come back in five minutes, but I got distracted. Two hours later I remembered and rushed downstairs. The lacy things were ripped and tangled while the sweaters and blouses were all shrunk down to size twos. I was sick inside. My first thought was to put these things back in the washer and start the cycle again. No, that would be dishonest—but it was very tempting.

Then I remembered that humor can defuse anger. So I came up with something I thought would be funny.

I approached Norma and announced that I had good news and bad news. Which did she want first? She gave me that what-have-you-done-now? stare I had seen many times.

She asked for the bad new first. I blurted, "I dried your clothes."

She gasped and ran for the basement to assess the damage. But I caught her arm and said, "Wait, you haven't heard the good news. Our granddaughter Taylor has a whole new wardrobe." Norma never even cracked a smile. So much for humor. I suggested that we jump into the car and head for the outlet mall and replace everything.

"Don't you understand anything?" she snapped. "It will take hours to find each of these items. They don't all come from the same place."

"Oh really," I replied. I thought surely at a big department store we could find everything in about fifteen minutes.

At this point the meltdown began. I thought she was overreacting and making a big thing out of a minor incident. Furthermore, she didn't even seem to appreciate my good intentions in trying to help her. She accused me of wrecking her day, and in response I accused her of being too concerned about material things. Then she started lecturing me about things that had nothing to do with the current incident, like how I never remember anything. Now, that really hurt. So I lashed back and accused her of caring more about her clothes than about me. That went over big. So big, in fact, that she turned and stalked out of the room, and the next thing I heard was the door slamming and the car roaring out of the driveway and screeching down the street.

I was glad she was gone. Here I had made just a simple little mistake and she treated it like a seismic crisis. Where was forgiveness? If she really loved me as she should, she would have forgiven me. Now she had wrecked *my* day. Sure, I shouldn't have forgotten the dryer and ruined her things, but she should have considered my intentions and my feelings. I was angry and miserable for hours, and it was all her fault.

We inflicted this kind of misery on ourselves time and again until we began learning one of the greatest truths of our lives: *we* didn't make each other miserable; our *beliefs* made us miserable. What she did that day had nothing to do with my happiness or sadness. What I believed and how I responded had everything to do with it. This is not a new idea; Solomon said it a few millennia ago: "For as he thinketh in his heart, so is he" (Proverbs 23:7 KJV).

What made me angry at that moment was the belief about her that I harbored in my heart. That belief was that Norma was a key source of my happiness; therefore, my emotional equilibrium depended on her actions. So it's no wonder I thought Norma should be understanding and forgiving. It had to happen or I wouldn't be happy. When her actions did not meet the expectations of my belief, I was miserable.

Had I not held the belief that she was the source of my happiness, what she did would not have had so much effect on my emotional equilibrium. My expectations were wrong because my beliefs were wrong. I had to learn that meeting my needs and expectations was not the reason God had placed her on earth.

A similar belief to the one that Norma did not hold my happiness in her hands was that "difficult experiences are good, not bad." I had wrongly believed that life's circumstances had to be going well in order for me to be happy. I covered this belief in chapter 12: all trials are good because they are used by God to continually transform us into his image of love.

As I learned and studied both truths—God is my main source of love and life, and all of my trials are good for me—I began to realize how I had placed a tremendous burden on Norma by expecting her to be the source of my happiness and not to be a burden to me because that would make me unhappy. I can hardly overstate how life changing it was to find that my beliefs, not her actions, determined my emotional equilibrium. When I took my beliefs seriously and began to examine and change them, it did wonders for me by giving me a way to manage my emotions and form all of my actions. Look at some of the benefits to our marriage that came from taking this belief into my heart:

1. I stopped complaining about what my wife did. I slip once in a while from a forty-plus-year habit.
2. I stopped judging her.
3. I stopped trying to change her when I realized that her behavior did not control how I felt and acted.
4. Instead of pointing that accusing index finger at her, I folded it in and pointed all four fingers at myself while my thumb pointed to God. Why? Because the only person I can change is me—not my mate.

My beliefs in God determine my happiness.   **Others determine my happiness.**

And this brings me to my next point.

Right Belief Number 2:
I Cannot Change My Mate Even If I Want To

Gwyn, a close friend of mine, wondered what had happened to Danny since they married. In the first few weeks, he seemed to do everything right. He knew she loved a clean house, and he did his share of keeping things straight and tidy. And when he said he would do something, such as carry out the trash, he would do it. But not anymore. He no longer followed through on his promises, and he didn't even notice when things were dirty and cluttered. He just came home from work, grabbed the remote, and plopped down, ignoring the need to keep things straight. On Friday, they were expecting friends for dinner. Danny had promised to clean out the garage, but it was already Tuesday, and he hadn't even touched it. Gwyn was getting more and more irritated. She considered cleaning it herself, but the garage was his area, and she was not going to clean it. If she did it once, he would expect her to do it the next time, and she would never get his help on anything.

Danny came home from work whistling and happy. Holding up a rented DVD, he grinned and said, "Surprise! Look what I have! And popcorn too. You'll love this movie. It'll make us want to cuddle all night long!"

She glared at him and scowled as she backed away from his attempt to embrace. "I can't believe you!" she cried. "How do you expect to clean the garage tonight and watch that movie at the same time? It will take two days to clean it, and our company is coming in three days. Did you totally forget this?"

Utterly taken aback, Danny threw the DVD across the room, pitched the popcorn toward the kitchen, and stalked out of the room. Tears of anger and frustration welled up in Gwyn's eyes. *He's not the man I married*, she thought, *and to tell the truth, I'm sometimes not really sure that I love him anymore.*

Gwyn and Danny's problem was based on a wrong belief about change. If you embrace this wrong belief, you will make a serious mistake about what is really going on in your marriage. You can feel that you are falling out of love with your mate when, in fact, you can have unrealistic expectations about what you can and cannot do to change your mate's behavior.

Thanks to our own marriage research center, we now have a high degree of certainty about what makes marriages work and what keeps them from working. We know that love doesn't last; you have to *make* it last with the power of God's love within you. After the marriage passes through the infatuation stage, many couples find loving each other unconditionally to be extremely difficult. No one marries a perfect partner. Negative traits and behaviors soon pop up, and some of these are difficult to live with. Without those euphoria-producing chemicals to help us see the magic in our mate, we begin to think the deflation of our feelings is due to some defect in him or her, a problem we think we can solve by changing our mate's behavior.

But that's not only a false belief, it's also unrealistic. God designed us to control ourselves, not each other. Using intimidation, aggressiveness, manipulation, guilt, or any number of other methods of persuasion seldom works to change another person. Such tactics may seem to accomplish minor changes now and then. Some mates attack the other or play the victim so effectively that the partner feels bludgeoned or shamed into changing. But the victory is hollow because anything we get as a result of manipulation is far from unconditional love and is sure to be counterproductive in the long run.

Let's go back to Gwyn and Danny. The day after Gwyn's confrontation with Danny, she came to me, told the whole story, and asked, "What can I do? I've tried to change Danny time and time again and nothing seems to work. Can you give me a really effective way for a wife to change her husband?"

"Gwyn, may I speak frankly to you?" I asked.

"Yes, absolutely," she replied.

"I know that you don't realize this, but the reason Danny irritates you is because you are guilty of the same thing that you are accusing him of. How about your own cleaning habits? How responsible are you about following through? You complain about Danny's wasting time; do you spend your time productively? I have a tough time getting you on the phone because either you're not home or I get a nonstop busy signal. It seems as though you are busying yourself with a lot of things."

My words hit home. Gwyn lowered her head and said, "You are so right. There are so many things I should be doing around the house, but I do other things to avoid them, such as shopping with my girlfriends or staying on the phone constantly. I don't follow through on what I know I should be doing every day."

"Now, Gwyn, let me tell you something else," I said. "You may not want to hear this, but I don't have any great insight to help you change Danny because it's impossible for you to do it. That's God's job. The changes Danny makes are between him and God. The same Holy Spirit is also in you, Gwyn; so what does that mean in terms of who you can change?"

"It means that the only person God gives me the power to change is myself?"

"Let the Holy Spirit through his words change you; let him do the work that he needs to do in you. Let him empower you to become more responsible and forget about changing Danny. You need to change so significantly that Danny sees the change and it motivates him to want to be more like you.

"Scripture verses such as Matthew 22:37 and 39 and 1 Thessalonians 5:18 will transform you in just weeks if you memorize them and chew on them day and night. Gwyn, this is what I do every day. I look at my life and see what needs to change to become more like God, and these same three verses I'm suggesting for you are in my heart now, and I couldn't be happier."

Gwyn got the point. In fact, she left me utterly motivated and thrilled at her new insight. That evening she apologized to Danny through tears: "I've been so wrong in trying to change you, trying to push you into becoming more responsible and cleaning out the garage. In fact, I want you to know that I am guiltier of this kind of behavior than you are. Will you forgive me?"

That night they had a great time together, and the next morning he woke her up gently, saying, "Honey, I have a surprise for you." He led her downstairs and opened the door to the garage. It was sparkling clean. After she had gone to sleep the night before, he had gotten up and spent three hours cleaning up the mess. The humility of Gwyn's confession—admitting her own faults and promising not to ride him anymore—softened his heart and motivated him to change.

This is the key to lasting love in your marriage: *change yourself* first and accept your mate unconditionally just the way he or she is. Then as you work with God to become more like him, watch how your mate will eventually try to emulate you. But don't do this just to change your mate; do it for yourself and for your own personal relationship with God. By taking responsibility for your actions and changing even small behaviors, you demonstrate unconditional love and thus create an emotionally secure and safe atmosphere in which your marriage can thrive.

Pushing your spouse to change in order to make you happy is hardly the way of unconditional love. When you want to change your mate, 99.99 percent of the time there's a selfish motive behind it. Expecting him or her to change to meet your expectations is putting self first. And if your mate does the same thing, then you have two selves in conflict, each fighting the other to fulfill his or her own needs.

The only way to improve the relationship is to shine the spotlight on yourself and expose your own faults and weaknesses. Your mate may not want to deal with his or her problems, but you will be surprised at how great an impact your own example can have when you deal with your own. You must not give in to hopelessness and helplessness, no matter how convinced you are that your partner is the real problem. Even if that is true, by changing yourself you can affect things dramatically and positively.

Right Belief Number 3:
God Supplies the Humble with Love

When Dave and Susie's marriage melted down after his affair, which I told you about in chapter 6, I watched them apply all four of the godly beliefs you've been reading about, starting in chapter 10 of this book. They both branded within their hearts 1 Corinthians 13, known as the love chapter. That's when their hearts began to change, and I could see them developing into a loving and forgiving couple. The best example of this came when one evening Dave came home from work much later than normal and Susie greeted him seething with anger.

"Where in the world have you been?" she demanded. "You're an hour late."

"The traffic was horrible," Dave responded. "There was a wreck on the freeway, and cars were backed up for over a mile."

"Likely story!" replied Susie. "You've been with that woman again. I just know it."

Dave immediately felt an impulse to blow up and tell her to get off his case. Why did he have to defend himself all the time? Wouldn't she ever forgive him? How long was she going to hold his sin over his head? But he told me that James 1:19 came to his mind from where he had embedded it deeply in his heart. "My dear brothers, take note of this: Everyone should be quick to listen, slow to speak and slow to become angry." And instead of exploding, he took the golden steps of pausing to listen deeply to what Susie was really saying. And, believe me, just doing that one thing can bring about amazing changes in your marriage and your life.

Dave paused to listen to what God's words were telling him. *Keep your mouth shut, Dave. God will give you his power to discern the meaning of this situation and give you his love to help you respond in a constructive, understanding, and loving way.* That's what James 1:19 is all about. When that verse reaches your heart as a belief, you'll find yourself punching the pause button instead of reacting impulsively on the basis of your immediate surge of negative emotion.

This pause action is a safety feature for preserving a relationship. Pausing is the key to listening to what's in your mate's heart. It's the key to listening to your friends or coworkers when conflict arises. But most important, it's the key to listening to God. Pausing provides a moment of stillness in your heart where the voice of God can speak to you and illumine the meaning behind the words of the other person. Or to put it another way, pausing allows you to listen to the heart of God before you respond. It allows time for his words that you have hidden in your heart to flow into your mind. And from his words you can form your response.

Just as your heart is the wellspring of who you are and what you have become, God's heart is also the wellspring of who he is. He is love, and love can flow from his heart to yours. Pausing allows time for that flow to occur. Just think of the superpower of connecting to the heart of God and receiving his love to pass on to the other person.

When Susie accused Dave of seeing that other woman again, he stifled his prideful impulse to blow up and defend himself. He remained silent and listened humbly. His pause gave him time to hear the truth coming out of his wife's heart, and he listened, not to her words but to her feelings (Philippians 4:8–9). He realized that she was still hurting, and she was fearful that his affair might resume again. Her angry accusation was really a cry of pain telling him how much hurt she had felt and expressing fear that she could feel it yet again.

So when Dave did open his mouth, he responded with deep humility to what he had heard—not from Susie's mouth, but from her heart. "Honey, I can see that you are still feeling pain from what I did. I am so sorry that you've had to suffer so much, and even sorrier that you are still suffering. I can hardly even believe that you are still standing here, willing to allow me in this house after what I did to you. I don't deserve you. I don't deserve your love and forgiveness. I love you and am so grateful to God just for the privilege of having you back in my life. Thank you so much for forgiving me and letting me stay with you and our precious little girl."

Susie burst into tears and fell into his arms, clinging to him as never before.

Dave's pause and response showed that he had embedded into his heart one of the most valuable beliefs one can have for a marriage to heal and flourish. When his wife jumped on him in anger, his impulse was to angrily defend himself. He was, after all, innocent of the indiscretion of which she accused him. He had repented of his sin and begged forgiveness. He had never repeated the sin and had done his best to rebuild her trust. She did not seem to appreciate it, and that hurt his pride. He felt angry, unjustly accused, and belittled. Why couldn't she quit harping on the past?

When he hit the pause button he realized that his angry impulse was due to a wrong belief. He saw that his pride was preventing him from hearing what she was really saying. But he paused long enough to allow God's truth in his heart to reach his mind. He remembered his new belief found in James 4:6: "[God] gives us more grace. That is why Scripture says: 'God opposes the proud but gives grace to the humble.'"

Dave humbled himself, forgot his own feelings, and empathized fully with the pain of his wife. He felt her hurt and in humility recognized his own culpability in hurting her. He applied his new belief from 1 Corinthians 13—that he should love her unreservedly and unconditionally instead of seeking self-justification.

Right Belief Number 4:
God's Love Makes My Home a Safe Place

In Scotland, about twenty miles southeast of Edinburgh, stands a small but beautiful castle built in 1430 by a nobleman named Lord Borthwick. The backside of the *keep* (the main tower or living quarters) of Borthwick Castle bears a huge scar high in the wall, where missing and broken stones create an indention perhaps three feet deep. The cause of the damage was cannon fire in the mid-seventeenth century when Oliver Cromwell attacked, intent on punishing the Borthwick residents for harboring Catholics during his Puritan sweep of Britain.

Many castles would have been breached after a three-foot penetration of their walls. But not Borthwick. Its walls range from ten to twelve feet thick. No doubt Cromwell eventually could have penetrated the castle with continual bombardment, but he chose to stop and let its inhabitants go free, leaving the castle to Borthwick, rather than expend the time and ammunition it would take to bring down the castle.

In fact, Borthwick's walls are so strong that in World War II, when all Britain was under threat of German air attack, Scotland's most precious records were moved out of government offices in Edinburgh and stored in Borthwick Castle.

Don't you long for a marriage that secure? A place of utter safety with strong walls of love surrounding and protecting you and your mate, instead of walls of deception standing between you? A place where you can relax and be yourself, unafraid to open your heart, unafraid that your love will suffer the ravages of anger, criticism, judging, backbiting, and all of the other tricks couples use to *demand* change so that each person can finally be happy? This false belief that they or it must change in order for spouses to be happy is tearing marriages apart all around you.

In this final section of the book, I want to show you how to build your marriage on a solid foundation of security that will protect both of you and enable your marriage to grow into the kind of blissful intimacy you've always dreamed of having. I want to show you the belief that will enable you to feel a ten-foot-thick secure wall around both of you, strong enough to make you feel safe in opening up the innermost recesses of the heart. The only way to enjoy a close, open, intimate marriage is to create a safe environment where two people who want to stay in love feel utterly secure with each other.

Many of us enter marriage with the wrong belief that our mate should be the source of all our satisfaction. We think, *Now that I have this person in my life, I am really going to have my needs met and be happy.* We soon find, however, that our mates do not meet this expectation. Husbands and wives can be tremendous sources of help and encouragement to each other, but if they expect to be the source of each other's happiness, disappointment looms just around the corner.

When that disappointment comes, many people assume they must have married the wrong person. Some may resort to an affair to recharge their batteries. The stolen charge may light up the circuits for a moment, but after the glow fades they will feel more miserable and empty than before. Even if they divorce and remarry the "right person," they will encounter the same frustration. The problem is not in the person they marry; it's in their wrong belief that that person will make them happy and keep them fulfilled.

Sooner or later we run headlong into an inescapable fact: no person on earth is capable of giving us the fulfillment we crave. By depending on people to make us happy, we saddle ourselves with the very negative emotions we want to avoid—deep frustration, disappointment, hurt feelings, worry, anxiety, fear, unrest, uncertainty, and confusion.

The bottom line is that we were not designed to find our ultimate fulfillment in each other. That is reserved for our relationship with God. Only he is meant to be the ultimate source of our love, fulfillment, and satisfaction (Deuteronomy 6:5).

As wonderful and delightful as the relationship between the sexes can be, Eve was not given to Adam as a substitute for God. He designed us to be in love with him first, and to obey his will, which was designed to lead us to life. And then from the overflow of that love, he gives us the power to love others. So when we take a mate, we simply extend our love for God to include another person in our life. When you open yourself to be filled by God, you draw your mate within your love for God.

At first, this may not sound altogether pleasing to you. The idea of your mate looking to God for fulfillment may seem like a personal rejection. If your partner's first relationship is with someone other than yourself, you may feel relegated to second place. You may wonder how close and secure the two of you can really be when your mate's first love is someone else, even if that someone is the God of the universe. After all, love triangles are deadly to marriages, aren't they?

When God is the third party in the triangle, it is anything but deadly; it is absolutely vital. To illustrate, picture a triangle with God at the apex and the husband and wife at the two lower corners. If the husband and wife remain at their corners, they are at a maximum distance from God and also from each other. If the husband moves laterally along the base of the triangle toward the wife, or the wife toward the husband, they get closer to each other but not closer to God. On the other hand, if both the husband and wife move upward along the sides of the triangle toward God, the movement automatically brings them closer to each other. The distance between them closes as they move up the triangle. Their increasing closeness with God increases their fulfillment, and their increasing closeness with each other increases their satisfaction with each other.

We can see by this illustration that God in the relationship is not an intrusion between the husband and wife, but rather his Spirit enables them to love each other and becomes a catalyst for drawing them together in the closest possible bond.

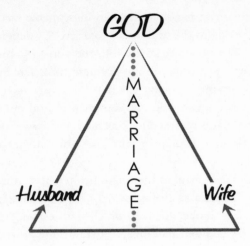

While each marriage partner is on a separate journey toward God, drawing near to him creates oneness and security between them. It reduces their separateness. When they reach God at the apex of the triangle, they become one with him and also with each other.

What do I mean by *oneness*? Ephesians 5 says that oneness is a divine mystery, something that can't be expressed in a formula or an equation. Oneness in marriage reflects the oneness that believers experience with God. It is a relationship of holy union and intimacy—"I in you and you in me," as Jesus put it (John 17:23). It is a shared life, a one-flesh relationship in which two souls and two hearts become inextricably bound together. You possess, you are possessed; you know and you are known. You are separate fibers woven together.

The Bible gives us the ultimate expression of oneness when it tells us , "The man and his wife were both naked, and they felt no shame" (Genesis 2:25). This is the heart of oneness, the very core of what God wants us to experience in marriage. This state of being naked and unashamed indicates that Adam and Eve were completely exposed, vulnerable, transparent, and open with each other. They hid nothing from the other. They could see each other for who they were, with all their limitations. Yet they had no shame, no guilt, no fear of being completely seen and known, no fear of being rejected. The first couple experienced complete acceptance and freedom together. They were safe and secure with each other because they were secure in their relationship with God.

That's the key belief we must hide in our hearts if we want a secure marriage with ten-foot-thick walls that will withstand bombardment from any enemy. We can feel safety in marriage only when we root our relationship with each other in our relationship to God. When we commit to him as our source of connection and fulfillment, we enfold our mate within that relationship.

The foundational security of this relationship enables you to open up to your mate verbally and reveal who you really are inside. It frees one mate to say to the other, "I want you to know my soul. I want to be open to you. I want to tell you who I am emotionally, psychologically, spiritually, and mentally." Mates who feel safe with each other will be willing to unzip their souls and trust who they really are in the hands of the other. The kind of security that fosters such intimacy is impossible unless it's rooted in the ultimate security of a relationship with God.

I suggest that you pick one or two of the following scripture passages and memorize them together as a couple. But over the years, like me, you may want to hide at least seventy key Bible verses in your heart and watch your nature become more and more like God's.

Scriptures to Hide in Your Heart

If I speak in the tongues of men and of angels, but have not love, I am only a resounding gong or a clanging cymbal. If I have the gift of prophecy and can fathom all mysteries and all knowledge, and if I have a faith that can move mountains, but have not love, I am nothing. If I give all I possess to the poor and surrender my body to the flames, but have not love, I gain nothing.

Love is patient, love is kind. It does not envy, it does not boast, it is not proud. It is not rude, it is not self-seeking, it is not easily angered, it keeps no record of wrongs. Love does not delight in evil but rejoices with the truth. It always protects, always trusts, always hopes, always perseveres.

Love never fails. But where there are prophecies, they will cease; where there are tongues, they will be stilled; where there is knowledge, it will pass away. For we know in part and we prophesy in part, but when perfection comes, the imperfect disappears. When I was a child, I talked like a child, I thought like a child, I reasoned like a child. When I became a man, I put childish ways behind me. Now we see but a poor reflection as in a mirror; then we shall see face to face. Now I know in part; then I shall know fully, even as I am fully known.

And now these three remain: faith, hope and love. But the greatest of these is love. (1 Corinthians 13:1–13)

The husband should fulfill his marital duty to his wife, and likewise the wife to her husband. (1 Corinthians 7:3)

I pray that out of his glorious riches he may strengthen you with power through his Spirit in your inner being, so that Christ may dwell in your hearts through faith. And I pray that you, being rooted and established in love, may have power, together with all the saints, to grasp how wide and long and high and deep is the love of Christ, and to know this love that surpasses knowledge—that you may be filled to the measure of all the fullness of God.

Now to him who is able to do immeasurably more than all we ask or imagine, according to his power that is at work within us, to him be glory in the church and in Christ Jesus throughout all generations, for ever and ever! Amen. (Ephesians 3:16–21)

Submit to one another out of reverence for Christ.

Wives, submit to your husbands as to the Lord. For the husband is the head of the wife as Christ is the head of the church, his body, of which he is the Savior. Now as the church submits to Christ, so also wives should submit to their husbands in everything.

Husbands, love your wives, just as Christ loved the church and gave himself up for her to make her holy, cleansing her by the washing with water through the word, and to present her to himself as a radiant church, without stain or wrinkle or any other blemish, but holy and blameless. In this same way, husbands ought to love their wives as their own bodies. He who loves his wife loves himself. After all, no one ever hated his own body, but he feeds and cares for it, just as Christ does the church—for we are members of his body. "For this reason a man will leave his father and mother and be united to his wife, and the two will become one flesh." This is a profound mystery— but I am talking about Christ and the church. However, each one of you also must love his wife as he loves himself, and the wife must respect her husband. (Ephesians 5:21–33)

Wives, submit to your husbands, as is fitting in the Lord.

Husbands, love your wives and do not be harsh with them. (Colossians 3:18–19) (This is submitting to each other out of love for God and using his love for each other. Love is serving each other.)

Marriage should be honored by all, and the marriage bed kept pure, for God will judge the adulterer and all the sexually immoral. (Hebrews 13:4)

Wives, in the same way be submissive to your husbands so that, if any of them do not believe the word, they may be won over without words by the behavior of their wives, when they see the purity and reverence of your lives. (1 Peter 3:1–2)

Husbands, in the same way be considerate as you live with your wives, and treat them with respect as the weaker partner and as heirs with you of the gracious gift of life, so that nothing will hinder your prayers. (1 Peter 3:7)

Eighteen

My Final Prayer for You and Our Country

Why did I write this book? To answer that question, let me summarize what I've pounded over and over in these pages. It was because I am so excited about the dramatic changes I experienced in my own life when I changed my beliefs that I couldn't wait to share what I have learned with you. The concept is so simple that it's easy to miss. When you change your beliefs to conform to God's two major commands—to love him and love each other—you gain peace, joy, and contentment, and you experience barrels full of overflowing love from God himself. It's all a matter of living the way he designed us to live. And all you have to do to gain this glorious way of life is take his words into your heart as your deepest beliefs and let your life flow out from that wellspring.

I won't pretend it doesn't take some effort, but what worthwhile goal doesn't? I repeat over seventy Bible verses every day in order to keep the most deadly beliefs rooted out of my heart. After memorizing your favorite scripture verses, it's all too easy to think, *I have already placed God's words in my heart, so what's the point in reviewing them every day?* The Scriptures themselves warn us about neglecting his words and not keeping up a daily habit of reviewing them. Especially Deuteronomy 6:4–9, a passage I've repeated many times in this book. Oh, how easy it is for the weeds—the cares of life, the problems, and our own desires—to choke out God's words and turn our hearts back to the wilderness of the three deadlies. The world's beliefs and our natural flesh can take over our lives very quickly if we don't carefully guard our hearts daily.

Remember Christ's parable of the sower and the seed in Luke 8:4–15. You want your mind to be the deep, rich soil in which God's words can take root and flourish. You want a heart that retains what God wants to sow in it, which is his own love, his own nature. That means you must till the soil, prepare it, and keep it turned, well watered, and fertilized. That means memorizing and cultivating God's words daily, which retain the seed he plants and produce a hundredfold crop of love, peace, joy, and righteousness in your life.

"I would dearly love to do this," you may say, "but I simply can't find the time. It's a hectic world today, and just keeping up with the minimal demands of work, family, church, and necessary errands consumes everyone these days." I completely understand what you're saying. I fight the same battles. Your boss demands overtime to meet impossible deadlines. Your mate is so demanding you hardly have time to think. Between school, little league, youth night at the church, sleepover parties, and school events, keeping your kids on their schedules is almost a full-time job. I get the picture. Been there, done that.

Yet there are many ways for you to find time to memorize and chew on scriptures, even in your crazy schedule. Here are just a few:

- *Having daily quiet times.* Many people have developed the good habit of reading a devotional, reading through the Bible, or using a host of other readings or meditations to keep their minds on God's words. I strongly encourage this because each person will find his or her own way of remembering God and his teachings daily.

- *Attending your Bible-believing church regularly.* Follow the scripture readings in the assembly or in class. Read those that speak to you personally again and again.

- *Listening to Christian radio or watching Christian TV.* Christian media can remind you of God and his words. Not all Christian media is good, but there are many excellent Christian teachers, dramas, and discussion programs available.

- *Learning and singing Christian songs.* Much Christian music is consistent with the message of Christ, and the lyrics of many songs are exact quotes from Scripture.

- *Placing reminders printed on cards or pictures on the wall of your residence.* Be creative with reminders of scripture passages in your home or in your car. You can find ways to create visual reminders of your most relevant verses.

- *Exercising, hiking, and visiting your favorite places to meditate.* You can review the main Bible verses that God has led you to remember while doing other useful activities that don't require engaging your mind.

As you can see after reading this book, sharing what I've learned in order to help others replace the deadly beliefs in their hearts with God's words of love has become my deepest passion. I see this as vital to the well-being and survival of our nation. It pains me deeply to see our culture slipping away from God's values and drifting into deadly hedonism. My passion is to call us back to God and his words of life, so that we can renew our commitment to him and find life again.

I urge you to share this passion with me. Start by changing your own heart, which will develop in you a love for God and others that will impel you to reach out and share this vital message. Join me in my dream of helping a whole nation return to God and his words by changing the beliefs in their hearts, one heart at a time. It's the difference between a life filled with misery and pain and a life filled with joy, peace, and love overflowing. That choice is really a no-brainer, isn't it?

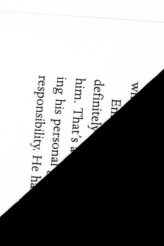

Appendix One
Kari's Letter

This past April, two and a half years after starting to hide God's words inside my heart, my mom wrote my grampa an e-mail, answering a question he had about my progress. He mentioned to her that he just wanted an update on how I was acting at home and how I was treating my sister. This can give you a lot of hope about yourself as a kid like me, or if you're a parent, it may motivate you further to start memorizing your most important or favorite sections of Scripture and begin hiding them in your heart along with your children.

Here's my mom's report card on me.

—Michael Gibson

OK . . . I know a lot of typical teenagers, boys and girls, and as a public school teacher if I was to compare them to Michael, here's what I would have to say.

Emotionally, I can see the five verses that he's hiding daily in his heart are changing his life. He's comfortable in his skin and who God made him. A huge growing-up step for a teenager. He's (on his own) creating goals and tasks for school, golf, and TKD, taking personal responsibility. He's shown great *perseverance* hanging in there with you on his book. He's begged for this opportunity for three years . . . WOW! Most kids would have given up!

He's connecting daily with friends and is a *leader* and *encouragement* to his friends. I told him he's like a chameleon lizard—anyone who is around him feels at ease and comfortable. He's living out Philippians 4:8–9. He stands up for the movies and music he will or will *not* listen to, regardless of what they may say (he has a friend who gives him a tough time for his movie standards). He's putting into practice this verse—computer, movies, TV, music, future dating standards, modesty in language—this is *huge* for a young man!

Michael *never* throws a temper tantrum. I still see kids his age not able to *respond* in a mature way when things don't go their way. Roger and I really see growth in that area. He's applying "quick to listen, slow to speak, and slow to become angry." He's really growing James 1:19 in his heart. This goes hand in hand with Galatians 5:13. He is not indulging in sinful nature but desires to live in freedom with obeying God and his parents. He's willing to *serve* us when we ask him to do a task. Not a lot of flack back either. We give him an 8.5 on obeying the first time we ask him to do something! :)

He does an *excellent* job obeying his parents and teachers. He has proven himself admirable, pure, noble, right, lovely, and true at school, church, and home. He shows patience and forgiveness when Rog or I mess up as parents. He never wavers with forgiving us and giving out grace.

Michael lives Romans 5:3–5 daily. He is able to look at the sufferings he has gone through and rejoice . . . treasure hunting! He hears daily from you and his parents that all pain produces perseverance, character, and hope. He hasn't dealt with a lot of serious pain, but with the little bumps, so far, he has shown real character on how he responds.

He has shown respect and trust in the Lord, responding to our upcoming adoption. I've watched him grow from 0 to an 8.5 in opening up his heart to a new sister. This is huge!! Look how he is responding . . . so precious to his mom :)

Matthew 22:37–39 . . . as a thirteen-year-old, Michael has shown tremendous development applying these verses to his heart. He *loves* God and *loves* others with all his heart! He is meeting weekly in a Bible study and attends FCA at school. He's a light in the public school system. His principal picked Bubby out of hundreds of kids to join him on a special outing . . . big stuff!

Grandpa, you've done a tremendous job teaching him the Word of God. I encourage you to continue to build him up. (His love languages are physical touch and verbal affirmation. He needs to hear every day how proud you are of him and what he is accomplishing . . . with a big hug!)

Overall, I love sharing what God and his Word have done in my son's life. My son is *not* perfect and has years of growth and training ahead of him. I see with my own eyes his growth and hard work applying these truths in his *everyday* life.

Michael's life consists of typical teenager stuff: playing, school, golf, TKD, studying, homework, church, family time, golf cart, friends, cell phone, computer, shopping, and hanging out with his grandpa—his best friend! I love watching him *love* being a kid yet also growing up and learning so much! He's learning what it means to be personally responsible.

I hope this helps. You may share any of this. I'm honored to be Bubby's mom and able to brag :)

— KIKI GIBSON*
Love you!

* Gary Smalley's daughter

Appendix Two
Materialism Test

This test was designed by Dr. Greg Smalley
with help from assistants at John Brown University.

Please indicate the extent to which you agree or disagree with each of the following statements. Using the following scale, place the appropriate number in the space to the left of each statement. Try to be as honest as possible in giving the *first* impression you have for each statement about your life right now.

1 = Strongly Disagree
2 = Disagree
3 = Uncertain
4 = Agree
5 = Strongly Agree

	Compared to the average person, I am financially wealthy.
	I enjoy watching home remodeling shows.
	I regularly eat out.
	Having money is the same as having power and prestige.
	I love spending time at the mall.
	I would like to drive a car that people admire.
	I'm not really attracted to the idea of living a simple life.
	It would be difficult to be happy if I were poor.

	Having more money would be a great solution to my problems.
	I get very attached to the things that I own.
	I enjoy looking at new homes or reading house-plan books.
	I'd love to own a big home.
	I own a lot of stuff.
	I enjoy owning things that people admire.
	I get pleasure from buying things.
	I like luxurious things.
	There are certain things that would make my life better if I owned them.
	I enjoy looking for new vehicles in person, online, or in magazines.
	It bothers me that I can't afford to buy all of the things I want.
	I have many assets and can afford more luxuries than most people.
	I hate the way it feels to be financially unstable.
	There's nothing wrong with spending significant time and effort on one's personal appearance.
	I like to take a lot of photographs when I travel.
	I love to be applauded, to win awards, or to be recognized for my accomplishments.
	Money is important to me.
	I like to go shopping.
	I regularly purchase things at garage sales or flea markets.
	I like to dress nice.
	I think about ways to earn more money.
	I can afford more luxuries than most people.
	I like to buy things when I'm feeling stressed out or depressed.
	It would be difficult to be happy if I had less money.
	I would describe myself as elegant.
	I am driven by success.
	I would like to be wealthy someday.
	I'm afraid at times that I won't experience the good life.
	It's hard for me not to buy my kids the things they ask for.
	Add up all of the numbers to get your total score.

WHAT DOES THIS MEAN?

The above statements are aimed at helping you identify the extent to which you have a belief deep in your heart that the accumulation of material things is a primary pursuit of life. In general, most people find themselves somewhere between a desire to acquire more possessions and a desire to give away more and serve others. When you naturally feel compassion toward others and have a desire for their welfare to improve, you are loving others. The balance is very important because if you are not taking care of your own welfare adequately, you can become less effective in caring for others. A key section here is 1 John 2:15–17. If you have more love for the ways of the world, you'll find yourself drifting away from God and his love. In fact, you can't know God's love if you continue to love the world more than him. The man who does the will of God by loving him and others lives forever, but the man who loves the world more than God will fade away.

Keep in mind that God rewards those who crave him day and night. So you may be financially rich by knowing God, but you'll find yourself still seeking him daily and expressing gratefulness to him for your riches.

Green Light: Score of 37–74

If you scored in the 37–74 range, you probably have a great balance between lust of the eyes, or materialism, and allowing God to fill and sustain your life. I emphasize "at this time" because life never stands still. In the next twelve months, your heart will either be overflowing with God's love—completely sustained and fulfilled by him—or you will be sliding in the other direction toward the need to accumulate more stuff to fill an empty heart. If you scored in this range, think of it as a green light for now and continue to devote yourself to finding your true source of life in Christ Jesus.

Yellow Light: Score of 75–129

If you scored in the 75–129 range, think of it as a yellow caution light. While you may feel you are relying upon the Lord as your source of fulfillment, your score reveals warning signs, pointing to materialistic tendencies and patterns. The worst thing about materialism is that it can divert you from loving God and others. The pursuit of more stuff absolutely undermines your dependence upon

Christ. He wants you to find true wholeness, joy, fulfillment, and satisfaction. But he knows this can only be found by becoming like him. Becoming like him means to love as deeply as he does. If you want your focus on holiness and not happiness, you must make your highest pursuit not about accumulating worldly possessions but about loving and serving Christ and others. For me, I'd rather have joy than happiness because it lasts even in trouble.

Red Light: Score of 130–185

If you scored in the 130–185 range, think of it as a red light. Stop and look at where you are headed. Your score indicates a person whose happiness is found in the accumulation of things. It points to a belief deep in your heart that reflects the notion that worldly possessions constitute the greatest good and highest value in life. The presence of this materialistic pattern could put you and your relationships at significant risk. You may be heading for trouble—or perhaps you're already there. When you try to find fulfillment and a higher quality of life through things, you face massive disappointment. It's inevitable, because God tells us that the only thing we need for quality living and well-being is him. He gives us *all* we need by giving us himself.

But there is good news! When you have God at the center of your life, whatever else you gain in material goods is simply overflow. When you're serving God and serving others in love, sometimes you get rewarded with more stuff than you ever dreamed of. That's okay because you can give away the excess. Whether you have more stuff or not doesn't really matter. The important thing is to get filled up with God alone. The other stuff that's added to your life is simply the run-off.

Begin by replacing your possession-seeking beliefs by hiding God's precious words in your heart found in Colossians 3:1–17, Galatians 5:13, and Matthew 6:33. Watch as God's Spirit takes control of your beliefs and turns you away from a life dedicated to materialism toward a life of real fulfillment, which is found in loving God and serving others. I can't say it enough: God's words are alive, "powerful, and sharper than any two-edged sword" (Hebrew 4:12 NKJV).

Appendix Three
Hedonism Test

This test was designed by Dr. Greg Smalley
with help from assistants at John Brown University.

Please indicate the extent to which you agree or disagree with each of the following statements. Using the following scale, place the appropriate number in the space to the left of each statement. Try to be as honest as possible in giving the *first* impression you have for each statement about your life right now.

1 = Strongly Disagree
2 = Disagree
3 = Uncertain
4 = Agree
5 = Strongly Agree

	I don't have enough fun in my life.
	Pleasure should play a central role in life.
	I have no concern about the level of my credit card debt.
	Childhood is the best time of life.
	People have accused me of being crude at times.
	I have addictive tendencies.
	I have been reckless with money.
	I am unpredictable.

	It is very important for me to be physically attractive.
	I enjoy taking high risks.
	I'm at my best when doing something adventurous.
	Compared to most people, I am a thrill-seeker.
	I am above the weight I should be.
	At times, I engage in excessive or uncontrolled eating.
	Having fun is the main passion in my life.
	I have workaholic tendencies.
	I don't like the thought of growing up.
	I have lustful thoughts throughout the day.
	I am driven by having fun.
	I have been accused of avoiding my responsibilities.
	I would rather live in my head than in the real world.
	My life lacks direction.
	I struggle with knowing what to do next.
	I consider myself lazy.
	I am a very sexual person.
	I am accused of having fun at the expense of others.
	I do things without thinking.
	I tend to ignore or put off problems.
	Having fun is more important than people and relationships.
	I often forget scheduled appointments.
	Pleasure is my ultimate goal in life.
	The way I look physically is an important part of getting what I want in life.
	I am pretty impulsive.
	I am accused of being a charmer.
	People have suggested that I fail to utilize my talents and gifts.
	I seek out exciting activities.
	I tend to avoid boring activities even if a friend invites me.
	Add up all of the numbers to get your total score.

WHAT DOES THIS MEAN?

The above statements are aimed at helping you identify the extent that you believe life is mainly for seeking a never-ending flow of thrills, fun, excitement, and pleasures in order to be happy and satisfied in life. In general, most people find themselves somewhere between a desire to gain more pleasures and a desire to love and serve others.

Green Light: Score of 37–74

If you scored in the 37–74 range, you probably have a great balance between seeking pleasure and serving others through love at this time. I emphasize "at this time" because life never stands still. In the next twelve months, you'll be either a better servant or sliding in the other direction toward hedonism. If you scored in this range, think of it as a green light for now, but depending upon how many pleasure thoughts you focus on in the future, you could deepen your beliefs in "life is for fun and thrills." You can stop now and learn ways to take on the living words of God (Galatians 5) to continue transforming you into the free and loving person whom God designed you to be. Then you'll find yourself naturally continuing to devote yourself to others in brotherly love, preferring others in honor.

Yellow Light: Score of 75–129

If you scored in the 75–129 range, think of it as a yellow caution light. While you may feel you are devoted to others in brotherly love and preferring others above yourself, your score reveals warning signs, pointing to hedonistic tendencies and patterns. You ought to take action to protect your mind and guard your heart. The best thing you can do is to walk in the power of God's spirit, hiding his powerful, living words within your heart. When you do this, his Spirit will lead you in exercising self-control and overcoming the lusts of the flesh.

Red Light: Score of 130–185

If you scored in the 130–185 range, think of it as a red light. Stop and look at where you are headed. Your score indicates a person who probably has beliefs hidden deep in his heart that the way to get the most out of life is to seek a never-ending flow of pleasure, fun, thrills, and excitement of any kind. The presence of this hedonistic pattern could put you and your relationships at significant risk. Don't be surprised if your spirit and soul seem dull. You may be finding that your interest in God is so faded that you can't seem to reach him. Take a break for a moment and read Ephesians 4:17–19 and Galatians 5. You'll be able to understand more clearly why you may be heading for trouble—or perhaps you're already there. But there is good news! You can stop now and learn ways to take on the living words of God to transform you out of hedonistic selfishness into the freer and more loving person whom God designed you to be. If your dream is turning into a nightmare, don't just pull the sheets over your head. Wake up and take action! Begin by hiding these scriptures in your heart and watch your beliefs change. Watch as God's Spirit takes control of your life and turns you away from a life dedicated to hedonism toward a life of real pleasure, which is found in loving God and serving others. You'll find that there's nothing in the world like the satisfaction you'll receive when you make love and service to others the new reality in your heart.

Appendix Four
Self-Interest Test

This test was designed by Dr. Greg Smalley
with help from assistants at John Brown University.

Please indicate the extent to which you agree or disagree with each of the following statements. Using the following scale, place the appropriate number in the space to the left of each statement. Try to be as honest as possible in giving the *first* impression you have for each statement about your life right now.

1 = Strongly Disagree
2 = Disagree
3 = Uncertain
4 = Agree
5 = Strongly Agree

	Thinking of yourself first is not a sign that you are a selfish person.
	I have accomplished a lot and I am proud of my achievements.
	I am somewhat into myself.
	Being ignored is intolerable.
	My feelings influence me more than the feelings of others.
	I think other people are envious of me.
	It's important to look after my personal interests.
	People make emotional demands on you when you get too close with them.

	My feelings come first.
	I get very frustrated if I have to wait to get what I want.
	It's difficult for me to empathize with people.
	It's very difficult to engage in self-fulfilling activities after you have children.
	It's sometimes necessary to worry less about other people to reach one's true potential.
	I prefer to give orders rather than follow orders.
	Since no one else is going to look out for me, I need to first look out for myself.
	I hate to be controlled and would like to live in real freedom.
	I believe that we should live for the present and stop worrying about tomorrow.
	You have to sell yourself if you're going to get ahead in life.
	It's difficult for me to accept other people's ideas when I feel right.
	I am swayed by my emotions.
	I am able to charm anyone.
	I have exaggerated my own importance when talking to others about myself.
	I am confident in my abilities to be successful.
	I am good at getting the attention of others by my behavior and attire.
	I am driven by success.
	I rely on myself to achieve my goals.
	I do what I want even if it is different from what others do.
	I would describe myself as ambitious.
	I would say that I'm better looking than the average person.
	I believe that I am special.
	I would describe myself as more of a leader than a follower.
	I have embellished details about myself to others.
	I am able to convince people about almost anything.
	I believe that my way of behaving is in the best interest of others.
	I'm a very private person and I don't like to share personal information with others.
	I secretly gloat when one of my enemies makes a mistake or fails.
	I usually get my own way.
	Add up all of the numbers to get your total score.

WHAT DOES THIS MEAN?

The above statements are aimed at helping you identify the extent that you have taken into your heart a pride-of-life belief. When adopted, the extreme end of this belief is an attitude that says, "It's all about me. I'm in charge of my life and I get the credit for what I accomplish." A person who creates his own beliefs from his own thoughts is likely to center on what he wants, what he wants to accomplish, and what makes him look good. In general, most people find themselves somewhere between a pride-of-life philosophy and a desire to love and serve others. Keep in mind that God only gives his grace (power) to those who humbly seek him and his ways and who recognize how much they need him daily. The proud are resisted by God and a loving, deep friendship with others is much more difficult.

Green Light: Score of 37–74

If you scored in the 37–74 range, you probably have a great balance between pride of life or self-centeredness and serving others through love at this time. I emphasize "at this time" because life never stands still. In the next twelve months, you'll be either a more effective servant or sliding in the other direction toward self-centeredness. If you scored in this range, think of it as a green light for now and continue to maintain God as your standard and on serving others. Again, daily chewing on Matthew 22:37–39 is essential.

Yellow Light: Score of 75–129

If you scored in the 75–129 range, think of it as a yellow caution light. While you may feel your primary focus is on serving others, your score reveals warning signs, pointing to independence and self-sufficiency tendencies and patterns. You ought to take action to protect your mind and guard your heart. The best thing you can do is make sure you are adopting God's beliefs by hiding his powerful, living words within your heart. This will assure you that your beliefs and desires are right, true, and promote your well-being. God knows you and loves you, and reliance on his words will give you the best possible life.

Red Light: Score of 130–185

If you scored in the 129–185 range, think of it as a red light. Stop and look at where you are headed. Your score indicates a person who errs on the side of being mainly concerned with or focused on yourself and your advantage. Often, this self-focus is to the exclusion of others. This person usually has beliefs hidden deep in his heart that attribute his success to his own superiority and abilities. The attitude is usually, "I'll plot my own path, and don't you get in my way or suggest that God knows what's best for me or that I should follow his teachings on any level. It's my life, and I'll live it as I please." When this belief gets out of balance it becomes very self-centered. It's the "me first" belief that we live in a dog-eat-dog world, and I intend to be the eater instead of the eaten. I intend to get mine first, and if I have to, I'll run over others to get it.

The presence of this self-focused pattern could put you and your relationships at significant risk. You may be heading for trouble—or perhaps you're already there. But there is good news! You can stop now and learn ways to take on the living words of God to transform you out of selfishness into the loving person that God designed you to be. If your dream is turning into a nightmare, don't just pull the sheets over your head. Wake up and take action!

Begin by hiding these scriptures (Hebrews 11:6, Matthew 22:39, Philippians 2:3) in your heart and watch your beliefs change. Watch as God's Spirit takes control of your life and turns you away from a life focused on self toward a life of "other-seeking," or a servant's heart, which is found in loving God and serving others. You'll find that there's nothing in the world like the satisfaction you'll receive when you find your status, recognition, and security only in God.

Appendix Five
Gary's Top One Hundred–Plus Bible Verses to Hide in Your Heart

The main reason why we chew on God's words every day is to see a hundred-fold increase in God's character within our lives. In the parable in Mark 4:1–20, Jesus says to his disciples in verse 11, "To you has been given the mystery of the kingdom of God, but those who are outside get everything in parables" (NASB). This is another reason why we should meditate on Scripture daily.

In the parable, the farmer sows the word:

1. With some people, the word is like seed sown along the path. As soon as they hear the word, Satan comes and takes away the word that was sown in them (stolen by Satan . . . Wow!).

2. With others, it's like seed sown on rocky places. They hear the word and at once receive it with joy. But since the seed has no root, they last only a short time. When trouble or persecution comes because of the word, they quickly fall away (not grateful).

3. Still others hear the word like seed sown among thorns; the worries of this life, the deceitfulness of wealth, and the desires for other things come in and choke the word, making it unfruitful (shopism).

4. With other people, the seed is sown on good soil; they hear the word, accept it, and produce a crop—thirty, sixty, or even a hundred times what was sown. (This happens when people hide his Word in their hearts.)

Six Priority Beliefs: God, Jesus Christ, Holy Spirit, Gratefulness, Serving Others, and Spiritual Heart

1. God

Ten Commandments and Laws

Then God spoke all these words, saying, "I am the LORD your God, who brought you out of the land of Egypt, out of the house of slavery. You shall have no other gods before Me. You shall not make for yourself an idol, or any likeness of what is in heaven above or on the earth beneath or in the water under the earth. You shall not worship them or serve them; for I, the LORD your God, am a jealous God, visiting the iniquity of the fathers on the children, on the third and the fourth generations of those who hate Me, but showing lovingkindness to thousands, to those who love Me and keep My commandments. You shall not take the name of the LORD your God in vain, for the LORD will not leave him unpunished who takes His name in vain. Remember the sabbath day, to keep it holy. Six days you shall labor and do all your work, but the seventh day is a sabbath of the LORD your God; in it you shall not do any work, you or your son or your daughter, your male or your female servant or your cattle or your sojourner who stays with you. For in six days the LORD made the heavens and the earth, the sea and all that is in them, and rested on the seventh day; therefore the LORD blessed the sabbath day and made it holy. Honor your father and your mother, that your days may be prolonged in the land which the LORD your God gives you. You shall not murder. You shall not commit adultery. You shall not steal. You shall not bear false witness against your neighbor. You shall not covet your neighbor's house; you shall not covet your neighbor's wife or his male servant or his female servant or his ox or his donkey or anything that belongs to your neighbor." (Exodus 20:1–17 NASB)

Hear, O Israel: The LORD our God, the LORD is one. Love the LORD your God with all your heart and with all your soul and with all your strength. These commandments that I give you today are to be upon your hearts. Impress them on your children. Talk about them when you sit at home and when you walk along the road, when you lie down and when you get up. Tie them as symbols on your hands and bind them on your foreheads. Write them on the doorframes of your houses and on your gates. (Deuteronomy 6:4–9)

Blessed is the man
   who does not walk in the counsel of the wicked
   or stand in the way of sinners
   or sit in the seat of mockers.
But his delight is in the law of the LORD,
   and on his law he meditates day and night.
He is like a tree planted by streams of water,
   which yields its fruit in season
   and whose leaf does not wither.
Whatever he does prospers. (Psalm 1:1–3)

"Teacher, which is the greatest commandment in the Law?" Jesus replied: "'Love the Lord your God with all your heart and with all your soul and with all your mind.' This is the first and greatest commandment. And the second is like it: 'Love your neighbor as yourself.' All the Law and the Prophets hang on these two commandments." (Matthew 22:36–40)

How precious to me are your thoughts, O God!
   How vast is the sum of them!
Were I to count them,
   they would outnumber the grains of sand.
When I awake,
   I am still with you. (Psalm 139:17–18)

But seek first his kingdom and his righteousness, and all these things will be given to you as well. (Matthew 6:33)

Sanctify them by the truth; your word is truth. (John 17:17)

Do not be deceived: God cannot be mocked. A man reaps what he sows. (Galatians 6:7)

Faith

For it is by grace you have been saved, through faith—and this not from yourselves, it is the gift of God not by works, so that no one can boast. (Ephesians 2:8–9)

Now faith is being sure of what we hope for and certain of what we do not see. (Hebrews 11:1)

And without faith it is impossible to please God, because anyone who comes to him must believe that he exists and that he rewards those who earnestly seek him. (Hebrews 11:6)

The Beatitudes

When Jesus saw the crowds, He went up on the mountain; and after He sat down, His disciples came to Him. He opened His mouth and began to teach them, saying, "Blessed are the poor in spirit, for theirs is the kingdom of heaven. Blessed are those who mourn, for they shall be comforted. Blessed are the gentle, for they shall inherit the earth. Blessed are those who hunger and thirst for righteousness, for they shall be satisfied. Blessed are the merciful, for they shall receive mercy. Blessed are the pure in heart, for they shall see God. Blessed are the peacemakers, for they shall be called sons of God. Blessed are those who have been persecuted for the sake of righteousness, for theirs is the kingdom of heaven. Blessed are you when people insult you and persecute you, and falsely say all kinds of evil against you because of Me. Rejoice and be glad, for your reward in heaven is great; for in the same way they persecuted the prophets who were before you." (Matthew 5:1–12 NASB)

The Lord's Prayer

Pray, then, in this way: "Our Father who art in heaven, hallowed be Thy name. Thy kingdom come. Thy will be done, on earth as it is in heaven. Give us this day our daily bread. And forgive us our debts, as we also have forgiven our debtors. And do not lead us into temptation, but deliver us from evil. [For Thine is the kingdom, and the power, and the glory, forever. Amen.]" (Matthew 6:9–13 NASB)

2. Jesus Christ

Then he said to them all: "If anyone would come after me, he must deny himself and take up his cross daily and follow me. For whoever wants to save his life will lose it, but whoever loses his life for me will save it. What good is it for a man to gain the whole world, and yet lose or forfeit his very self?" (Luke 9:23–25)

In the beginning was the Word, and the Word was with God, and the Word was God. He was with God in the beginning. (John 1:1–2)

Yet to all who received him, to those who believed in his name, he gave the right to become children of God. (John 1:12)

The Word became flesh and made his dwelling among us. We have seen his glory, the glory of the One and Only, who came from the Father, full of grace and truth. (John 1:14)

For God so loved the world, that He gave His only begotten Son, that whoever believes in Him shall not perish, but have eternal life. (John 3:16 NASB)

To the Jews who had believed him, Jesus said, "If you hold to my teaching, you are really my disciples. Then you will know the truth, and the truth will set you free." (John 8:31–32)

You are already clean because of the word I have spoken to you. (John 15:3)

For the wages of sin is death, but the gift of God is eternal life in Christ Jesus our Lord. (Romans 6:23)

That if you confess with your mouth, "Jesus is Lord," and believe in your heart that God raised him from the dead, you will be saved. For it is with your heart that you believe and are justified, and it is with your mouth that you confess and are saved. (Romans 10:9–10)

I have been crucified with Christ and I no longer live, but Christ lives in me. The life I live in the body, I live by faith in the Son of God, who loved me and gave himself for me. (Galatians 2:20)

Instead, speaking the truth in love, we will in all things grow up into him who is the Head, that is, Christ. (Ephesians 4:15)

I can do all things through Him who strengthens me. (Philippians 4:13 NASB)

And my God will meet all your needs according to his glorious riches in Christ Jesus. (Philippians 4:19)

Since, then, you have been raised with Christ, set your hearts on things above, where Christ is seated at the right hand of God. Set your minds on things above, not on earthly things. For you died, and your life is now hidden with Christ in God. When Christ, who is your life, appears, then you also will appear with him in glory.

Put to death, therefore, whatever belongs to your earthly nature: sexual immorality, impurity, lust, evil desires and greed, which is idolatry. Because of these, the wrath of God is coming. You used to walk in these ways, in the life you once lived. But now you must rid yourselves of all such things as these: anger, rage, malice, slander, and filthy language from your lips. Do not lie to each other, since you have taken off your old self with its practices and have put on the new self, which is being renewed in knowledge in the image of its Creator. Here there is no Greek or Jew, circumcised or uncircumcised, barbarian, Scythian, slave or free, but Christ is all, and is in all.

Therefore, as God's chosen people, holy and dearly loved, clothe yourselves with compassion, kindness, humility, gentleness and patience. Bear with each other and forgive whatever grievances you may have against one another. Forgive as the Lord forgave you. And over all these virtues put on love, which binds them all together in perfect unity.

Let the peace of Christ rule in your hearts, since as members of one body you were called to peace. And be thankful. Let the word of Christ dwell in you richly as you teach and admonish one another with all wisdom, and as you sing psalms, hymns and spiritual songs with gratitude in your hearts to God. And whatever you do, whether in word or deed, do it all in the name of the Lord Jesus, giving thanks to God the Father through him. (Colossians 3:1–17)

This is how we know what love is: Jesus Christ laid down his life for us. And we ought to lay down our lives for our brothers. (1 John 3:16)

3. Holy Spirit

But I tell you the truth: It is for your good that I am going away. Unless I go away, the Counselor will not come to you; but if I go, I will send him to you. When he comes, he will convict the world of guilt in regard to sin and right-eousness and judgment: in regard to sin, because men do not believe in me; in regard to righteousness, because I am going to the Father, where you can see me no longer; and in regard to judgment, because the prince of this world now stands condemned.

I have much more to say to you, more than you can now bear. But when he, the Spirit of truth, comes, he will guide you into all truth. He will not speak on his own; he will speak only what he hears, and he will tell you what is yet to come. He will bring glory to me by taking from what is mine and making it known to you. All that belongs to the Father is mine. That is why I said the Spirit will take from what is mine and make it known to you.

In a little while you will see me no more, and then after a little while you will see me. (John 16:7–16)

But you will receive power when the Holy Spirit has come upon you; and you shall be My witnesses both in Jerusalem, and in all Judea and Samaria, and even to the remotest part of the earth. (Acts 1:8 NASB)

That He would grant you, according to the riches of His glory, to be strength-ened with power through His Spirit in the inner man, so that Christ may dwell in your hearts through faith; and that you, being rooted and grounded in love, may be able to comprehend with all the saints what is the breadth and length and height and depth, and to know the love of Christ which surpasses knowl-edge, that you may be filled up to all the fullness of God. Now to Him who is able to do far more abundantly beyond all that we ask or think, according to the power that works within us, to Him be the glory in the church and in Christ Jesus to all generations forever and ever. Amen. (Ephesians 3:16–21 NASB)

4. Gratefulness

Not only so, but we also rejoice in our sufferings, because we know that suf-fering produces perseverance; perseverance, character; and character, hope. And hope does not disappoint us, because God has poured out his love into our hearts by the Holy Spirit, whom he has given us. (Romans 5:3–5)

And we know that in all things God works for the good of those who love him, who have been called according to his purpose. (Romans 8:28)

Do not conform any longer to the pattern of this world, but be transformed by the renewing of your mind. Then you will be able to test and approve what God's will is—his good, pleasing and perfect will. (Romans 12:2)

But he said to me, "My grace is sufficient for you, for my power is made perfect in weakness." Therefore I will boast all the more gladly about my weaknesses, so that Christ's power may rest on me. That is why, for Christ's sake, I delight in weaknesses, in insults, in hardships, in persecutions, in difficulties. For when I am weak, then I am strong. (2 Corinthians 12:9–10)

We are taking every thought captive to the obedience of Christ. (2 Corinthians 10:5 NASB)

This you know, my beloved brethren. But let everyone be quick to hear, slow to speak and slow to anger. (James 1:19 NASB)

Be anxious for nothing, but in everything by prayer and supplication with thanksgiving let your requests be made known to God. And the peace of God, which surpasses all comprehension, will guard your hearts and your minds in Christ Jesus. Finally, brethren, whatever is true, whatever is honorable, whatever is right, whatever is pure, whatever is lovely, whatever is of good repute, if there is any excellence and if anything worthy of praise, dwell on these things. The things you have learned and received and heard and seen in me, practice these things, and the God of peace will be with you. (Philippians 4:6–9 NASB)

Be joyful always; pray continually; give thanks in all circumstances, for this is God's will for you in Christ Jesus. (1 Thessalonians 5:16–18)

5. Serving Others

Greater love has no one than this, that he lay down his life for his friends. (John 15:13)

Be devoted to one another in brotherly love. Honor one another above yourselves. (Romans 12:10)

You, my brothers, were called to be free. But do not use your freedom to indulge the sinful nature; rather, serve one another in love. (Galatians 5:13)

Then make my joy complete by being like-minded, having the same love, being one in spirit and purpose. Do nothing out of selfish ambition or vain conceit, but in humility consider others better than yourselves. Each of you should look not only to your own interests, but also to the interests of others. Your attitude should be the same as that of Christ Jesus: Who, being in very nature God, did not consider equality with God something to be grasped, but made himself nothing, taking the very nature of a servant, being made in human likeness. And being found in appearance as a man, he humbled himself and became obedient to death—even death on a cross! (Philippians 2:2–8)

6. Spiritual Heart

How can a young man keep his way pure?
By keeping *it* according to Your word.
With all my heart I have sought You;
Do not let me wander from Your commandments.
Your word I have treasured in my heart,
That I may not sin against You. (Psalm 119:9–11 NASB)

Above all else, guard your heart, for it is the wellspring of life. (Proverbs 4:23)

For as he thinks within himself, so he is.
He says to you, "Eat and drink!"
But his heart is not with you. (Proverbs 23:7 NASB)

"But the things that come out of the mouth come from the heart, and these make a man 'unclean.' For out of the heart come evil thoughts, murder, adultery, sexual immorality, theft, false testimony, slander." (Matthew 15:18–19)

Notes

Chapter One: Hope for You in All Circumstances

1. James 1:19 and Philippians 4:8–9.
2. See Appendix 1 for Kari's letter to me along with an introduction from Michael.
3. These are my paraphrase of the four key beliefs from Scripture:
   Love the King, your God, with all of your heart, soul, mind and strength.
   [Matthew 22:37]
   Love your neighbor in the same way you want to be loved. [Matthew 22:39]
   Give thanks to God in all circumstances for this is his will. [1 Thessalonians 5:18]
   Forgive those who trespass against you so that your heavenly Father will forgive
   you. [Matthew 6:12]
4. Viktor Frankl, *Man's Search for Meaning* (Boston: Beacon Press, 2006).

Chapter Three: The Amazing Power of Your Beliefs

1. William Backus, *Learning to Tell Myself the Truth* (Minneapolis: Bethany House
   Publishers, 1994), 15.
2. Gary J. and Carrie Oliver, *Mad About Us* (Minneapolis: Bethany House Publishers,
   2007).
3. Albert Ellis and Windy Dryden, *The Practice of Rational Emotive Behavior Therapy*,
   2nd edition (New York: Springer Publishing Company, 2007).
4. 2 Corinthians 12:9–10; 1 Thessalonians 5:16–18.
5. For more on beliefs that can help you manage your eating problems, see chapter 14.
6. Philippians 4:6–9.
7. Paul Pearsall, *The Heart's Code* (New York: Broadway Books, 1998).
8. See chapter 14.

Chapter Four: Preparing Your Heart for Powerful Changes

1. Archibald Hart, *Habits of the Mind* (Dallas: Word Publishing, 1996), 39.
2. See Psalm 1.
3. Galatians 5:14.
4. John 15:10–14.
5. Judson Wheeler Van DeVenter (1855–1939), "I Surrender All," 1896.
6. *Oprah After the Show*, Oxygen TV, November 18, 2005.
7. Luke 8:4–15; Psalm 119:9–11; Psalm 1.
8. Matthew 12:33–35 and 15:18–20.
9. Summarized from Christine Gorman, "Six Lessons for Handling Stress," *Time*, vol. 169, no. 5, January 29, 2007, 82.
10. Matthew 6:33.
11. Matthew 10:29.
12. Matthew 6:21.
13. David Roher, "Patterns of the Old Life Left Behind," bible.org, www.bible.org/illus.php?topic_id=1588.
14. George MacDonald, "The Golden Key," *The Gifts of the Child Christ*, ed. Glenn Edward Sadler (Grand Rapids: William B. Eerdmans, 1973), 171.
15. In chapter 18, I have a list of ways you can immerse yourself in God's Word.

Chapter Five: Five Steps to Changing Your Beliefs

1. Ed Wheat, *Intended for Pleasure* (Grand Rapids: Fleming H. Revell, 1977, 1981, 1997).
2. C. S. Lewis, *Perelandra* (New York: The Macmillan Company, 1944), 88.
3. Matthew 12:43–45.
4. Matthew 15:18–19.
5. See Psalm 1.
6. Jeremiah 15:16.
7. James 4:6.
8. See Psalm 1.

Chapter Seven: The Deadly Lust of the Eyes

1. *The Weight of Glory* by C. S. Lewis © C. S. Lewis Pte. Ltd. 1949. Extract reprinted by permission.

Chapter Ten: The High Value of Loving God

1. Quoted in Bruce Larson, *The Communicator's Commentary: Luke* (Waco, Texas: Word Publishing, 1983), 59.
2. James Packer, *Keep in Step with the Spirit* (Old Tappan, New Jersey: Fleming H. Revell Co., 1984), 64–65.
3. "Only One Bible," bible.org, www.bible.org/illus.php?topic_id=159.
4. *Ends and Means* by Aldous Huxley. ©1937, 1964 by Aldous Huxley. Reprinted by permission of Georges Borchardt, Inc., for the Estate of Aldous Huxley.

5. *Mere Christianity* by C. S. Lewis © C. S. Lewis Pte. Ltd. 1942, 1943, 1944, 1952. Extract used by permission.

Chapter Eleven: The High Value of Loving Others

1. Dean Ornish, MD, *Love and Survival: 8 Pathways to Intimacy and Health* (San Francisco: Harper Perennial, 1999), 21, 42, 132.
2. Romans 8:37–39.
3. Romans 5:8.
4. Matthew 7:12.
5. *The Weight of Glory* by C. S. Lewis © C. S. Lewis Pte. Ltd. 1949. Extract reprinted by permission.
6. *Mere Christianity* by C. S. Lewis © C. S. Lewis Pte. Ltd. 1942, 1943, 1944, 1952. Extract used by permission.

Chapter Twelve: The High Value of Trials

1. Doc Lew Childre and Howard Martin, *The HeartMath Solution* (HarperOne: San Francisco, 2000), 105–14.
2. Philippians 4:6–9.
3. Romans 5:3–5; 8:28; 2 Corinthians 12:6–10; James 1:2–5.
4. Reprinted with the permission of Simon & Schuster Adult Publishing Group from *The Road Less Traveled* by M. Scott Peck, MD. © 1978 by M. Scott Peck, MD.
5. 2 Corinthians 12:9–10.
6. Daniel G. Amen, MD, *Change Your Brain, Change Your Life* (New York: Three Rivers Press, 1999).
7. Used by permission.

Chapter Thirteen: The High Value of Forgiveness

1. Michael Gibson, *Five Smooth Stones* (self published).
2. 1 John 2:9–11.
3. John Eldredge, *Waking the Dead* (Nashville: Thomas Nelson, 2006), 132–35.

Chapter Fourteen: How Your Beliefs Affect Your Eating Habits and Addictions

1. Gerald G. May, MD, *Addiction and Grace* (HarperOne: San Francisco, 2007).
2. Dean Ornish, MD, *Love and Survival: 8 Pathways to Intimacy and Health* (San Francisco: Harper Perennial, 1999).
3. Max Lucado, *A Gentle Thunder* (Dallas, TX: Word Publishing, 1995), 122.

Chapter Fifteen: How Your Beliefs Affect Your Vocation

1. Bob Buford, *Halftime* (Grand Rapids: Zondervan, 1997) and Bob Buford, *Finishing Well* (Nashville: Integrity, 2005).
2. Lee Iacocca and William Novak, *Iacocca: An Autobiography* (New York: Bantam, 1988), quoted in *Lifeline*, Summer, 1997.

The Smalley Relationship Center provides conferences and resources for couples, singles, parents, and churches. The Center captures research, connecting to your practical needs, and develops new tools for building relationships.

resources include:

- More than 50 best-selling books on relationships
- Small Group curriculums on marriage and parenting
- Church-wide campaign series with sermon series, daily e-mails, and much more
- Video/DVD series
- Newlywed kit and premarital resources

www.garysmalley.com web site includes:

- Over 300 articles on practical relationship topics
- Weekly key truths on practical issues
- Daily devotionals
- Conference dates and locations
- Special events
- Weekly newsletter
- Free personality and core fear profiles
- Request a SRC Speaker

To find out more about Gary Smalley's speaking schedule and conferences, and to receive a weekly e-letter with articles and coaching ideas on your relationships, go to www.garysmalley.com or call 1.800.848.6329

Attend our live **I Promise Marriage Seminars** taught by

DRS. GARY & GREG
SMALLEY

A six-session marriage seminar based on the new
I Promise book and Purpose Driven Curriculum

free resources: go to **www.garysmalley.com**

• **Weekly e-letter** 🗟

Receive articles, coaching tips, and inspirational encouragement
from Gary Smalley, which will help you build a more effective and
stronger marriage.

• **Profiles** ①

The overall theme of I Promise is security, and you can take a 20-
question test on how secure your most important relationship is.

(Bonus: After you take that profile, consider taking our personality profile that gives you even more insight into what kind of personality styles
you and your spouse fall into.)